Co

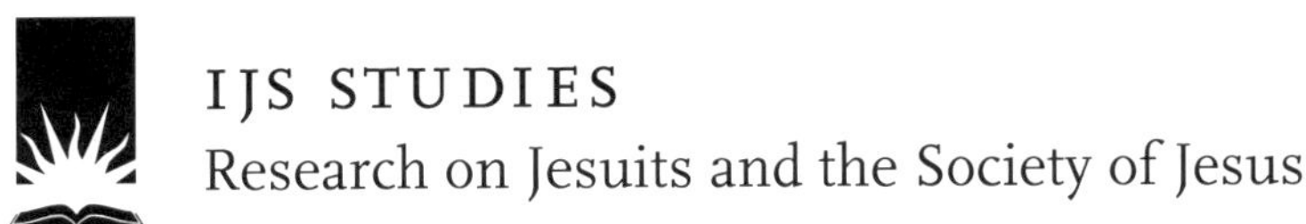

In the School of Ignatius

STUDIOUS ZEAL AND DEVOTED LEARNING

Claude Pavur, S.J.

Institute of Jesuit Sources
Boston College

Cover: *Educatio*, a 1914 painting by Br. Francis Schroen, S.J., which hangs in the rotunda of Gasson Hall at Boston College. The painting depicts Ignatius of Loyola and other students in a classroom in Paris. According to a contemporary account of the painting, Ignatius "is reciting his Latin lesson while the students gaze admiringly."

Photography by Gary Wayne Gilbert, University Photographer, Boston College

Cover design by Keith Ake, Office of University Communications, Boston College

Library of Congress Control Number: 2019947892

ISBN: 978-1-947617-02-5

Institute of Jesuit Sources
at the Institute for Advanced Jesuit Studies
Boston College
140 Commonwealth Avenue | Chestnut Hill, MA 02467 | USA

email: iajs@bc.edu
http://jesuitsources.bc.edu

Fees are subject to change

INSTITUTE FOR
ADVANCED JESUIT STUDIES
BOSTON COLLEGE

IJS Studies is an imprint of the Institute of Jesuit Sources

In the School of Ignatius:
Studious Zeal and Devoted Learning
Claude Pavur, S.J.

Institute of Jesuit Sources
Boston College

IJS Studies

Research on Jesuits and the Society of Jesus

With this book, the Institute of Jesuit Sources is inaugurating an imprint—*IJS Studies–Research on Jesuits and the Society of Jesus*. This imprint will provide a solid and reputable addition of academic works to the rich catalogue of source materials that the Institute has been publishing since its foundation.

The imprint publishes double-blind, peer-reviewed scholarship, and focuses in particular on studies in the fields of Jesuit history, spirituality, and pedagogy.

IJS Studies is edited by the Institute for Advanced Jesuit Studies. It will feature a variety of widely accessible and interdisciplinary titles, produced by Jesuit and non-Jesuit scholars whose work assists the initiatives of the Institute for Advanced Jesuit Studies at Boston College, the home of Jesuit Sources.

Casey Beaumier, S.J.
Director, Institute for Advanced Jesuit Studies

More information about this imprint can be found at http://jesuitsources.bc.edu.

Foreword

Walter Benjamin (1892–1940) once remarked that there has never been a progressive movement in history that did not claim to act in the name of origins. French revolutionaries, for example, often justified their actions as a reenactment of ancient Rome. They wanted a noble legacy to fill the void of meaning they found in an illogical present and to illuminate their new world with better (or possibly, the best) practices. It was only by returning to the roots, they thought, that we could be led reliably into the future.

One can track the same interplay between past and future in the crucial moment of church history that was the Second Vatican Council (1962–65). The Italian word *aggiornamento*—which the council adopted to indicate its main goal—was closely connected with the theological movements that paved the way for the *ressourcement*. Binding these two concepts together, the council sought to re-envision the mission of the church in modern times by looking back at the most original sources, those of the early church.

Jesuit education exists within a similar kind of dialogue between past and future. If one wishes to find a distinctive and constant trait in it, it could well be the Jesuits' endeavor to keep reflecting on education in their schools, on how to improve it, on how to make it "distinctively Jesuit." These concerns were present in the motivations of Ignatius of Loyola (*c.*1491–1556) in his early governance of the order and were fundamental in the long-labored efforts behind both the first *Ratio studiorum* (1599) and its proposed "modernizing" revised version (1832), and they became increasingly evident during the second half of the twentieth century with the production of documents such as "Go Forth and Teach: The Characteristics of Jesuit Education" (1987), "Ignatian Pedagogy: A Practical Approach" (1993), and many other related compositions, talks, homilies, conference addresses, and so on.

The peculiarity of this more recent debate on the distinctiveness of Jesuit education is that the *Ratio studiorum* has faded away from the sources Jesuits previously regarded as inspirational and authoritative. In order to envision the mission, identity, and methods of Jesuit schools for the future, Jesuit schools have focused more and more on Ignatian spiritual writings and the Constitutions of the Society of Jesus as the "origins" and fundamental "sources." The link between the present and future of Jesuit schools and the past of the Society of Jesus has often been connected with (and often limited to) its founder, Ignatius of Loyola.

With this engaging volume, Claude Pavur raises a question of fundamental importance for those who care about the future of Jesuit education: Is it really helpful to retire the *Ratio studiorum* from discussions over the identity of Jesuit schools and to avoid referring to its content when engaging with the question of Jesuit education in the present day?

As Pavur argues in this book, neglecting the *Ratio* in current debates over Jesuit education would only be helpful if it were not a foundational document, one embedded in the very identity of the Society of Jesus. Yet, over time, these aspects of the *Ratio studiorum* have often been overlooked, thus diminishing the importance of the *Ratio* in the real operations of Jesuit schools: at the beginning of this process, the *Ratio* was still respected as a venerable document from the early years of the Society, and though its content was discarded as a useless relic, many felt that its underlying spirit should continue to be followed in modern times. At the end of this same process, however, the *Ratio studiorum* had been transformed from a vital and effective set of rules into a mute monument covered by the weeds of history and segregated from the living tradition of the Society of Jesus.

Pavur's discourse stands as a challenge to scholars, Jesuits, and educators in a manner very much reminiscent of Michel Foucault (1926–84): it is an invitation to deconstruct and reconstruct the mission of Jesuit education, returning the *Ratio* to the pantheon of original sources for Jesuit education, with all its foundational power and historical fertility. Pavur's invitation is nothing but a claim for *ressourcement*: a source that has been neglected in more recent times is still standing today, as it has done for centuries past, as a pillar for the educational enterprise of the Society.

Pavur invites us to consider the foundational dimension of the *Ratio*, its roots in Ignatius's own plans for the Society, its value as a team-built project (the most Ignatian of things!), its focus on humanities and on an ordered plan of studies that envisions as its goal the formation of the whole person beyond the mere technical instruction of a student. He also emphasizes how the *Ratio* itself wisely introduced the need to adapt its rules to circumstances—so that what has sometimes been wrongly considered a rigid set of prescriptions bound to an early modern mentality is actually a powerful text that retains meaning and vision today.

Volumes such as this are bound to trigger a debate. As *disputatio* has always been an important part of Jesuit pedagogy, I am sure that the author will be doubly pleased to have been provocative in this regard. Pavur's message, with which I could not but wholeheartedly agree, is that such debates have positive outcomes provided that they are informed by the sources, which alone offer sufficient depth to a conversation whose goal is to navigate Jesuit schools through the unknown waters of the future.

It is with great satisfaction that with this book the Institute of Jesuit Sources is inaugurating a new imprint, *IJS Studies–Research on Jesuits and the Society of Jesus*, one intended to provide a solid and reputable companion to the editions of sources the institute has been publishing since its foundation. That the first book published by this new imprint is devoted to Jesuit pedagogy stands also as a clear sign of the continuing relevance of such a ministry for the Society of Jesus. Let me express the wish that this volume is the first of a long list of such studies, one of many useful instruments for deepening the knowledge of how the Jesuits and their associates have successfully educated youth for over half a millennium. I also wish to personally thank Claude Pavur for his friendship and highly erudite scholarship: *Vivat et floreat.*

Cristiano Casalini
Chair of Jesuit Pedagogy and Educational History
Boston College

Prefatory Note

This book argues for the ongoing relevance of the Jesuit plan of studies of 1599, generally known as the *Ratio studiorum*. It seeks to contribute first to the educational efforts of the Society of Jesus and its allies; second to the labors of all other educators looking for viable relevant ideas. The point of these researches is *not* re-instituting Renaissance particularities that do not fit our age but rather our prudent anchoring in the tradition and a competent, commonsense leveraging of that founding charter's wisdom and vision.

But the issue is not merely "relevance." Nor is it the mining of a document famous in the history of education for some productive pedagogical notions. The argument is that the *Ratio studiorum* emanates from deep in the very *core concept* of the Society of Jesus, from its earliest history, from its spirituality; the *Ratio* helps to constitute, perpetuate, make effective the Jesuit order itself. Apart from the document and all that it represents and implies, the Society simply *cannot be what it is.* If some disagree, the argument remains an essential one to have in full, because without the right self-concept, the Society will necessarily be alienated from its real identity and utterly unable to fulfill its real mission.

The most important lines of argumentation will be found in the fifth chapter, "The *Ratio studiorum* of 1599: Inescapably Foundational." The other chapters comprise relevant materials that fill out various aspects of the picture or that approach it from different angles. These chapters may be especially useful for those who still feel vague about the conceptual, structural, and historical underpinnings of Jesuit education proper and its relation to the Society. The penultimate chapter, "Toward a Revised *Ratio studiorum* for Jesuit Colleges" looks toward a new configuration that might be confidently undertaken after the old dispensation is adequately understood. The afterword tries to correct a widespread and major deficiency in the understanding of both Ignatian *and* Jesuit spiritualities: there is a certain dimension without which one does not really "have" *either* Ignatius *or* the Society of Jesus. This book with all its apparatus will, I hope, provide a handy guide to the idea of Jesuit education, sufficient background for informed discussion about it, and a trustworthy basis for developments that are both faithful and creative.

Should these essays provoke better ideas, or even merely sound and convincing refutations, that will be entirely to the author's satisfaction. Time is short, the crisis pressing. Simplistic errors, deep-seated biases, and shaky ideologies abound. All too easily conversations can go on interminably while vital goods again and again fail to be delivered. Talk when cheap is quite costly. The age is contrary, often oblivious, and not so eager to listen, much less to act. So may grace abound all the more. The "dearest freshness deep down things" can burst forth again. Let wisdom be justified by all of her children (Luke 7:35).

Claude Pavur, S.J.
Chestnut Hill, MA
September 1, 2019

1. Defining Jesuit Education

Especially for those who are unfamiliar with the Jesuit educational tradition, we might best begin with an overview of its primary charter, the *Ratio studiorum*, surveying its chief contents and qualities, its status and relevance.[1] What is that document? What are its main features? How might we variously read and apply that content? How might such a document relate to Ignatius of Loyola's (*c.*1491–1556) *Spiritual Exercises*? What might we most profitably take from the *Ratio* for Jesuit education today? This chapter gathers as a kind of prelude many major themes that will later receive a more detailed treatment.

An Overview of the *Ratio studiorum*

The *Ratio studiorum* (hereafter, RS) is a celebrated educational plan published in 1599 by the Society of Jesus to be the official guide-book for the running of Jesuit schools. It gives no extended account of the philosophy of Jesuit education, but it presents specifics of that education, by detailing the aims and the directives for all the main agents, units, and operations in and of the school. There are rules for administrators, teachers, students, grades, classes, and "academies," which are formal study clubs. Teachers are told what the scope of their responsibilities includes; how to hold examinations, public disputations, and contests; what books and authors to teach; in what order they should be taught; in what school exercises should consist; what each grade should have as a goal; how the school day should be structured; when the vacation-times will be for different levels; under what conditions students should be admitted and promoted and disciplined or dismissed. The RS was a brilliant organizational advance in its day, standardizing education from grammar school to graduate school more completely than it ever had been before. The RS's impact stretched across hundreds of Jesuit schools for hundreds of years, well into the twentieth century.

You can learn much about the RS just by surveying its headings. Here are a few striking features, expanded with some commentary based on other historical knowledge:

---

1 This essay has been adapted from a talk given at the Ignatian Heritage Celebration, Gonzaga University, Spokane, Washington, on September 29, 2011. The task on that occasion was not simply restricted to a description of what made up the RS; it was also to sketch out the RS's current relevance and possible contribution. Some points are given fuller treatment elsewhere, but this lecture may serve as a simple overall view of the terrain and some essential questions, particularly for the uninitiated. Also, this presentation contains unique material like the five different interpretive approaches that may be adopted in employing the RS today.

1. *The content of the RS is structured by the offices and their responsibilities.* It is very clear what the various parties are supposed to be doing. There is a "large idea" in place and there are many interrelated parts. The success of the larger project depends on each piece doing well what it is supposed to be doing. There is unity and coherence through the whole, as the parts are linked in a certain order.

2. *The content proceeds from "top-down."* The first set of rules has to do with the provincial, or the Jesuit who is the key authority for a given geographical domain. The last rules deal with the academies. In between, the order goes from the most advanced classes down to the beginning ones. There is something telling about this structure. *De arriba* (Spanish "from above") has a special significance in Ignatian spirituality: graces flow from above.[2] Proper authority is a good and helpful thing. The attitude seems to be "Why would we not want to be in harmony with the right authority?" This is not the place for individual assertion or rebellion against established norms, but rather for mining and profiting from the wisdom of the elders in the most efficient and helpful way. Freedom and happiness come from being in harmony with the best wisdom and ultimately with "who we are meant to be."

   We might find here a reflection of the Society's distinguishing characteristic in Ignatius's eyes: obedience. It is something with deep roots in the Judeo-Christian tradition. Proverbs 29:18 says: "Where there is no vision, the people perish: but he that keepeth the law, happy is he" (King James Version). The Douay–Rheims version has: "When prophecy shall fail, the people shall be scattered abroad: but he that keepeth the law is blessed." Some translations render the first part as "With no vision or prophecy, the people run wild/are unrestrained/cast out restraint/are scattered." The RS was meant to serve as a kind of vision that unifies people and helps them to get the most out of their efforts and experience; it was meant to be a kind of helpful and inspired "law" or set of guidelines.

   But what may escape notice here is the *bottom-up dynamic* that led to the drafting of the RS: it was in fact not merely the result of a top-down "imposition." There was extensive consultation with experienced teachers about what is most beneficial for their students. Before the final version of 1599, there were earlier documents circulated in 1586 and 1591, the first being for review and comment only, the second for a three-year trial. After the trial, a committee of six chosen Jesuit educators sent out a set of survey questions to all the provinces and then sifted through the teachers' responses before drafting the final version of 1599.

2 Hugo Rahner, *Ignatius the Theologian* (New York: Herder & Herder, 1968), 3–10.

3. *There are three programmatic tiers or stages.*
A favorite Jesuit idea is that the ends guide our actions. We are to act with our ultimate purposes, our final destinations, our goals in mind. In the plan of the RS, there is a definite hierarchy implied, with the theological sphere at the top, philosophy in the center, and Letters at the foundation. The implication is that theology (which includes scripture) is the peak toward which everything inclines. Each of the stages is essential in Jesuit education, and the structure was imagined as a normative dynamic: become competent in Letters first, then in philosophy, then in theology. Do not mix these stages together.

4. *Oversight is a leading value, especially for the sake of the students.*
There is a superstructure (made up of provincials, rectors, prefects) who are to follow their own rules in order to ensure that the plan is being properly followed and attaining the right results. Why this emphasis? Ultimately, it is for the sake of the students and for the quality of the education that all the students are receiving. The students find their place in the outline as well (the academies or study clubs, the beadles or teacher assistants, the decurions or academic team-captains). Students therefore can collaborate in the educational process, becoming part of the oversight structure. Even pedagogically, there is a "reaching up" that the student must do: everyone has mastered the material when he has learned how to teach it. The education works in humanistic fashion, through the deep absorption and imitation of good models in writing, speaking, and acting. The students are free to enter the program or not, but once in, they are not free not to cooperate. There are precious resources of time and space: they are for those who are willing to devote themselves to the effort.

5. *The overriding goal of Jesuit education is clearly presented at the outset and repeated in several passages.*
Early in the RS, in the first rule for the provincial, we find a most important statement:

> The final goal of Jesuit education. Since one of the leading ministries of our Society is teaching our neighbors all the disciplines in keeping with our Institute in such a way that they are thereby aroused to a knowledge and love of our Maker and Redeemer, the provincial should consider himself obliged to do his utmost to ensure that our diverse and many-sided educational labor meets with the abundant results that the grace of our calling demands of us. (RS, no. 7)

Notice the result clause: the teaching takes place *so that as a result* a certain spiritual result takes place. What is first intended is not competence, prestige, honor, excellence, but *a rousing of the soul toward a knowledge and love of God*. Consider a second locus:

> The function of the prefect. The prefect's function is to act as the rector's general agent for achieving good academic order, and to direct and regulate the classes, according to the power received from the rector, in such a way that those who attend those classes make as much progress as possible in moral integrity and in the liberal arts and learning, for the glory of God. (RS, no. 99).

Here again there is the desire for a particular result: "In such a way [...] that [...]." Moral integrity is an essential part of a liberal education. This is a Christian view, but the ancient Greeks and Romans had it too. The perfect orator was "the *good* person speaking well."[3] The vision of the RS includes an unambiguous affiliation to this tradition of "good letters and good character." The students must realize that this is the guiding vision:

> First rule for non-Jesuit students. Learning should be joined with devotion. 1. Those who attend Jesuit academic institutions to get an education should realize that, with God's help, there will be no less intense an effort to steep them in devotion and the other virtues than there will be to steep them in the liberal arts. (RS, no. 466)

"Devotion" translates the word *pietas*, which is a very rich concept, one not limited to the religious sphere. It means the good and wholesome bondedness you have with God, parents, country, and with any benefactor who has enriched you in a way far beyond your abilities to compensate. Or, from the other side of things, it means that kind of bondedness that you have with those whom you yourself have enriched in such a way—your spouse, your children, your students, your fellow-citizens.

6. *Pointedness is preferred.*
   The items are concise. The text of the RS was honed down so that there was not much excess verbiage. It is clear, sharp, focused. This allows for creativity and adaptation around the bare point that is made. It means that there is freedom, even though there is also a definite desideratum to be attained. The RS "gets to the point" and does not belabor it. In this way, it reflects the giving of "points" in the *Spiritual Exercises*: God is given ample room to work. A Jesuit retreat master once pointed out that "Ignatius could tell a retreatant to pray for five hours and he might use only three sentences to indicate the matter."

7. *The RS took a long while to emerge.*
   A timeline for the RS would show that it required generations to emerge. There was a very careful sifting and testing in experience over a fifty-one-year

3 *Bonus vir, dicendi peritus* is found in the *Institutio Oratoria* 12.1.1 of Quintilian (*c.*35–*c.*100), who attributes this phrase to the Elder Cato (234–139 BCE).

period, starting with the school in Messina (1548). The teachers were involved in the process. Various breakthroughs were taken up and refashioned as needed. The Society's schools were happy to find and share the successes that others had discovered. This is part of the secret of the phenomenal success of Jesuit education. Education is sometimes challenged today because the responsible parties may not be sufficiently historical in their understanding and not ready or eager enough to mine the past for what it might contribute. The prevailing humanism in the era of the RS was also operating on a similar principle: first make a careful sifting of what has already been done very well; then make an advance on it if you can.

The Status of the *Ratio studiorum*

If you can say that the book of the *Spiritual Exercises* is an essential document for Ignatian spirituality, and that the book of the *Constitutions* of the Society of Jesus is essential in a similar way for the Jesuit order, then you might say that the RS is likewise essential for Jesuit education. It does not matter that it comes from a far off time and place. Compare it with the New Testament, which is so basic for Christian existence although it comes from an even further off time and place; many of us use it daily. If you want to be a mature and informed Christian, you need these scriptures. Of course, the *Spiritual Exercises* and the *Constitutions* of the Society of Jesus are both even older than the RS, and Jesuit circles have been happy to return to them repeatedly for direction and nourishment. Why shouldn't that be the case with the RS as well? A little closer to home, the Constitution of the United States of America comes from more than two centuries ago, but we seem to have no problem invoking it repeatedly and reverentially in our political deliberations.

But the situation is more complicated than I have implied. The RS is essential for "Jesuit education," but it was written as a document for training Jesuits and non-Jesuits together. There is a special significance in the fact that all the scholastics who were to make up the core of the Society had to rely on the RS as the defining document for their Jesuit academic-spiritual formation. This formation in fact made up most, even almost all, of the years of their very extended period of training in the Society. Then, having gone through that academic formation from bottom to top, they were all the more able to pass on that Jesuit education competently to others, both inside and outside the Society. The mystique and the strength of Jesuit education probably derive in good measure from the focus and identity and continuous tradition that was established by means of this document and its evolving practical interpretation through the centuries.

The RS has therefore been foundational not just for the schools, but for Jesuit formation and therefore for the Jesuit order itself, insofar as the Jesuit order is significantly constituted by those who pass through this kind of training.

To put it baldly: *the RS helps to constitute the Jesuit order*. It is not just a guiding document for one particular apostolic activity that the order undertakes.

Does this point perhaps make the RS less relevant for the running of Jesuit schools? After all, there is a broad consensus that that Jesuit schools today are not meant to be seminaries, so the fact that the RS also trained seminarians seems to make it less useful for a wider population. But that would be a misdirection, because there is also a broad consensus that Jesuit schools, even if they are not seminaries, should not be purely secularistic either. Therefore, we cannot escape the other side of the question: How do we work the *religious* voice into the conversation about the identity of Jesuit schools? How do we make their essential fabric quite clearly different from institutions based on entirely secular norms? The RS offers a balance. It points to the fact that a solid Christian, liberal arts education is in large measure one that both seminarians and non-seminarians should get. It has to do with a spiritual-intellectual goal that is so essential that it is for everyone. This vision grounds collaboration, unity, fellowship in vision and understanding.

Secular examples of higher education are abundant and ubiquitous. Most faculties have many of their credentials from such sources. But is there a parallel current of distinctive Jesuit dynamics, in which we might hear the "voice of the Institute of the Society of Jesus"?[4] Working out the chemistry of the right balance of elements is the task of Jesuit educational leadership today. The RS can help us to recover the voice of the Institute in which lay and Jesuit formation are distinctively united.

One Mystery Solved, Others Raised: The Locus of Leadership

So the RS has been a foundational document, but people have neglected it.[5] This solves a mystery for me, namely: "Why have discussions of Jesuit education so often seemed to be so vague?" The answer is most probably that knowledge of the foundational document and its tradition has been missing. If you have no fixed reference point, and no authoritative text (like the New Testament, for example, in Christian theology), then of course you are going to be wandering in a very large wilderness. The RS can serve at least as an important fixed point.

But here another mystery opens up: If the RS was so important, why did it get neglected? Why was it apparently considered irrelevant? Why, *particularly* when

4 In Latin, *institutum* can mean "what has been formally established." This word carries a special meaning in reference to the Society of Jesus: it is the distinctive idea of the Society itself, how it understands itself as expressed in certain key founding documents and charters. The Society's "Institute" points to the totality of the Society's way of being, its formation and mission and governance structures and overall meaning and purpose.

5 The foundational character of the RS is the subject of extensive argumentation and reflection in the fifth chapter of this volume, "The *Ratio studiorum* of 1599: Inescapably Foundational."

Vatican II (1962–65) asked religious orders to return to and update their original charisms, did the Society not re-establish an effective modern version of the RS? It is clear that there was some desire to do this. At least from the earlier half of the twentieth century, in the face of the pressure to switch to the elective systems and academic major programs, there were discussions that kept raising the importance of the RS: some of these were recorded in the *Jesuit Educational Quarterly*. But this line of approach apparently proved unworkable at the global level. And yet one should doubt that it is really helpful to abandon something that has been constitutive of one's order and that has been an integral part of its identity. Perhaps the authorities simply did not see that the RS was a foundational kind of document, and they despaired too soon of framing a modern equivalent.

A second great mystery also arises here, namely: In whose hands does the leadership of Jesuit education lie today? Yes, it is in the hands of God, as Ignatius would no doubt emphasize. But more immediately, where does the responsibility lie? Where precisely is the stable, perduring, thinking, planning organizational unit working out the details of Jesuit education, if not globally then locally? Who is at what table using what kinds of documents and thinking together with what others, with what transparency, and on what schedule? Is that conversation well informed and broad and deep enough? Do the discussants have the requisite linguistic, historical, and institutional knowledge and authority, not to mention the existential commitment? Who is going to critique their work if it is lacking? And who has the oversight of the directive conversation that should be a standing feature of any particular school or set of schools? In mechanics, a device known as a "governor" keeps the processes going smooth and steady. Is there any such equivalent in the administration of Jesuit schools?

You might rightly point out that we live in an age of decentralization at least in this respect: there is no one authority speaking for the Society's Institute. And might this not be a major part of the challenge today? I remember that once, at a meeting run by the Heartland group (which works with Jesuit identity questions in higher education), I was told by a faculty member from another school: "I feel like I'm being dragooned into this process, but what I want to know is: Who are the generals? I'd like to know some names and faces." There is a question of leadership. It does not necessarily have to reside in any kind of single imperial figure or in a cadre of "generals," but the leadership will have to be there somehow and identifiable as such. There will at some point need to be some names and faces. Behind the RS were Superior General Claudio Acquaviva (1543–1615, in office 1581–1615) and an international committee of six whose names we do know.

I said a little while ago that Jesuit educational leadership means working out the chemistry of various aspects like the balance of the religious and the secular aspects. To carry this metaphor a little further, you need a think-tank to plan the experiments and a lab in which to work out that chemistry. In the past, the leadership resided ultimately with the provincial and then with rector and then with the president/principal and then with the general prefect of studies. But these were not lone, tyrannical individuals. They worked within a community with its traditional understandings and practices and norms and documents like the RS.

Perhaps it is still the case that Jesuit education will simply never be what it is meant to be without clear, sure-footed, directive, ongoing support and leadership from the provincial's office, which itself must be in touch with a wider circle of practices and meanings. That is a question quite worthy of its own discussion: Can Jesuit education be soundly constituted apart from that leadership? It seems to me that not to have such leadership certainly takes you in a distinctly different direction. It endangers, even annuls, the whole schema.

The argument now might be that greater autonomy is given to schools, to make them "free" from external agencies. But merely to view the provincial as an external agency is already to abandon the horizon of the RS at step 1. Schools are in fact beholden to many external agencies like the government or accrediting agencies or the presses that choose which books they want to publish and therefore which professors are going to be eligible for tenure. But the provincial is not external to the Jesuit school. I see no reason for the provincial not to have a place on the administrative flowchart for a Jesuit university and to take an active role in determining the things that bear upon the essentials of Jesuit identity. At the very least, if boards of trustees want to have Jesuit presidents, they must want what goes with being a Jesuit: accountability to Society authorities, ideas, character, tradition, mission, and development that are consonant with these aspects. Though there may be flexibility and latitude in various respects, there is no *laissez-faire*, no "self-constitution" on the spot, no break in the chain of oversight and responsibility.

For the sake of argument and realism, let us suppose that substantively directive leadership in matters that bear critically on the mission is simply not forthcoming from the provincial's office, for whatever reasons. Certainly, nothing prevents a school from using its own resources to get in touch with and to develop the core structures and directions that have historically come from the Jesuit order. It is a daunting project, but it is possible. The school would still have to have its own authoritative directive center and local oversight structures. And it would have to have competent, qualified, well-informed, and well-formed people in those roles. They would really have to know what they are doing.

Here, then, is a practical suggestion for any Jesuit university wanting to be authentically Jesuit in circumstances prevailing today: establish a perduring executive structure, one that is well informed, well credentialed, and officially responsible for the conversation, the analysis, and the practical decisions that achieve, maintain, and develop Jesuit educational identity. The larger community and the higher leadership should ensure that this executive board deals with the most radical and relevant questions in an effective and timely way.

Reading the RS Today: Major Hermeneutical Approaches and the Question of Justice

This question of informed and competent leadership is essential because there always has to be a discerning, sensible use of tradition. The leaders must be well prepared to know and act on a legitimate understanding of the Institute. And yet even when you do have leaders in position, there are various approaches that may be taken. Here is a brief survey of a range of interpretive options.

Modernist: We might say that Ignatius himself was essentially interested in a Christian liberal education appropriate for his day. The old is out-of-date. Let's make it new and fit it to modern times, do for our own day what Ignatius did in his.

> **Difficulty:** How do you do this? What are the elements? It is not so easy to see what we must do for the same effect. How do we save what is good not just for one generation but for many, including our own? If you discount what is old, you may be violating an essential tenet of the RS that favors well-tested approved contents.

Formalist: Renaissance Jesuit education in letters consisted mostly in learning the arts of communication and the grounding for professional and leadership positions in society, so we might just put the focus on those communicative skills most helpful for success now, and we might just strive for excellence in whatever field.

> **Difficulty:** Merely to focus on rhetorical expertise for leadership in various areas can end up subordinating the main inspirations and goals of Jesuit education to a secularizing program.

Postmodernist: Style is what matters. Surpass the modernist tendency even to look back at the old forms in order to remake them. Break all molds. Raise the hearts and minds of the youth to the mystery of being–or better, experience—and excite their wonder; then you do not need to worry too much about particular content.

> **Difficulty:** The tradition is one of definite content and history. You cannot, for example, simply use Buddhist approaches to transcendence to raise people's wonder and still claim that you are a Jesuit school. Details matter. Content matters. Take these away and you radically change the chemistry and the outcomes and the meaning of the education.

Restorationist: The RS enshrines values that go beyond its own day, and this is proven by the fact that it was used for several centuries. Let us restore as much as we can of the original program, even with the specific sources that were used.

> **Difficulty:** This education does not seem to prepare students for the world as it is now. They may learn to write excellent Latin prose and to read Greek very well, but are they going to be well-informed citizens who have the power to make good, well-informed decisions in the present age? And won't we be losing sight of a great deal that has developed since the Renaissance if we engage in a restorationist approach?

Traditional-Adaptive: keep some continuity with the past, with the RS-tradition as a kind of guide, but adapt the education to the present age.

> **Difficulty:** How shall we achieve, in a pluralist or hyper-pluralist age, a vital and deep consensus on what kind of continuity to keep and what kinds of adaptations to make? Perhaps the world has changed so much that only the modernist solution is workable. Some kind of faculty-administrative unit will have to be trained and established as an important executive agency. But people resist having "new" authorities over them.

Any oversight group re-shaping an institution will have to be aware of these possible approaches toward contemporary Jesuit education. It will have to deliberate well and deeply enough to come to its own decision about what is most promising for the given situation. This is not so easy. Deliberative processes are themselves fraught with dangers, particularly if different members have read different materials and not only vary in their interpretations but also cannot achieve a timely and workable resolution. It is all too tempting to leave major decisions in abeyance or to settle for specious solutions. Yet just because there will never be a total agreement on the contents of the curriculum, an educational institution is not entitled to ignore the question of curricular contents or to excuse itself from the effort to attain as much consensus as may be possible. Too much is at stake. Too many students could be short-changed in the essentials. That would be one of the worst injustices that a university could commit. Such a moral and practical failure would in effect undermine the weight of any other justice-discourse that it would try to establish. To speak this way is to say nothing against diversity, but to give a definite priority to the substance and quality of the mission, where we find the more radical justice-questions that many would avoid.

The *Ratio studiorum* and the *Spiritual Exercises*

There is an entirely different dimension of interpretation implied in another question to which I would like to turn now: "How does the RS relate to the *Spiritual Exercises* of Ignatius of Loyola?" This is very important material to consider because there seems to be a bit of confusion here, even at the highest levels.[6]

6 See the fuller discussion of this question in "The Historiography of Jesuit Pedagogy," chapter 4 below.

Some assume that a grounding in or an orientation toward the *Spiritual Exercises* is essential for the health and identity of the school. And since the *Exercises* (originally written by the Christian "Iñigo" and not the theologian and presbyterally ordained cleric "Ignatius") are not just for Jesuits, people perhaps easily assume that they can better ground the reorientations of Jesuit higher-educational institutions across a wider base. At least that is apparently the hope. The Ignatian Colleagues Program sponsored by the Association of Jesuit Colleges and Universities (AJCU) looks like an abbreviated novitiate experience for selected personnel (though everyone still seems to agree that universities are not seminaries).[7]

The *Spiritual Exercises* and the RS are certainly "of a piece." Both of them have specific content, given in a specific sequence, with different stages. There is a strong grounding structure and yet ample freedom to elaborate on the contents under the inspiration of the Spirit and in light of the particularities of various situations. Both programs include stages that should not be mixed up, and fixed moments that cannot be left out (like the study of humanities in the RS or the passion of Christ in the *Exercises*). There is a strong sense of the importance of details in the operations undertaken (whether in prayer or in classroom procedure). There is also a sense of goals: there are specific graces to be obtained, or specific academic outcomes to be attained. The spiritual-religious vision is key: the RS says the point of Jesuit studies is helping to rouse our neighbors to a knowledge and love of our Maker and Redeemer; and the *Spiritual Exercises* helps us individually to dispose ourselves freely for God's praise, reverence, and service.

The documents seem harmonically linked, particularly with the Society's aim of learned devotion (*docta pietas*). Nevertheless, the RS is a far more proximate source for leadership in the Jesuit educational enterprise than is the book of the *Exercises*. If you give everyone in the school a profoundly moving thirty-day Ignatian retreat, the committed faculty will still want and need to know what they should do from day-to-day in the school *qua* Jesuit educational institution. It is partly that desire for the concrete details of successful apostolic service that led to the RS in the first place.

A seminal paper of Fr. Peter Schineller, first delivered at a conference on the Jesuit *Constitutions* in Rome in October of 2006, is entitled "From an Ascetical Spirituality of the *Exercises* to the Apostolic Spirituality of the *Constitutions*: Laborers in the Lord's Vineyard."[8] The title itself makes the essential point; namely that there is a move from an *ascetical* spirituality, which is more about

7 On the Ignatian Colleagues Program, see https://www.ignatiancolleagues.org/ (accessed October 22, 2018).

8 Peter Schineller, "From an Ascetical Spirituality of the *Exercises* to the Apostolic Spirituality of the *Constitutions*: Laborers in the Lord's Vineyard," in Ite inflammate omnia: *Selected Historical Papers from Conferences Held at Loyola and Rome in 2006*, ed. Thomas M. McCoog (Rome: Institutum Historicum Societatis Iesu, 2010), 85–108.

the maturation and development of the individual's spiritual self, to an *apostolic* spirituality, which is no longer so much about how you should try to cooperate with dynamics leading to your own salvation, but rather how you should go about caring for your neighbors in a corporate endeavor. What I might add to Fr. Schineller's analysis is simply that the RS is even a step further in the direction of concreteness regarding the apostolic activity of schools. The educational work too has a spirituality and a definition of activity that is not entirely encapsulated within the scope of the *Exercises*.

What Might We Derive from the RS Today?

It helps to state some particular goods that can result from careful attention to the RS and from prudent use of its tradition:

1. *A concrete historical sense that is necessary for the authentic continuance of the Jesuit tradition.*
   If we do not know our origins, we will have a hard time knowing who we are. We do not create the Jesuit identity "on the spot" or on the basis of one or two moments or documents in the tradition. Ideological or partisan adherences are not enough to provide authentic grounding for Jesuit education. In fact, they would likely simply truncate or distort that very concept.

2. *The importance of the formational attitude within a body of belief.*
   Remember the first rule for the provincial: the point of the education is to achieve a spiritual effect in the souls of the students. It implies a theology of creation and salvation, leaving all other doctrinal details assumed in the background. A distinguishing trait of Ignatius and the early companions' approach to theology is that it was to nourish their souls. It was not simply a professional enterprise, even in the advanced academic professional sphere. There is a sense of community, allegiance, and ethos that transcends the merely academic.

3. *An orientation to thinking about the curriculum as a whole, and a sense of the importance of order and progression in the educational scheme.*
   Our times are especially challenged in this respect. In the RS, things are laid out in stages; one builds in a certain direction, with certain fixed points. Teachers and students know where they are according to a construct, which is, yes, artificial as all educational plans are, but this construct provides a sense of measure and proportion and direction. It also promotes humility since it is harder to have a sense that "I already know it all." No, there are other authors to be encountered, other ideas to be examined, before you can feel that your education is complete. Even then, you stand in some awe of the achievements of great minds and personalities.

4. *An awareness of the worth of particular educational pursuits, namely those of Letters (i.e., language, composition, rhetoric, culture, and literature), philosophy, and theology.*
   These subjects help to define our intellectual horizon, and they can ensure that the larger questions of meaning and purpose in life are not ignored (thus providing an answer to the issue posed by a recent subtitle: *Why Our Colleges and Universities Have Given Up on the Meaning of Life*).[9] Certain authorities are given special attention in the RS, notably Cicero, Aristotle, Aquinas, and scripture. These are long-standing commonly approved standards of excellence that serve to sharpen understanding and create community. The RS can help us focus on a specific core that gets to the heart of humanistic education. Today, we can incorporate a more complex series of focal points, without just abandoning ourselves to "open grazing." But there have to be limitations somewhere. As Ignatius said about prayer: it is the deep relishing, not the coverage of every possible detail, that makes all the difference.[10] There is that guiding maxim, *Non multa, sed multum*: do not aim for coverage of vast amounts of content, but rather for depth in the appreciation and understanding of the important material that is taken up.

   So what are our focal points, who decides them, who develops them, oversees their delivery and its improvement? This is a job for the educational leadership in collaboration and consultation. What if there are no pre-eminent authorities that we all acknowledge today? There is an entire history of pre-eminent authorities from which one can select the authorities and traditions of thought that are more in keeping with the spirit and aims and the concrete unfolding of the Institute. People with the right judgment and authority and commitment will have to be responsible for making the selections and for overseeing their delivery.

5. *The RS highlights the importance of cultural self-appropriation for the students.* These focal points of the tradition are so deeply understood and absorbed that through our study of them we come to know better who we are in a corporate sense. College is for discovering who we are, but not merely in a narcissistic or individualistic way. There is a wider community. *Affiliation* is key, and it is arguably far more important than the much-praised (but fragmentational) value of "diversity." The affiliation to the whole complex that includes the best aims, perceptions, struggles, and hopes of the greatest

---

9 Anthony Kronman, *Education's End: Why Our Colleges and Universities Have Given Up on the Meaning of Life* (New Haven: Yale University Press, 2007).

10 "For what fills and satisfies the soul consists, not in knowing much, but in our understanding the realities profoundly and in savoring them interiorly." George E. Ganss, ed. and trans., *The Spiritual Exercises of Saint Ignatius: A Translation and Commentary* (St. Louis, MO: Institute of Jesuit Sources, 1992), no. 2 (22).

thinkers of the tradition immediately and necessarily opens upon a greater appreciation for diversity while providing for the commonality needed to build an intellectual-spiritual community.

6. *The RS helps us to see the importance of delivering what for the Jesuit educational tradition is the most valuable content.*
   In the Jesuit tradition, there is always an eye to scripture and the Gospel. The fifth rule for the provincial states that "he should very diligently promote the study of sacred texts." This is one of the defining moments that a Jesuit education should help us understand. We need to be sure that students are educated spiritually and religiously, with attention to the dominant specific sources of our tradition.

7. *The RS offers a model for faculty agency and collaboration.*
   The tradition of the RS suggests the value of cooperative investment and ownership by the faculty under the proper leadership: the RS was largely a faculty document that emerged from the contributions of many voices, even though it was promoted, overseen, and promulgated by a central authority. The RS also suggests the importance of lay and Jesuit/Catholic and wider formation since it was not purely a seminary document but one intended to give *all* students the best total formation possible.

Conclusion: A Story and an Experiment

I would like to end by recounting a telling moment from my time as a visiting professor at a Jesuit university. Though I had arrived there for a short stint as a veteran teacher, I was asked to go through the orientation process at the beginning of the year with the rest of the new hires. There, I met a first-year member of my department. At the end of the year, this person had gotten an appointment at another university. Before we parted ways, I asked her for her candid assessment of her experience and the university. She said,

> I am not Catholic, but when we were there in that orientation session and [the Jesuit mission and ministry officer] was speaking about the vision of the school, I was thrilled and I felt that what he was saying was exactly what I wanted. That was what I was looking for. But after that day of orientation—it was exactly like everywhere else.

This is precisely the point: we all can rightly expect that Jesuit schools should be identifiably and self-consciously and concretely different in the day-to-day details, and that difference should be especially known to and communicated by the faculty and the programs. It should be obvious. Ultimately, the faculty has to be the guardian of an organically developing tradition, because the curriculum is in its hands. But faculty members need leadership. And they need to be informed. The RS is a kind of document that used to help to define the features of the school and orient the new faculty on specifics. It is a document that can inspire us to build a new identity, more complex than the schools of the Renaissance, but just as effective in arousing the students to "a knowledge of and love for our Maker and Redeemer."

Thought Experiment on Jesuit, Catholic Identity

If you are working in a Jesuit and Catholic university that is coming to terms with its mission and identity, I propose this thought experiment:

Imagine a loyal, open-minded, faithful, sensible Catholic in your college or university. What specifically do you think would make such a person feel that the school was doing what it could to achieve its essential goals specifically as a Jesuit, Catholic educational institution? What would be such a person's bottom line about the specifics of Jesuit and Catholic identity, that is, what are those particular elements without which there would be no substantial core-difference from secular educational institutions? What is the absolute minimum that such a person would allow for the designation as Jesuit and Catholic to be meaningful with regard to the education? Second, what documents or authorities do you imagine such a person using as the basis of his/her position? And lastly, imagine being part of a team of educators in which everyone had made his or her position known to the rest of the group. Wouldn't that be a good start?

Postscript: The Bottom Line

If someone should ask for my own "bottom line" on the specifics of Jesuit college education, here is what I propose as essential:

At every Jesuit college, there must be guaranteed for each student a mature confrontation with the Jesus Christ of the scriptures. All students should know the contents, meaning, and impact of the scriptural bases of the Christian tradition. I propose this as the one essential, bedrock element of a universal RS for our times. I am not talking about proselytization nor about academic knowledge that explores, for example, the special questions of biblical scholarship. I am more interested in the positive core content, that is, the person and words and mission of Jesus as portrayed and interpreted and lived.

I would proceed to ask: "What are the elements that help us to understand that core better?" Once you have the understanding of the Gospels as a goal, other subjects start to find a place in the curriculum. From the written Gospels that foreground the person of Christ and his identity and mission, you can easily see the need to know how to handle texts and languages and literature; the Hebrew scriptures; Paul and other interpreters of Christianity; theological fields of discourse; rhetoric and hermeneutics; ancient Mediterranean culture; the dynamics of mythical, religious, and historical life and understanding; implications for ethics and politics and economics; questions of God; atheism; evolution; science and faith; questions of meaning and culture and spirituality. In other words, you are quickly brought into the wide range of humanistic, philosophical, and theological studies, including humanistic approaches to science.

Taking the goal as a fully mature understanding of the Gospel and its chief purveyor is the beginning of a very large crystal of human and religious understanding. Jesuit education should allow that crystal to grow steadily. In this way, the school can do both its "evangelizing" and its "general education": the Christian students need an adult understanding of the grounds of their tradition and faith; and even those who profess no religion at all still need to know the foundations of our common culture and so much of our history. Such an education, rightly instituted and maintained, will likely lead to immense contributions to justice and spiritual fulfillment.

2. In the School of Ignatius: Studies, Spirituality, and Service in the Society of Jesus

> The learning acquired in this Society aims at spiritually benefiting its own members and [our] neighbors, on the strength of God's favor. (*Doctrinae quae in hac Societate addiscitur hic scopus sit suis et proximorum animis, Dei favore aspirante, prodesse [...]*)
>
> —The Constitutions of the Society of Jesus, *part 4, chapter 5, no. 1 [351]*

The early Jesuits did not speak of "Jesuit education" but of the "studies of the Society" (*studia Societatis*).[1] This difference is significant. There are two things that need to be distinguished and then properly related to each other: (1) the studies Jesuits undertake in their "academic formation" to prepare themselves for ministry and to reach that state in which they can be approved for a fuller incorporation into the Society; and (2) the education that Jesuits and their helpers undertake to prepare others who are *not* in the Society for those individuals' particular paths in life as part of a larger community of faith and culture. Both of these have been called the *studia Societatis*. Historically, the first of these was underway before the second was formally undertaken.

In this essay, I propose what I hope are direct, handy, and coherent answers to several questions that bear on the Society's studies, spirituality, and service. The first question concerns how the first Society-sponsored school arose. The response will raise other questions that take us back to the academic character of the Society, to its origins in Paris, to features of Ignatius's own particular story and spirituality, and on to important aspects of Christian culture and history. The academic training of Jesuits will be shown to be understandable as spiritually formative of Jesuits, as aboriginally constitutive of the Society, and as essential grounding for the Society's service of caring for souls, a major aspect of which care includes the Society's leadership and maintenance of "Jesuit education." Certain conclusions seem to follow. For the Society to serve effectively and to become what it is, it must give its program of studies a high priority and ongoing, well-deliberated oversight. Correspondingly, for schools to be effectively "Jesuit," they must be organically and robustly linked to the Society's foundations, vision, and leadership.

---

1 This chapter is based on the version that appeared online as "Ignatius at School: Studies, Spirituality, and Service in the Society of Jesus," *New Jesuit Review* 3, no. 12 (2013). The author gratefully acknowledges Fr. Leo Nicoll, S.J., of Loyola University of the South, for his helpful challenges and encouragement.

What Led the Society into Education?

The Society organized its first school for non-Jesuits (Latin *externi*; English *externs*) as a result of requests from civic leaders who wanted to make their community more virtuous and prosperous. The beginning of an organized public kind of "Jesuit education" (as opposed to various *ad hoc* classroom involvements, the adoption of responsibilities in already-established schools, and the creation of "residential colleges" for the training of Jesuit recruits) is usually taken to be the school in Messina (1548). According to the account we have from Pedro de Ribadeneyra (1526–1611), an important early witness to the developmental years of the Society, the school there can be traced to the initiative of Juan de Vega (1507–58), the viceroy of Sicily. It is worth quoting at length the entire passage, as it is rarely reproduced, much less studied:

> Also at that same time, the island of Sicily embraced our Society. James Lhoost, a Fleming of remarkable modesty and learning, first carried our name there. Rodolfo Pío de Carpi, cardinal-protector of our Society and bishop of Agrigento, prevailed upon Ignatius to send James to Agrigento. Jerome Doménech followed him shortly thereafter. Juan de Vega, the viceroy of the Kingdom of Sicily, brought him along in 1547 from Rome, with Ignatius's approval, for his assistance and advice in pastoral administrative matters. These he provided quite amply and comprehensively. Thinking that it would be too little merely to surround his towns with walls and guards, to open the highways after eliminating brigandage, and to establish trust and security in that kingdom, de Vega wanted his subjects' hearts filled with virtue and devotion, and he wanted to make a good start by spreading the divine name. Those other elements just mentioned would be all the more splendid and solid to the extent that they had been set on this stable foundation. Since he had gotten very familiar with Ignatius in Rome and had seen our manner of life and our Institute, he selected for the project those that he thought would be fit for his designs and useful to him.
>
> For longer-lasting results, de Vega used his authority to get the town officials of Messina to seek out Ours and call them in, and to set them up in a permanent residence after the founding of a college. That city—cultured, wealthy, and especially interested in promoting religious life—followed the judgment of this very influential and wise prince: it began to love those whom it had not yet seen, and to desire those who it was hoping, on his word, would be helpful to it. Both the Viceroy de Vega and the city of Messina had written to the pope and to Ignatius about this matter.[2]

2 Pedro de Ribadeneyra, *The Life of Ignatius of Loyola*, trans. Claude Pavur (St. Louis, MO: Institute of Jesuit Sources, 2014), nos. 286–87, slightly adapted here. The original Latin and Spanish texts are found in MHSI 93.

Spiritually rooted ethical, socially implicated conversion was the aim. The presence of the Jesuits was linked with a permanent residence connected with a school. But why not just a residence? The viceroy had not only seen the Society's manner of life but had gotten some familiarity with its "Institute." Educational involvement seemed right not only in terms of the design for moral civic reform but also for the Society's kind of presence. The career of the first companions had already informed the *self-concept*, the *abilities*, and the *undertakings* of the early Society in such a way that later Jesuits both *seemed to others* and *in actuality were* suitable to run a school. Even before the opening of the college in Messina, Jesuits had occasionally taught in the classroom and given scholarly lectures. The way had already been prepared for this development.

Even in terms of its own self-concept, taking up educational work was in fact an altogether natural and organic development in the Society's history. Some kind of readiness to lecture and to teach is already expressed in the earliest official expressions of the Society's chief purpose. The *Formula of the Institute* appeared in the papal bull *Regimini militantis ecclesiae* (1540). There it was stated that the Society's chief purpose was to strive especially for (1) "the progress of souls in Christian life and doctrine" and (2) "the propagation of the faith by the ministry of the word, by spiritual exercises and works of charity, and specifically by the education of children and unlettered persons in Christianity." Note that "doctrine" (in Latin, *doctrina*, i.e., teaching or learning) and "education" are both already mentioned as elements in the core purpose of the Society, though neither expression implies anything like a distinctive network of schools with a specially cultivated system of education; furthermore, in this text, the educational contents are explicitly related to Christianity rather than to a general course of studies.

When the papal bull *Exposcit debitum* (1550) presented the *Formula* in revised form, it reversed the order of the two items and changed the wording a bit to describe the twofold chief purpose of the Society of Jesus: to strive especially (1) "for *the defense and* propagation of the faith" and (2) "for the progress of souls in Christian life and doctrine, by means of public preaching, lectures, and any other ministration whatsoever of the word of God, and further by means of the *Spiritual Exercises*, the education of children and unlettered persons in Christianity, and the spiritual consolation of Christ's faithful through hearing confessions and administering the other sacraments." At this point, it adds: "Moreover, he should show himself ready to reconcile the estranged, compassionately assist and serve those who are in prisons or hospitals, and indeed to perform any other works of charity, according to what will seem expedient for the glory of God and the common good."[3]

---

3 These translations from the original documents and both versions of the *Formula of the Institute* can be found in parallel format in John W. Padberg, S.J., ed., *The Constitutions of the Society of Jesus and Their Complementary Norms: A Complete English Translation of the Official Latin Texts* (St. Louis, MO: Institute of Jesuit Sources, 1996), 3–14.

The education of the members and the educational dimension of their striving are implicit but necessary components here; later, they are made explicit in both versions of the *Formula*. They are necessary because both parts of the Society's "chief purpose" demand solid learning, received and communicated. Even catechetical instruction involves concepts that call for understanding and explication beyond rote learning. In fact, memorization itself is often oriented toward giving the students a handle on basic concepts. It is one thing merely to list the holy days of obligation, another to understand the meaning of what is being celebrated on those days, and yet another to begin to understand the concepts involved in answers to questions like the following: What is venial sin? What are virtues? What are sacraments? What are the gifts of the Holy Spirit? What is meant by revelation? What are the sources of authentic church teaching? Nor could the other essential tasks of *defending and propagating the faith* succeed on the basis of prayer or naïve scripture-reading alone. Explicating what is believed and defending one's beliefs from real or possible adversaries both demand some reliance upon studies, some serious engagement with languages, rhetorical skill, a learned tradition, and an accurate knowledge of terms and concepts and their usages, along with practice in using those terms in disputation.

Thus the apostolic orientations and the self-understanding of the Society from the very beginning required a certain kind of educational investment. At that time, theological competence was not typically certifiable without some prior study in philosophy, which itself depended on a background in "Letters," or a study of classical languages and literature through courses of grammar, the humanities, and rhetoric. Conscientiously operating along a tripartite structure of Letters, philosophy, and theology, the Society eventually found itself managing a large-scale enterprise that was to have wide cultural and religious impact.[4] Its own program for formation—and the plan it instituted for its schools—ended up replicating the broad lines of Ignatius's own academic path. One easily senses a deep connection here: it was Ignatius's turn to academic work that made all the difference in the Society's character, self-understanding, and apostolic choices. And these were all part of a much larger web.

What Had Led Ignatius to Studies?

The main proximate reason for Ignatius's emphasis on studies was the desire to serve the church and his neighbor, especially in *cura animarum*, the care of souls.

4 The triad of Letters–philosophy–theology has ancient roots: Philo Judaeus (*c.*20 BCE–*c.*50 CE) set a hierarchical pattern for early Christian understanding: "The liberal arts should serve philosophy, which should itself serve the revealed wisdom of Scripture." See Stephen B. Brown, "Theology and Philosophy," in *Medieval Latin: An Introduction and Bibliographical Guide*, ed. F. A. C. [Frank Anthony Carl] Mantello and A. G. [Arthur George] Rigg (Washington, DC: Catholic University of America Press, 1996), 267–87, here 273.

This would involve understanding the spiritual life, the dynamics of virtues and vices, the graces of Christ and the church. Passionately involved in the ministry of the Word in various forms (particularly that of spiritual conversation), Ignatius soon found that he needed to attain a formal and public credibility in matters touching on the faith. It was a time of such turmoil in the church that this should not have appeared to him to be an unusual expectation. He was, after all, making an implicit claim to authority by operating as a kind of spiritual guide, instructor, adviser, or director. He therefore desired the church's seal of approval to support his ministry of the Word and to keep himself free from suspicion.

Some may say that Ignatius's turn to studies was merely a "second best," occurring after the failure of his Jerusalem venture (1523–24), his primary apostolic dream being to spend the rest of his days in the Holy Land converting souls and strengthening them in faith. But this view is problematic. He did not jettison the Jerusalem project until much later, after his studies had been completed, when the early companions had waited in Venice for a year to make that journey (1537). Second, Ignatius may have been interested in studies even before his journey to the Holy Land: we read, for example, that he had put "his books" on a ship that he did not finally board.[5] What were these books? They were being carried to the Holy Land by Ignatius at a time when he was cultivating poverty scrupulously, so any possessions he had must have been considered essential. In addition, Ignatius's early attention to the literary world (before and after his wounding at the battle at Pamplona in 1521), his eagerness to write his own handbook of spiritual exercises, and the tradition of the educated courtier from which he came—all these suggest an early disposition toward the "world of Letters" and educated discourse (the term "Letters" here standing as a synonym for education).[6] In addition, there was a larger context whose point of view Ignatius could not have escaped: the age-old church perspective on the nature and value of studies. This understanding would have been reinforced by any learned clergy he had met along the way in the role of preachers or confessors or counselors (for example, the Dominicans in Manresa).

Why Did the Church Think Credibility Could or Should Be Attained This Way?

Reformation movements heightened the need for oversight and for credentialing. Oversight traditionally fell within the purview of the bishop (*episkopos*; "overseer"); credentialing had long been done through the medieval institution

---

5 Ribadeneyra, *Life of Ignatius*, no. 61.

6 For the topic of the "educated knight," see Martin Aurell's *Le chevalier lettré: Savoir et conduite de l'aristocratie aux XIIe et XIIIe siècles* (Paris: Fayard, 2011); Jean-Charles Khalifa and Jeremy Price, eds., *The Lettered Knight: Knowledge and Aristocratic Behaviour in the Twelfth and Thirteenth Centuries* (Budapest: Central European University Press, 2017).

of the university. But there is a larger background here too: education ("Letters" in the larger sense) and *ethos* were linked from the times of ancient Greece's *paideia*, and then in both the rhetorical and the philosophical traditions that spread throughout the tri-continental Mediterranean sphere. They were also interconnected from the times of ancient Judaism, when study of the Torah accompanied and promoted righteousness. The Renaissance humanism that was coming into full flower in Ignatius's day famously championed the ethical, civic, and spiritual values of the right kind of attention to the *bonae litterae*, "good letters" (i.e., ethically relevant humanistic rather than technical writings, or written discourse that offered students personal improvement). Furthermore, there is a simple widespread, commonsense, perennial line of logic that connects *authenticity of life* with a *correct understanding of reality*, correct understanding of reality with *informed reflection*, and informed reflection with a *conscientious study of authorities or models and a testing of ideas*. In Judeo-Christian traditions, the dynamics of revelation and transcendence have often collaborated with those of immanence and reason.

How Did Ignatius (and Later the Society) Understand Studies?

Given this long-standing cultural heritage and the assumptions of his age, did Ignatius perhaps understand that studies might not only give him *formal credibility* in the eyes of theological authorities, a pathway to his preferred apostolate of helping souls, but also *in themselves* actually advance him spiritually and thereby improve the quality of his apostolic performance or versatility or effectiveness? Were studies not just an extrinsic institutional "filter" established to weed out confusion, heresy, misrepresentations, and oversimplifications—not just a path to theological conformity, but part of *a positive way to God*, toward a greater spiritual breadth and depth of understanding, and therefore also toward a greater capacity to help others? Did they enhance the spiritual life that he was living? Were they a way to come into consonance with the church and into greater communion with God's Spirit and his will? Were the studies in themselves, done correctly, *authentic spiritual formation*, just as Ignatius's early mystical experiences had been, although studies had to involve different dynamics and procedures, "natural means" rather than "supernatural" ones?

The history suggests that the answer is yes. It is true that Ignatius had to struggle to "turn off" the distractions of certain spiritual insights during his academic efforts and that this might indicate some kind of disjunction between study and the spiritual life, but any idea of a dichotomy is misleading. There is very good reason why the German word for "spiritual," namely *geistlich* (related to the word *Geist* as in *der Heilige Geist*, the Holy Spirit), can also refer to events of intellect, interiority, and cultural creativity. Since the "spiritual" is not at all foreign to what happens in the domain of culture or Letters or intellectual-academic formation, it would be quite misleading to set up any complete opposition between the two terms. Letters can form, inform, express, and motivate the soul. Athens, Jerusalem, and Rome all agree on this. The Latin phrase used to describe both a leading experience of the early Society and a desideratum for all the members of later times, *unio animorum*, can be translated as "the union of minds and hearts." Likewise, the Latin word *sententia* suggests feeling (*sensus*) as well as intellectual judgment.[7]

We must remember that the earliest Society of Jesus did not aim most for *pietas* (a devoted goodness) but for "docta" *pietas* (a *learned* devoted goodness). Hence the fullest level of profession for priests in the Society, for almost all of its history, required advanced academic achievement:[8] "If there were any doubt about St. Ignatius' attitude towards scholarship, it would be dispelled by the fact that he founded a Society in which definitive and full-fledged admission (the solemn profession) is restricted to men who give proof of knowledge ('outstanding and choice') of both philosophy and theology."[9]

It is significant that the formula for the highest possible level of profession in the Society includes, immediately after the mention of the vows constitutive of religious life, a promise to have special care for the education of the young: "(I vow [...]) perpetual poverty, chastity, and obedience in the Society of Jesus, and, moreover, special care of the instruction of youth." The spiritual coadjutors as well vow a "special care of the instruction of youth." Note that these formulae do not explicitly limit instruction to religious or catechetical teaching. Furthermore, the academic trappings of birettas and the title *magister* (master) were significant markers in its early years. It is *prima facie* extremely unlikely that the founders' were interested in badges and distinctions that they perceived to be "worldly." Thus it was that the order that had been founded entirely by individuals who happened to be studying for advanced degrees at the University of

7 For the physiological basis of the mind–feelings connection, see António Damásio, *Descartes' Error: Emotion, Reason, and the Human Brain* (New York: G. P. Putnam, 1994).

8 One eyewitness of mid-twentieth-century Society life in the United States, Fr. Thomas Joseph Casey, S.J. (1927–2018) of the Missouri province, told the author that for the full profession of the four vows, the Society in effect required the equivalent of a doctoral degree. This was a general rule to which there might be occasional exceptions. Further testimony to the Society's high-pitched academic self-concept can be found in the well-known case of Fr. Joseph Fichter, S.J. (1908–94) of the New Orleans province. Not having the requisite academic credentials for formation in the New York province, it is said, he went to the South where the requirements were less stringent. Having gone through the "short course" (a less rigorous curriculum than the "long course" that was typically prerequisite for full profession), Fichter died not as one of the "fully professed" but as a "spiritual coadjutor"—even after he had held the Chauncey Stillman Chair of Catholic Studies at Harvard University (1965–70) and had written many books and articles in the field of sociology.

9 Miguel Bernad, "The Ignatian Way in Education," *Philippine Studies* 4, no. 2 (1956): 195–214, here 206.

Paris soon found itself staffing colleges that became "the principal centers for all Jesuit ministry."[10] Such practices and such a history are quite telling. They point to *something essential in the idea of the Society*.[11]

What Is the Larger History of Ignatius's Connection with "the World of Letters or Education"?

Early in his converted life (and likely before it), Ignatius was already hearing sermons preached by people who had been well educated. He presumably had the occasion to converse with religious and confessors and fellow-believers who stood at various levels of literacy and academic experience. So even the Ignatius of Manresa was not outside the sphere of the church's investment in studies as something consonant with and supportive of Christian spirituality.

In addition, consider the implications that passages such as the following have for the status of the *intellectual* aspects of Ignatius's mystical experiences:

> One day as he was standing on the steps of the stairs into the Dominican church, reciting the Office of the Blessed Virgin, his *understanding* was so carried away into God that it was as if he could perceive the Most Holy Trinity in some kind of visible form that represented externally what he was *understanding* internally. This happened with such overflowing abundance of divine consolation that he could not keep from sighing and weeping even during the public prayers that he went on to attend, all the way to the midday meal. After that meal, he could not refrain from thinking or talking about anything other than the Most Holy Trinity, *with such a variety and number of reasons, comparisons, and examples* that he became an object of wonder to everyone who listened to him.[12]

Reason, comparisons, examples—these put us in the domain of discursive thought rather than mystical silence. Ignatius himself parallels studies and spiritual illuminations when he wants to mark out as especially distinctive his mystical vision at the Cardoner River:

> Moreover, this *mental illumination* was so abundant and advanced that Ignatius himself claimed that all the rest of the illuminations and divine helps that he had gotten from God throughout his life to his sixty-second year heaped up into one, could not be compared with this single one. He said that *whatever he had learned at other times, either by study or effort or supernatural light* was less than what he received at that moment.[13]

---

10 John W. O'Malley, *The First Jesuits* (Cambridge, MA: Harvard University Press, 1993), 206.

11 For a fuller corroboration and development of this idea, see chapter 5, "The *Ratio studiorum* of 1599: Inescapably Foundational."

12 Ribadeneyra, *Life of Ignatius*, no. 41. Emphasis added.

13 Ibid., no. 45. Emphasis added.

The point here is that he does not say that it was *outside* of learning or *beyond* all reasoning, but an especially great experience of illumination compared with other illuminations he had gotten. He is using the same "scale," as it were, not saying that the scale makes no difference in this case.

Books and reading were significantly implicated in Ignatius's conversion, particularly Ludolph of Saxony's (*c.*1295–1378) *Life of Christ* and Jacobus de Voragine's (1228/30–98) *The Golden Legend.* We might instinctively tend to put these texts at an altogether "non-scholarly" level in modern discourse, assuming that they were narrative entertainments that are popular and pietistic, even folkloristic—and not at all academic and intellectual. Perhaps we might think that they were light and fanciful creative works written primarily for edification. But the categories of that time allowed "Letters" to cover quite a wide range of material, and the lines were not drawn as we might draw them now. Books of "legends" were not merely that, as we might read them now. Consider, for example, the opening of de Voragine's *Golden Legend:* "The whole time-span of this present life comprises four distinct periods: the time of deviation or turning form the right way, the time of renewal or of being called back, the time of reconciliation, and the time of pilgrimage."[14]

The first section also begins with a larger vision in mind: "The Lord's advent is celebrated for four weeks to signify that his coming is fourfold: he came to us in the flesh, he comes into our hearts, he comes to us at death, and he will come to judge us."[15]

Such passages suggest that the text involves real learning and reflection, and they invite the reader to enter upon the same. We are beyond fables and folklore here. As for the other work that impressed Ignatius in 1521, I cite a well-known expert's description: Ludolph's *Vita* was "profound and scholarly."[16]

Thus in at least one sense Ignatius's "scholarship" began long before he got to Paris. In any case, "Letters" were intimately bound up with the very first appearances of Ignatian spirituality. Even his memory of the romances of chivalry that he could not get as his preferred reading during his recovery was part of his story: books, reading, imaginative mental activities were not something separate from guiding ideals and life-choices. It was in the wake of reading Ludolph and de Voragine that Ignatius was moved to take an organized and thoughtful approach in the little book that he began to write as a new convert, the *Spiritual Exercises*, which he organized around the idea of four weeks. De Voragine's attention to the four periods and four weeks mentioned above suggests that Ignatius's own spiritual writings are at least partly derivative of his reading and study. If so, he was

---

14 Jacobus de Voragine, *The Golden Legend: Readings on the Saints*, trans. William Granger Ryan (Princeton: Princeton University Press, 1993), 1:3.

15 Ibid., 1:4.

16 George Ganss, ed., *Ignatius of Loyola: The Spiritual Exercises and Selected Works* (New York: Paulist Press, 1991), 19.

not working simply from his spiritual experiences, introspection, and personal ascetical journey. Certainly, the intellectual, systematic, philosophical elements of the "Contemplation for Attaining a Love for God" and those of the "First Principle and Foundation" were considered by the author to be quite at home in the pilgrim's little book of spiritual exercises.[17]

How Did the Faith-Tradition Shape Ignatius's Mentality Regarding Studies and Spirituality?

Ignatius's vision does not emerge in a vacuum. The intellectual tradition in the church was a large and perduring one, with many representatives following Justin Martyr (100–65) and Clement of Alexandria (150–215) in the second century to Ignatius's own day. The long monastic era was closely connected with libraries, the production of good manuscripts, and the careful study and spiritual appropriation of texts, particularly scriptural ones. Outside of monasteries, the Franciscans and Dominicans cultivated advanced thinking. The former had produced Bonaventure (1221–74) and the latter Thomas Aquinas (1225–74). In Ignatius's day, Erasmus's (1466–1536) *Enchiridion* and the older, widely read *The Imitation of Christ* were both contemporary models of "formation through letters." Ignatius greatly favored the latter, but he never said that the former was without merit.

Some might resist the general applicability of this point and assert the existence of a definite and strong "anti-Letters" tradition in the Christian spiritualities of the West—God's foolishness (1 Cor. 1:25) exceeding all human intelligence and capacity. But surely this has been to a considerable extent a question of avoiding the pride and errors of intellectualist, rationalist, gnostic, secularistic, or sophistical extremes rather than a wholesale condemnation of all literary and scholarly means of communicating and expanding upon the Gospel. Christianity, "religion of the Book" that it is, would not have gone very far without "Letters." It was immersed in them from the beginning.

Jesus himself, though his uncomprehending opponents at one point say he is not educated (John 7:15),[18] was remembered as always having the scriptures on his lips, from his time of temptations in the desert (Luke 4) right down to his citation of Psalm 31:5 on the cross: "Into thy hands I commend my spirit: thou hast redeemed me, O Lord, the God of truth" (Douay–Rheims version, cf. Luke 23:46). His great summary teaching on love of God and neighbor are direct citations from the scriptures (Deut. 6:4–5 and Lev. 19:18). Even after his

17 For example, on the Principle and Foundation, see Ganss, *Spiritual Exercises*, 148–50, where he stresses that this text is a foundational *thought* for Ignatius and from it flow various *conclusions*.

18 They "were astonished at it, saying, 'How does this man have such learning [*or* "know his letters"], when he has never been taught?'" (John 7:15, NRSVCE).

resurrection, he expounds the scriptures on the way to Emmaus (Luke 24:27). We can most reasonably assume that Jesus's first thirty years before his public ministry included significant study of sacred literature. Yes, "the letter kills, but the Spirit gives life" (2 Cor. 3:6)— but Paul, great student of the Torah and the prophets and the Writings, did not hesitate to express that insight in letters with spiritual aims in mind, and with great spiritual benefits as a result.

In any case, Ignatius's conversion did not at all dispose him to jettison his inclinations toward the importance of Letters. Long after he had passed from the scene in 1556, his own understanding of studies was reflected in the first rules for Jesuit students in the *Ratio studiorum* (1599):

> [434] Jesuit students should try above all to guard their purity of heart and to keep a right intention in studies, seeking in them nothing other than God's glory and spiritual benefit of souls [*nihil aliud in his nisi divinam gloriam et animarum fructum quaerentes*]; and in their own prayers, they should frequently ask for the grace to progress in learning so that one day, finally fit [*idonei*], they may go to cultivate the vineyard of Christ our Lord by their example and learning in just the way that the Society hopes of them.
> [435] They should resolve to apply their minds earnestly and resolutely to their studies. And as they should be mindful that they ought to keep the fervor of studies from dampening their love of the essential virtues and religious life, so they should persuade one another in turn that they are going to do nothing more pleasing to God in the colleges than if they apply themselves diligently to their studies with that intention about which we have spoken. And even if they never come to employ those things that they have learned, they should fix firmly in their hearts the conviction that the very labor of their study, undertaken out of due obedience and charity, must be of great merit in the sight of the divine and supreme Majesty.[19]

We can be sure that we are getting Ignatius's own mind here, in these citations from the *Ratio studiorum* of 1599, because the words have been largely taken from the *Constitutions*; if Ignatius did not directly compose the following paragraphs, he certainly approved them:

> [360] 1. In order to make good progress in these subjects, the scholastics should strive first of all to keep their souls pure and their intention in studying right, by seeking in their studies nothing except the glory of God and the good of souls. Moreover, they should frequently beg in prayer for grace to make progress in learning for the sake of this end.
> [361] 2. Next they should have a firm resolution to be genuine and earnest students, persuading themselves that while they are in the colleges they

19 Adapted slightly from Claude Pavur, trans., *The* Ratio studiorum: *The Official Plan for Jesuit Education* (St. Louis, MO: Institute of Jesuit Sources, 2005), nos. 434–35.

> cannot do anything more pleasing to God our Lord than to study with the intention mentioned above; likewise, that even if they never have occasion to employ the matter studied, the very toil of study, duly undertaken because of charity and obedience, is itself a very meritorious work in the sight of the Divine and Supreme Majesty.[20]

Studies themselves are a work of obedience and charity, the most pleasing service of God that the students can be accomplishing at that time. The academic efforts do not have to be somehow "combined" with something else in order to be accounted as service. What is being learned may be employed in a variety of apostolic labors to come, but even if not, the students have at that moment of study the opportunity to be doing something of merit, something for God's glory and for the good of others.

We find this vision completely coherent with what Ignatius told the scholastics at Coimbra:

> And do not imagine that during this interval of studies you are not being useful to your neighbor. Over and above the advantage to yourself (which is demanded by well-ordered charity: "Have pity on your own soul, fearing God" [Sir. 30:14]), you are serving God's honor and glory in many ways.[21]

Ignatius goes on to name four of these. The first way is the significance of their effort to prepare themselves for the service of their neighbors. If they offer themselves to God for the sake of their neighbor, they "might well be as much an instrument for helping the neighbor as [they] would through preaching or hearing confessions." Second, by becoming virtuous and good they are creating the necessary condition for helping neighbors to be good: "While you personally advance in every virtue, you are also greatly serving your neighbor." Third, they are giving the good example of their lives. Fourth, they are serving by their holy desires and prayers: even their academic labors undertaken for the service of God become a continual kind of prayer.

These passages do not so explicitly say that the very *contents* of the studies themselves are designed to change one's soul and bring one closer to God, only that one can pursue them with a sanctifying intention for the greater glory of God and the good of souls. The studies seem an important subsidiary means that will assist spiritual endeavors. But it is hard to see how this happens unless the connection between studies and service is not merely extrinsic or utilitarian, or simply one means by which to achieve an ascetical self-renunciation for the

---

20 Cited from the *Constitutions* 4, chapter 6, which is entitled "Means for Their Learning Well the Aforementioned Subjects."

21 For the citations given in this paragraph, see John W. Padberg and John L. McCarthy, eds., *Ignatius of Loyola: Letters and Instructions*, trans. Martin E. Palmer (St. Louis, MO: Institute of Jesuit Sources, 2006), 173–74.

sake of God's will. If knowing these studies can be used to good spiritual effect in helping others, they must also contain something wholesome for the students themselves. Could the "crown" of Jesuit education, theology, possibly be a merely indifferent thing, with no positive formational force for arousing the hearts and minds of the student to a greater love of the Creator and Redeemer (cf. *Ratio studiorum*, no. 7)? This is quite unlikely. Jesuit academic formation is rather better understood as an integral and vital part of the individual's spiritual formation, part of a larger apostolic dynamism and a service-oriented program.

The citation from the *Constitutions* (no. 351) used as the epigraph to this essay underlines the fact that Jesuit studies do look to spiritual benefits for the scholastics and for others: "The learning acquired in this Society aims at spiritually benefiting its own members and [our] neighbors, on the strength of God's favor." In sum, then, the studies are supposed to be good *both* for the scholars' souls *and* the souls of others. Any valid understanding of Jesuit education must build on this foundation.

What Is the Point of This Exposition?

In this essay, we have at the very least raised and started to answer some basic questions about the meaning and situation of the Society's program of studies, and we have brought forth various *loci classici* that bear on the answers. There seems to be enough of a basis to support this provisional conclusion: studies are spiritually formative and a central, aboriginally constitutive interest of the Society, both serving others in the labor of *cura animarum* and integrating itself and all those souls more deeply into a communion of hearts and minds in the church. Such an understanding is amply borne out by the history of the Society's investment in studies: this investment has led to the creation of a vastly influential tradition in Christian education, one organically linked with the larger web of the spiritual and intellectual traditions of the church. Part 4 of the Jesuit *Constitutions* speaks to this same point about the integral status of studies in the Society. Jesuits therefore must take their educational pursuits with utter seriousness in order to be who they are. They must know clearly what they are doing with the studies and how essential those studies are to their Institute.

Pope Benedict XVI (r.2005–13) highlighted this vision of the Society in an address that included this comment: "Naturally, the effort to promote a culture inspired by Gospel values in cordial collaboration with the other ecclesial realities demands an intense spiritual and cultural training. For this very reason, St. Ignatius wanted young Jesuits to be formed for many years in spiritual life and in study."[22] Service of the "urgent needs" of the church through "culture" (including philosophy and theology) and service of culture through the apostolate of

22 From the homily of Pope Benedict XVI, St. Peter's Basilica, Rome, April 22, 2006, at a Mass celebrating the Jubilee of Ignatius, Favre, and Xavier.

education—these are what Pope Benedict sees in the distinctive legacy of the Society. The educational dimensions (formational and apostolic) cannot be displaced or diminished if the Society is to remain what it is and render the service that the church expects of it.

A certain art and discernment and administrative prudence are needed, because if education can be (and ought to be) *formative* then it can certainly also be, when badly managed, *de-formative.* Scribes can be pharisees, and distortive, manipulative partisan or ideological dogmatism can emerge from any direction. Studies are not simply valuable in the abstract as such: they must be the right kinds of studies, taught in the right way, by the right kinds of purveyors, with the right kinds of intentions on all sides, and with the right kinds of self-correcting oversight. The Society could easily end up doing greater harm precisely where it is trying to do the greater good. Much is at stake. The educational apostolate and the formational studies that integrally support it deserve the Society's best attention, its best thinking, its best efforts, particularly now in this age of massive cultural confusion. There is much to be sifted. Quality material has to be gathered, vetted, cultivated, promoted, established, and set in the right proportions into an educational scheme—not for the sake of a new sacred and untouchable canon, but rather for the sake of the quality formation that is so necessary. An ongoing oversight is needed for updating, for the addition of new topics, for any necessary re-proportioning of the existing ones, and for the prevention of the adulteration or loss of essential contents and for the assurance of good management in their delivery.

The Society of Jesus faces great challenges now, and its response necessarily affects all its helpers and allies. The internal structures that have long supported both the formation of Jesuits and the Society's leadership of the educational apostolate are gone, or at least transformed beyond recognition. Juniorates, philosophates, and theologates do not exist as such any more, *qua* Jesuit formational entities with their own locations and governing faculties, procedures, and curricula under the guidance of Society leadership. *De facto*, at least in the United States, the period of Letters has been suppressed as a dedicated, integral period of formation; philosophy is often "out-sourced" to what is available *ad hoc* or elsewhere on campus; and theology is now studied not in "theologates" as such, but in consortial theology centers that hire faculty "on the open market" and look not so much to Jesuit formation *per se* but *ad extra* to many other aspects and needs of the church at large.

Undeniably, some goods, some advantages over the old system have been achieved by these innovations—and others have been quite lost. Jesuits in formation now learn from a wider range of faculties in which many professors may be quite excellent without having any direct investment in or understanding of or care about the Jesuit academic formational project or a standing place in a well-thought-out curricular program. So it is quite a fair question to ask if perhaps the pendulum has not swung too far the other way, into "openness" and "diversity" and "inclusion" and electives and an overall lack of definition. There is also the value of what might be called the canon of specificity: "Furthermore, it is good to determine in detail the books which should be lectured on and those which should not, both in the humanities and in the other faculties" (*Constitutions*, part 4, chapter 5, E [359]). The union of minds and hearts depends greatly upon shared points of reference, shared curricula, shared teachers, shared educational experiences in the context of stable programs that can be reviewed and improved by knowledgeable administrators, year after year.

The existence of specific formational structures in a more traditional shape does not necessarily suggest a radical, so-called "monastic" separation from the wider academic world or a lack of openness to partners in teaching or in learning. In fact, the Society's traditional "in-house" way of arranging a course of studies merely accepts the *standard secular norms used by professionals everywhere to train their own next generations.* To establish a professional school means setting up a distinctive course of studies managed by the same kinds of professionals and a set of norms geared to certain specific ends. The contents of the program cannot be determined primarily by a general principle of inclusion and democratic representation and "diversity." The Society is not really collaborating well with the world—or with "reason"—if it discounts this well-approved and widespread sensible *secular* arrangement. The non-existence of such formational structures as the ones just mentioned, however, is a cause for concern for the mission and identity of the Society of Jesus, for its helpers and allies, and for its leadership in the educational apostolate. At this critical time, the Society is called to attempt to build a new consensus, on the strength of God's favor, with a deeper, more informed awareness of the nature of its Institute and of the place of studies in it. Indeed, the service of the people of God demands it.

3. The Curriculum Carries the Mission: The *Ratio studiorum*, the Making of Jesuit Education, and the Making of the Society of Jesus

> It may be possible to study together without being able to go on the way together.
> It may be possible to go on the way together without being able to take a stand together.
> It may be possible to take a stand together without being able to plan together.
>
> —*Confucius,* Analects *9:31*[1]

It is a remarkable achievement of planning together, that famous Jesuit document known as the *Ratio studiorum* (abbreviated hereafter as RS).[2] For hundreds of years, it helped a larger community to study together, to go on the way together, and to take a stand together. Yet its full importance as a device for achieving a greater union of minds and hearts has long been underestimated. Against the widespread neglect, I will show that the RS in fact represents something that is quite integral to the charism of the Jesuit order, and I will propose an important way in which it can even today provide something of great value to both Catholic and secular higher education. I believe that in a certain way the RS is not only not antiquated but still beyond us.

Historical Context and Content

The full title of the document is the *Ratio atque institutio studiorum Societatis Iesu*. This might be translated as "The Official Plan for Jesuit Education."[3] It can be considered to be one of the great early achievements of the Jesuit order. I say early, because even though it was not issued until 1599, it had already been about fifty and more years in the making. The first Jesuit school had opened in Messina, Sicily, in 1548, eight years after the foundation of the order. By the time Ignatius died in 1556, there were thirty-nine colleges operating or soon to be operating under the care of the Society. These institutions were equivalent to American

1 Thomas Cleary, trans., *The Essential Confucius: The Heart of Confucius' Teachings in Authentic I Ching Order; A Compendium of Ethical Wisdom* (San Francisco: HarperOne, 1993), 131.

2 This essay has been adapted from the Edmund F. Miller, S.J., Lecture delivered at John Carroll University on March 26, 2008.

3 Claude Pavur, trans., *The* Ratio studiorum: *The Official Plan for Jesuit Education* (St. Louis, MO: Institute of Jesuit Sources, 2005).

high schools augmented by the first two years of a college curriculum. Those colleges that went on to add philosophy and theology faculties approached something that paralleled our universities. Two centuries brought the number of Jesuit educational institutions around the world to a total of eight hundred. Thus the Society was averaging four new or adopted schools per year before the suppression of 1773.

Every time a new school was started, it had to have a plan by which it would be run, that is, a *ratio*, a way of doing things. The Jesuits had to become quite adept at borrowing, inventing, adapting, and sharing principles and rules and structures that helped them to manage their schools well. After much sifting, they gathered what they had found to work best in most cases. The RS is the grand culmination of their experience, their reflections, and their well-considered judgments. The text stands as a kind of official guide-book for the running of Jesuit schools. It contains sets of rules for administrators, teachers, and students, and also for the management of the various grades, individual classes, and study-clubs. It offers directives about how to hold examinations, public disputations, and contests; what books and authors to study, and in what order; what the school day should be like; when the vacations will be; under what conditions students should be admitted or dismissed; and similar matters.

Rooted in Ignatius's Life

We can trace the germ of the idea of the RS back much earlier than the 1548 school in Messina to the person of Ignatius himself. First of all, he himself had a radically educational self-concept. We may think of Ignatius under the titles of ex-courtier, religious founder, retreat master, spiritual guide, beggar, pilgrim, evangelist, spiritual searcher, psychologically astute administrator, dedicated man of the church, mystic, ascetic, and saint, but he always carried another identity as well: student and learner. Fr. Howard Gray (1930–2018) has written about how "education for Ignatius antedated [his years of schooling] and persisted until his death."[4] He cites Ignatius's description of his months at Manresa as a time when

> God was dealing with him in the same way a schoolteacher deals with a child while instructing him. This was because either he was thick and dull of brain, or because of the firm will that God had implanted in him to serve him—but he clearly recognized and has always recognized that it was in this way that God dealt with him.[5]

---

4 Howard Gray, S.J., "The Experience of Ignatius Loyola: Background to Jesuit Education," in *The Jesuit* Ratio studiorum: *400th Anniversary Perspectives*, ed. Vincent J. Duminuco, S.J. (New York: Fordham University Press, 2000), 2.

5 Joseph N. Tylenda, S.J., trans., *Ignatius Loyola, a Pilgrim's Journey; The Autobiography of Ignatius Loyola* (Wilmington, DE: Michael Glazier, 1985), no. 27, 35–36. Cited by Gray, "Experience of Ignatius Loyola," 2.

If Ignatius always thought of God as a kind of educator leading him through a learning process, treating him as a schoolteacher does a child, then the educational metaphor is an integral part of his understanding of his nascent spirituality. This in itself would not necessary lead to the establishment of schools as a primary apostolic venture in the religious order that he would later found, but it may help us see why he so enthusiastically undertook such an apostolate when the opportunity arose. In his biography, we can identify two key moments that contributed to his vision: (1) when he saw that education was necessary for him to help souls, and (2) when he realized that a more ordered approach to education is far preferable to the alternative. When you put this self-concept and these insights together with the founding of the Society, you have the seeds of the RS.

Ignatius began to get the first idea, that education was necessary for him to help souls, when he was enthusiastically conversing with people about the spiritual life, largely on the basis of his own deep spirituality and the illuminations he had begun to receive after his conversion in 1521. He had a tremendous impact on other people because of his charismatic personality and his inner fire. Yet he had completed no course of training in theology, and it was a time of increasingly embittered religious controversy, the time of the reformers. Who, then, was to say this ex-nobleman-become-beggar was an authentic spokesperson for the church? What authority had reviewed his instruction and approved it? Ignatius found himself imprisoned, under suspicion, repeatedly forced to defend himself. He became increasingly convinced that he simply had to acquire solid academic credentials to win acceptance as a trustworthy guide in important spiritual questions. In fact, even before he had gotten embroiled in difficulties with the authorities in Alcalà and Salamanca, he had already realized that education was important for his spiritual ministry, and that insight had led him to enroll in a grammar school in 1524 in Barcelona, when he was in his early thirties. Grammar school was where you went to learn Latin grammar, and Latin was the *sine qua non* of intellectual, ecclesiastical, and cultural life in Western Europe at that time. Making a great effort, Ignatius eventually acquired enough understanding of the language and literature to begin his higher educational studies.

The second idea, that of the greater value of an ordered approach to learning, came to Ignatius through reflection on his experiences at the universities of Alcalà, Salamanca, and Paris. He discovered that what he called the "Parisian method" got him further along faster and it gave him a real mastery of the material. In Spain, at the universities of Alcalà and Salamanca, he had tried to do everything all at once. Soon, he felt that things were going nowhere for him academically. So he pulled back and made another start by going back to study the fundamentals of the humanities. One of his early biographers, Pedro de Ribadeneyra, summarized it this way:

> In Spain, responding to the advice of certain people and driven on by a kind of longing to help souls more expeditiously, he undertook a course of studies that was not very organized. He leapt into the study of logic, philosophy, and theology all at the same time. That headlong charge brought him a long delay. For this reason, to correct his pace by slowing it down, he first entrusted himself to good Latin instructors at the College of Montaigu to be retrained. He spent almost two years in that study. Then, sufficiently fluent in Latin, he entered the philosophy course in the year 1529, and he finished it quite successfully.[6]

Later, Ribadeneyra says that Ignatius put this experience at the service of those who were to follow him in the Society:

> At the start he took up many subjects at the same time, jumbling everything together. He wisely took precautions that this should not happen to us by ensuring that our studies would have nothing either out of order or chopped up or truncated. Everything was to be done correctly and in order. For precisely where he himself suffered and where he was challenged, he learned to help those who are being challenged.[7]

Here, Ribadeneyra directly connects the Society's studies with Ignatius's experience.

Like the *Exercises*

The RS also expresses Ignatius in another way: it reflects many of the characteristics and basic values that we find in the *Spiritual Exercises*. These works are twin products of the same interiority. First, both texts can be called pedagogical and both employ exercises as a way to sure improvement. The retreatant or student must engage in activity, repetitive activity, that yields deepening experience or progressive expertise. Second, the *Exercises* and the *Ratio* are divided into discrete, successive stages that are not to be mixed up. The *Exercises* has its four progressive weeks, and the *Ratio* gives us a definite movement from Letters to philosophy to theology. Each part has its own specific goal, and this is made explicit in both documents.

Third, there is both structure and freedom: one should be as faithful as possible to the exercises as they are laid out, but there is some leeway for creativity

6 Pedro de Ribadeneyra, *The Life of Ignatius of Loyola*, trans. Claude Pavur (St. Louis, MO: Institute of Jesuit Sources, 2014), no. 96. For the original Latin for this and the following citation, see *Vita Ignatii Loyolae*, Monumenta Historica Societatis Iesu, series quarta, vol. 93, Fontes Narrativi de Sancto Ignatio de Loyola et de Societatis Iesu Initiis, Vita Ignatii Loyolae, vol. 4, ed. Cándido de Dalmases, S.J. (Rome: Monumenta Historica Societatis Iesu, 1965): 206, 208.

7 Ibid., no. 98.

and choice, both on the parts of the director and retreatant and on the parts of the teacher and student. There is oversight, but there is also a range of ways of realizing the goals, the principle of adapting things to person, places, and times.

Fourth, there is great attention to details. In the *Exercises*, Ignatius talks about bodily position in prayer, diet, acts of reverence, and so on. In the *Ratio*, details fill the book, about the contents of classes, the particular Latin grammar to be used, how examinations are to be taken and graded, the manner in which students are to leave the room, and so on.

Fifth, there is an overriding investment in personal activity and engagement: in the *Exercises*, what happens is essentially a deep appropriation of and response to the Gospel, through imagination, memory, and will. The director gives some guiding points, but the Holy Spirit is expected to act directly on the soul of the exercitant. In the RS, the students are also guided by the teacher, but they are expected to actively engage and appropriate what they learn as individuals, even to the point of being able to teach it. The high points of the academic year are the public philosophical and theological Acts (*Actus*), where scholars show they they not only know the content thoroughly but can independently handle the material in a formal debate or public examination. Even at the first stage of Letters, students are asked to show what they know in class or in *academiae* (study clubs), in daily competitions with their classmates, in school-wide contests, and in ongoing efforts at composition in prose and poetry, the best of which was published on a display board for everyone to read.

Sixth, the *Ratio* and the *Spiritual Exercises* have a similar intentionality that they state at the outset: they both look primarily toward the promotion of a radically open disposition toward God. The book of the *Exercises* states its purpose as that of helping exercitants to conquer themselves and regulate their lives in such a way that they will not be influenced in their decisions by any inordinate attachment. Such a detachment or indifference is necessary for the freedom that will lead us to fulfill our human vocation, defined as the praise, reverence, and service of God. The RS opens with a rule for the provincial explaining the rationale for the entirety of Jesuit education. This is as important as anything else in the text, so I would like to quote it directly:

> *The final goal of Jesuit education.* Since one of the leading ministries of our Society is teaching our neighbors all the disciplines in keeping with our Institute in such a way that they are thereby aroused to a knowledge and love of our Maker and Redeemer, the provincial should consider himself obliged to do his utmost to ensure that our diverse and many-sided educational labor meets with the abundant results that the grace of our calling demands of us.[8]

---

8 RS, no. 7.

This rationale makes all the difference. It focuses not so much, as the *Exercises* does, on cooperating with God's work on our interiority in the quest to attain the *spiritual freedom* to allow *us* to praise, reverence, and serve God; rather, it looks to teaching in such a way that our *neighbors* are thereby *aroused* to a knowledge and love of our Maker and Redeemer. Notice that the aim is not just *teaching*, but teaching *in such a way that* there is a certain spiritual result in the souls of others, a stirring up of this knowledge and love in them. We might have excellent instruction; we might use all the finest techniques and methods, and cover all the exercises; we might even have a very correctly ordered system of education, and yet we might miss the essential meaning if we do not operate with this intentionality.

This parallelism between the RS and the *Spiritual Exercises* is not merely extrinsic, nor is it merely a coincidence: both studies and prayer were often thought to be integral parts of a single journey toward a state of spiritual fulfillment.[9] The two documents have two different sources in Ignatius's biography: the *Exercises* derive from Ignatius's Manresa and the RS from his Paris. Both, however, can be said to aim at *evoking a change in the souls of the participants* who have agreed to accept direction. The *bonae litterae* (literally "good letters" or "good literature") were supposed to support *pietas* or devotion, just as devotion would likely lead one toward a deep involvement with those texts that best informed the spirit (at minimum, the Gospels). Both Jerusalem and Athens could agree on this: first reading and then writing and speaking the right things in the right way impact and express one's character and spirituality.

Foundational to the Society

The points that the RS is rooted in Ignatius's experience and that it is of a piece with the *Spiritual Exercises* are certainly important because they will help determine the weight that some will be willing to grant to the document. In chapter 5, "The *Ratio studiorum* of 1599: Inescapably Foundational," I go further to claim that the RS is not just a significant factor in Jesuit history but even *a foundational document for the Society of Jesus*—foundational not just in the obvious sense that it grounded Jesuit education, which soon became one of the Society's major apostolates, but in the sense that it helped *to institute that very reality that we know as the Society of Jesus*. This understanding makes the RS not just an

9 See Peter-Hans Kolvenbach, "*Pietas et eruditio*," *Review of Ignatian Spirituality* 38.2, no. 115 (2007): 11–26, here 11: "The earnest desire to become an educated Christian while being as well a Christian intellectual has produced in pedagogical texts, as early as the 14th century, the binominal idea 'devotion and knowledge' with ever so many variations [...]. It is interesting to study the Jesuit theological learning from the point of view of this binomial idea of *pietas* and *eruditio*, because it seems to characterize our *minima Societas*." Fr. Kolvenbach points here to what could be called a spirituality of *docta pietas*, learned devotion, as characteristic of the Society at its original core.

achievement of the early Society, one among many, but something that is really part and parcel of the Society itself.

What is at stake in such a point? If it is correct, then not only does it help to order Jesuit resources and to direct the Society's major apostolic planning today, but, if the RS is truly taken to be a foundational document, then Vatican II's call to religious orders to return to their sources can be fulfilled by the Society only if the Society gives full weight to the RS as an integral part of its Institute.[10] The Society of Jesus cannot rest merely on a recovery of the *Constitutions* or the *Exercises* or both. It cannot simply return to Ignatius's pilgrim days at Manresa and be content with that. It has the unfinished business of an adequate recovery of the RS. We must always have Paris too.

Contemporary Consequences of the RS for Jesuit Education

What might this mean for Jesuit education? What does the renewal of the Society of Jesus have to do with the curriculum in a Jesuit school that is not training Jesuits? A great deal. We cannot have a good understanding of Jesuit education without knowing the document that is the Magna Carta of the tradition. This is true even if we reject its direct applicability to today. But in fact, the RS is far more than a museum-piece that helps to flesh out our historical understanding. It is closer to a long-lasting educational constitution. For several centuries, it prescribed the academic common ground, the shared horizons, and much of the educational vision of the membership of the Society, and that membership went on to exert a decisive influence on the structure, content, and direction of Jesuit schools. Why do most of them maintain language, philosophy, and theology requirements, and why did many of them until relatively recently have such a notable investment in Latin and Greek languages and literature? Because of the legacy of the RS. That legacy has shaped the living idea and the expectations that people have of the Society and its schools.

Of course, in this age of collaboration, what goes into the training of Jesuits is not irrelevant to what should go into shaping the consciousness and practices of the Society's partners. But the RS has from the beginning a *dual nature* that involves people in and outside of the Society, because it governed the training of non-Jesuits as well as that of Jesuits. It is not merely a seminary-plan, nor is it a plan for a more general, non-seminary education. It is both and it is more. It is a seminary plan that includes at the same time a general education; and it is a seminary plan that helps to keep delivering the goods that the plan offers by forming the people who will be carrying it out in the Jesuit schools of the next generation. This complex nature of the RS is no doubt part of the mystique of Jesuit education as well as part of the practical underpinning of its own success.

10 "Decree on the Adaptation and Renewal of Religious Life" (*Perfectae caritatis*), proclaimed by His Holiness Pope Paul VI on October 28, 1965.

Recognizing the RS as integral to the foundations of both the Society and its educational institutions makes reflection on it a relevant project for today, not only for the Jesuit order but also for the schools. The institutions need to consider what the role the document might play in the making of Jesuit education in their own cases. This is not an easy thing to do, because the task is not a matter of simple restoration. The RS was composed in and for the late Renaissance. As an early modern document, it does not fit postmodern times so easily. And yet, its importance and influence for hundreds of years point to the likelihood that it was successful not only because it fit its own times so well but also because it carried values that transcended its own time and may therefore fit our time too. What, then, are those elements of lasting value? And how might contemporary times read the RS in such a way as to become more authentic about what is happening today in Jesuit education?

The Curriculum Carries the Mission

The RS's most significant contribution to this educational tradition may well be the idea of the importance of *the curriculum as the primary vehicle for the mission.* Here, I am conceiving of the curriculum not as a static block of pre-fabricated contents that anyone might mechanically deliver, but rather as a meaningfully structured, engaged, dynamic, content-rich process involving the personalities of teachers and students within larger intentionalities and understandings that frame and motivate the entire enterprise. A living academic *culture* is at issue.

There are many great things that happen on Jesuit college campuses today: retreats; service projects; study-abroad programs; liturgies; social events; special lectures; workshops; meetings of student-and faculty-associations and of representative governance groups; extracurricular activities (including sports); musical and theatrical events; and the activities of clubs of all kinds. Even though many of these are vital to student growth and essential for the well-being and identity and life of the university, none of them, I would say in light of the RS, is as important as the curriculum, for the curriculum is where all the students *must* go and spend much of their time, whether or not they take part in any of these other enterprises. Without the everyday student–teacher events giving shape to a definite curricular journey, we would not even *have* a college or university. The RS says something about administration and liturgies and study-clubs and sodalities, but it puts the main accent on the curriculum: what to teach and what to learn, when and how. In the midst of an abundance of competing factors in college today, the curricular aspect needs to be recognized as the essential medium through which the mission is most critically communicated. This idea has major consequences if it is accepted. Consider the simple fact that in light of the RS, the Mission and Ministry Office in Jesuit colleges and universities should have a highly significant curricular impact. In fact, this is rarely, if ever, the case.

This idea also puts a special responsibility on the faculty to work out, manage, oversee, and constantly improve the curriculum. Of course, it obliges the students to follow their course of studies responsibly and get the most out of them; it also obliges the administration to oversee the project and keep it moving forward. But the main burden is on the faculty, which shares as a group a corporate responsibility for educating the next generation. Teachers therefore must devote quality-time to thinking about the curriculum as a whole. No discipline is an island. At some point, the dynamics of territoriality are self-defeating; they must yield to a commonality of purpose. The faculty is charged with engaging in a corporate effort to discover, to institute, and to refine a curricular wisdom. That entails a great ongoing labor. For example, it involves reviewing the major radical critiques of higher education that have been emerging, evaluating them, and working out the most appropriate responses.

Furthermore, at some level, the core has to be fashioned not so much with an eye to professional competency as to the education's larger purposes, namely to all that bears most significantly on the development of the students in their vocation to be fully humane, fully spiritual persons who are progressing toward wisdom—wisdom about God and the good, about nature, about ethics, about culture and society, about family, about relationships, about themselves, and about what it takes for them to live a truly good life. To achieve success, it will also be necessary to descend to the details of course-contents and make judgments about what should be guaranteed in the educational core. It is not enough to say that everyone should have one or two or three hours of economics or philosophy. A *Ratio*-inspired consciousness asks further questions about the details: What exactly are we going to put into those hours? What texts are better, more appropriate, more productive, more successful than others? What topics are most worth the students' time and attention? What best supports intellectual, cultural, moral, and religious conversion? It makes sense to pour energy into assessment practices if and only if we are agreed on what to assess.

How can the faculty achieve such an effect? It needs to develop an RS-like vision, and that cannot be done in a single year or even in a single decade. The RS was the product of many voices over time, and a similar investment may be necessary today. If the curriculum (as the organized and appropriate delivery of quality content) is the primary carrier of the mission, then some type of faculty "on-the-job" formation will be a high priority, making it clear to every teacher that the institution has a distinctive corporate approach. Such an effort supports the institution's academic freedom to be what it is supposed to be.

Part of the approach involves learning to think formationally. For example, a young philosophy teacher may emerge from graduate school very impressed with Friedrich Nietzsche's (1844–1900) *Twilight of the Idols* and eager to expound it. But there is a formational question that needs to be asked: Given the mission and character of our school, and even simply given basic pedagogical considerations, is this the best text to give freshmen as their introduction to philosophy? If this text is to be taught, how does it fit into the larger rationale? Where are we trying to lead the students with it? This decision in a *Ratio*-inspired regime would not simply be left to the individual teacher, as it often is today. There is a corporate wisdom and role and expectation that should at the very least be parts of the decision. Everyone is invested in the next generation's education. No one has a blank check.

The RS would never have succeeded without the existence of the right type of oversight structures and the *bona fide* agreement of a faculty to cooperate. For practical reasons, Jesuit college programs today probably also need a kind of internal governing board that goes far beyond the typical business of most curricular committees. They need to support ongoing reflection and work on the curriculum.

Order in the Curriculum

One of the main tasks would be the question of order in the curriculum. How does each year of college build on and extend the work of the previous year? Ever since my own college years, I have been awed by the vast variety of the course-offerings available today. I have been equally distressed by the fragmentary jumble that any curricular program seems to be forced to be. Alasdair MacIntyre put it very well in his *Commonweal* article of October 2006: academe has produced more and more fields and more and more specialists and therefore more and more possible courses; it has not been equally diligent about developing a habit of thinking about how the parts relate within a larger totality.[11] The freedom to choose from a great array of courses may feel very good to us when we are college students, but does it serve us well in the long run? Certainly, when I was in college I would have preferred to have been able to assume that the faculty had worked out a very solid, coherent, well-elaborated core, delivered with a consistent and even improving quality through the years. In fact, they had not done anything like this. There were simply generic distribution requirements, and the students had to fill them out as best they could. A particular teacher would have little knowledge of the various curricular options taken by the individual students. Curricular variables were all too numerous. In a *Ratio*-inspired dispensation, teachers would not only know the general lines of the plan but they would know much of the specific content as well.

It is time to go back to Ignatius's radical insight that it is better not to jumble things up in the curriculum but to take them in a certain sequence, with thorough preparatory grounding, and with a sense of how they fit into a larger educational plan. One of the timeliest and most essential improvements that the

11 Alasdair MacIntyre, "The End of Education: The Fragmentation of the American University," *Commonweal* 133, no. 18 (October 20, 2006): 10–14.

RS can offer to contemporary education is simply that very idea of a plan, a *ratio*. Electives need not be entirely eliminated, nor should they be superabundant. At minimum, there should always be, at the very least, a curricular option for the more ordered, integrated, and systematic approach, one that might more clearly be in the tradition that impressed Ignatius on his journey so many years ago. This option is usually not present today. We have lost the skill of constructing a humanistic curriculum architectonically.

There probably needs to be a standing team of faculty that is explicitly commissioned to work out and oversee a program that integrates the best of what might be covered in language and letters, scientific and social thinking, philosophy, theology, and spirituality. The inspired delivery of such a program constitutes the greatest promise of Jesuit education. It would allow for the establishment of a distinctive kind of university that would give students a real option in types of liberal arts curricula. Surely this kind of diversity will be a valuable thing to promote, and surely it is just the kind of diversity that this tradition should be most expected to promote.

Conclusion

> A disciple asked Confucius about the cultivated person.
> Confucius said, "Cultivate yourself by seriousness."
> The disciple asked, "Is that all?"
> Confucius said, "Cultivate yourself to make others secure."
> The disciple asked, "Is that all?"
> Confucius said, "Cultivate yourself to make all others secure. Even the sage kings had trouble cultivating themselves enough to make all people secure."
>
> —*Confucius,* Analects *14:44*[12]

Just so, the RS has a very large aim. It is not just about self-cultivation for some kind of possibly narcissistic personal security. Nor is it about leaping to just any kind of other-oriented action in some kind of naïve activism. Rather, the RS looks to a certain type of energized wisdom that involves a self-cultivation, a broadened and deepened consciousness that has undergone conversion and that can act through affiliation in a community for a universal and transcendent end. Recovering the spirit and the genius of the RS as a foundational document in the Society of Jesus is one of the most important things that the Jesuit order and its allies can do now for this vital tradition in Catholic higher education.

---

12 Cleary, *Essential Confucius*, 85.

4. The Historiography of Jesuit Pedagogy

Overview: Jesuit Pedagogy and the *Ratio studiorum*

Pedagogy here refers not to the didactics or methods of instruction but to the whole educational "concept"—the aims, ideas, methods, practices, structures, arrangements.[1] "Jesuit pedagogy" is therefore synonymous with "the idea of Jesuit education." It refers to what has typically been known as the *studia Societatis*, the studies of the Society. This essay selectively surveys some of the most important moments in the history of how this idea has been expressed.

For almost the entire history of the Society of Jesus, literature on the idea of its studies has been closely tied to the plan known as the *Ratio studiorum* (hereafter abbreviated as RS).[2] Jesuit education cannot be entirely reduced to what is expressly articulated in this document, nor can all teaching done by Jesuits be considered directly derivative of it, but it is nevertheless where we find the fullest, sharpest, most concrete, and most generally held notion of Jesuit education over the longest time period.[3] No other universal formal plan for Jesuit education has superseded it. Noteworthy also is the fact that the RS had a substantial pre-history: it followed a lengthy, well-deliberated sifting of many decades, stretching from the Society's first residential colleges (where, even in 1540, the Society had particular expectations of its younger members) and from *ad hoc* teaching, as in Goa (1542) and Gandía (1546), and from its first full institutional undertaking in Messina (1548). Even earlier there had been the experiences of Ignatius of Loyola (*c.*1491–1556) and the early companions in the 1520s at Alcalá and Paris, where the *ordo et modus Parisiensis* had made a lasting favorable impression on them.[4] In fact, the Parisian program could well be called the

1 This essay has been slightly adapted from Claude N. Pavur, "The Historiography of Jesuit Pedagogy," first published online in October 2016 in Jesuit Historiography Online, Brill Online Reference Works; http://referenceworks.brillonline.com/entries/jesuit-historiography-online/the-historiography-of-jesuit-pedagogy-COM_194129 (accessed October 1, 2018).

2 The original title was *Ratio atque institutio studiorum Societatis Iesu* (Naples: Tarquinio Longo, 1598). It was issued in January 1599, so it is often called "the *Ratio* of 1599" to distinguish it from the review-version sent out in 1586 and from the trial version produced in 1591. The English version cited here will be *The* Ratio studiorum: *The Official Plan for Jesuit Education*, ed. Claude Pavur (St. Louis, MO: Institute of Jesuit Sources, 2005).

3 There should be a distinction between the spiritual work of mercy and charity, "educating the ignorant" or teaching Christianity to children and unlettered people (mentioned in the Society's earliest formula) and the more systematic, institutionally integrated, corporately managed enterprise properly called "Jesuit education."

4 Gabriel Codina, "The *Modus Parisiensis*," in *The Jesuit* Ratio studiorum: *400th Anniversary Perspectives*, ed. Vincent J. Duminuco, S.J. (New York: Fordham University Press, 2000),

earliest form of Jesuit education: not only did all the founders take degrees at the University of Paris but, right after the founding of the Society, Ignatius preferred it as a training ground for his new recruits.

The RS was intentionally issued as an ever-present ideal rather than as an immutable set of laws: it prescribed what Jesuits should be trying to do in schools unless circumstances demanded adaptations.[5] Whatever the academic variations appearing over the next three and a half centuries, the RS was always considered the authoritative reference point. So when Superior General Jan Roothaan (1785–1853, in office 1829–53) sent out to the restored Society an updated version in 1832, his cover letter made it quite clear that the earlier plan, the *Ratio* of 1599, had such substance, status, and proven success that the new document should not in any way diminish the old one's authority.[6] Even as late as 1957, a general congregation praised the RS as something to be universally known, highly esteemed, and put into practice in the Society's programs for formation.[7]

The RS was more than a guide for running schools: it was simultaneously Jesuit education's defining charter and the Society's last great foundational document. It made educational concerns for both Jesuits and non-Jesuits an integral part of the Society's Institute, with a formational infrastructure that produced teachers and a supervisory superstructure that provided quality control.[8] Called for by the *Constitutions* as an extension of itself, particularly part 4, the RS governed both Jesuit schools and the academic formation of all scholastics in the Society for several centuries (that is, 1599–*c.*1965).[9] Jesuits and non-Jesuits were

---

28–49. Codina mentions that Ignatius and several who later went to Paris first discovered the *modus Parisiensis* at Alcalá (38).

5 *Constitutions*, no. 455: "[The plan of studies] ought to be adapted to places, times, and persons, even though it would be desirable to reach that order as far as this is possible." John W. Padberg, ed., *The Constitutions of the Society of Jesus and Their Complementary Norms: A Complete English Translation of the Official Latin Texts* (St. Louis, MO: Institute of Jesuit Sources, 1996).

6 For the Latin text of this document, see Georg Michael Pachtler, Ratio studiorum *et institutiones scholasticae Societatis Jesu per Germaniam olim vigentes collectae, concinnatae, dilucidatae*, ed. Karl Kehrbach, tomus 2, Ratio studiorum ann. 1586, 1599, 1832, Monumenta Germaniae Paedagogica 5 (Berlin: A. Hofmann & Company, 1887), 228–33.

7 "All should know well and greatly esteem the *Ratio studiorum*; and its method and rules should be carefully observed in the education of our young men." John W. Padberg, Martin D. O'Keefe, John L. McCarthy, eds. and trans., *For Matters of Greater Moment: The First Thirty Jesuit General Congregations*, Series 1: Jesuit Primary Sources in English Translations, no. 12 (St. Louis, MO: Institute of Jesuit Sources, 1994), 678 (decree 66, no. 85, paragraph 2).

8 The gathering of foundational documents in a volume entitled *Institutum Societatis Iesu* [The Institute of the Society of Jesus] (Florence: Ex Typographia A SS. Conceptione, 1892–93) included the RS, as did several similar collections before it.

9 Of course, there was a kind of *ratio*-plan *in nuce* before 1599, with fragments being put into place as early as 1548. The *de facto* expiration date of the *Ratio studiorum* in Jesuit formation might be fixed differently in various locations. In the late 1960s in the United

together engaged in the *studia Societatis*. The Society therefore used these *studia* not only as one way to fulfill directly its mission of helping souls but also as a replication mechanism in which younger generations attained the expertise needed to give freely again what they had received, whether directly, in their own participation in the apostolate of education, or indirectly, through what they brought to their other ministries. It turned out that the *studia* were also effective as a recruitment mechanism for the Society, even though such a use was expressly against the spirit and the letter of the code.[10] Young and idealistic men at an impressionable time of life had visible examples of one possible vocational path constantly before their eyes, and this option took shape in specific individuals—the Jesuits, with all their differences of personality and talent.

Thus an important part of the Jesuit educational system was inwardly directed (*ad intra*), ultimately for outward (*ad extra*) purposes. The order's identity and mission were explicitly invested in training people who would by that training be able to carry on its educational work. Such a commitment progressively bolstered the order's educational character as well as its achievement and wide geographical propagation. It was in the Jesuits' own *ad intra* formational program that the RS held sway for the longest time: up until the mid-1960s, all Jesuit scholastics were obliged to follow the traditional RS sequence of "Letters" (taking courses in classical languages and literature in institutions often known as "juniorates"), philosophy (following a Scholastic course in "philosophates"), and theology (learning Thomistic positions and approaches in "theologates").[11] Between the years of philosophy studies and those of theology there were usually

---

States, most of the juniorate programs (two years of study undertaken in a specific formational community and focused on classical languages and literatures) were terminated or radically reorganized. The closings of the Maryland and New Orleans juniorates have been reported by participants as 1966 and 1967, respectively. Another marker for the expiration of the RS might be the date of the last Latin disputation in philosophy studies: in the New Orleans province's philosophate at Spring Hill College (Mobile, AL), this has been reported by a participant as January of 1965.

10 See RS, no. 330: "In private conversations as well, he will impress on them the same things pertaining to devotion, but he will do this in such a way that he does not appear to be enticing anyone to our form of religious life. But if he does notice anything along this line, he should send the person off to his confessor."

11 And indeed even in 2016 (the time of the first publication of this essay) there are still alive some who can remember having had classical studies (Greek and Latin), the (philosophy) arts course (including the study of what was called cosmology), and Thomistic theology, with oral exams in Latin. Until shortly after mid-century, some works were still being published in Latin (for example, the early works of the Canadian philosopher Bernard Lonergan [1904–84]). One could not say that the RS was entirely a dead letter in 1960 despite the need for revision. The first full translation of the *Constitutions* from Latin into English was published only in 1970 (Ignatius of Loyola, *The Constitutions of the Society of Jesus*, trans., intro., and commentary George E. Ganss [St. Louis, MO: Institute of Jesuit Sources, 1970]).

three to five years of regency (called *magisterium*, in the Jesuit catalogs), during which the scholastics would practice teaching in the Society's mode, that is, within the ambit of the RS. These four periods of formation constituted the preponderant bulk of all the preparation for Jesuit priestly ministry. Only the two-year novitiate and the tertianship (usually done after ordination for six to twelve months) fell outside the scope of this plan. It is for good reason that to this day the term for Jesuits preparing for the priesthood is "scholastics," that is, "people who are going to classes (Latin *scholae*)."

Given the lasting dominance of the RS, we might handily map the entire career of the understanding of Jesuit education in these stages: (1) emergence of the RS; (2) practical adaptations of the RS; (3) late modernity's challenges to the RS; (4) deprecation and loss of the RS, with some attempts to re-conceive the Jesuit educational project. Now that the RS has celebrated its fourth centennial and received fresh translations into several languages, it is becoming again a topic of study and reflection, and we may be standing at the beginning a fifth period, (5) a revaluation of the importance of the RS.[12] The historiography of Jesuit pedagogy follows the lines of the career just outlined. It proceeds from the mostly internal Jesuit documentation in the early period to allied documents, again mostly internal, to support the proper appreciation and functioning of the RS. After the Society had become a subject of controversy, was suppressed, and then restored to run influential schools once again, adversarial secularizing and modernizing thought tended to produce tendentious representations of Jesuit education. These evoked some extended apologias and more comprehensive positive expositions of the educational concepts and practices cultivated in the Society's schools. Soon after the mid-twentieth century, however, there was again a reaction against the idea of the RS, a forgetting of it, diminishment of it, or even a flight from it. This time, the reaction occurred within the order itself in the name of adaptation. Circumstances had changed so radically as to require a thorough rethinking of the Society's educational work. Yet internationality, opposition to "Eurocentrism," and other cultural, social, and political changes, agendas, and diversity all cumulatively made the very idea of a single educational charter in the tradition of the RS look like a fantasy. Assumed to be irrelevant and antiquated, the RS faded further and further from view. Reflection on the contemporary practices of Jesuit education attempted to integrate current ideas and methods and to call up themes from the tradition as they appeared to be useful. But in the early twenty-first century, now that the RS is no longer "living," historical analysis may provide for new understandings and objective assessments of the RS and its tradition.

---

12 László Lukács's (1910–98) critical edition of the Latin text in MHSI 129 appeared in 1986; it was followed by translations in Spanish (1986), French (1997), Polish (2000), Italian (2002), English (2005), Japanese (2008), Ukrainian (2008), and Portuguese (2009).

Key Texts from the Earlier Literature on Jesuit Pedagogy

Official Expressions of the Idea

The *Constitutions* and the *Ratio studiorum* are the primary documents that officially both establish and express the idea of Jesuit education, and so they merit some attention in this context. Of the two documents, it is the RS that gives the most explicit and detailed view of Jesuit pedagogy by laying out the structure, contents, governance, and practices of *studia Societatis*, stating the rules for every office and for all the major procedures (admissions, corrections, exams, contests, disputations, study-groups) to be used for the entire program. But in the first rule for the provincial it also rises above details to give the larger idea of the education:

> The final goal of the Society's studies—1. Since one of the leading ministries of our Society is teaching our neighbors all the disciplines in keeping with our Institute in such a way that they are thereby aroused to a knowledge and love of our Maker and Redeemer, the Provincial should consider himself obliged to do his utmost to ensure that our diverse and complex educational labor meets with the abundant results that the grace of our calling demands of us.[13]

Jesuit education is seen here as a leading ministry of the Society especially entrusted to the provincials, helping neighbors by teaching them a range of certain relevant subjects in a manner designed to evoke a specific intellectual and spiritual effect. This description reveals a constitutive feature of the Society's spirituality: *docta pietas*. Learning the disciplines is to be in service of people's spiritual health or salvation (*salus*), and it is also something vital to the Society itself. The *Ratio* of 1586 put it this way: "Clearly two things are the safeguard and chief support of our Society, fervent zeal for devotion [*ardens pietatis studium*] and an outstanding studied knowledge of reality [*praestans scientia rerum*]."[14]

An earlier source for the idea of Jesuit education can be found in the fourth part of Ignatius's *Constitutions* (1558), which dealt with the academic formation of both Jesuits and non-Jesuits and the running of schools. The preamble to part 4 significantly situates the idea of Jesuit studies:

> The end steadfastly pursued by the Society is to aid its own members and their neighbors in attaining the ultimate end for which they were created. For this, in addition to the example of one's life, learning and skill in expounding it are required. Hence [...] it will be necessary to provide for the edifice of learning and of skill in employing it so as to help make God our Creator and Lord better known and served.[15]

---

13 RS, no. 7.

14 *Duo plane sunt Societatis nostrae praesidia ac firmamenta, ardens pietatis studium et praestans rerum scientia*; Pachtler, *Ratio*, 27; also MHSI 129:2.

15 *Constitutions*, no. 307.

The dual target is explicit: the service is for the Society's own members and for its neighbors. These words are partially restated in chapter 5, where a definite criterion and content are indicated (albeit with an "escape clause," that is, the words, "generally speaking"):

> Since the end of the learning which is acquired in this Society is with God's favor to help the souls of its own members and those of their neighbors, it is by this norm that the decision will be made, both in general and in the case of individual persons, as to what subjects ours ought to learn and how far they ought to advance in them. And since, generally speaking, help is derived from the humane letters of different languages, logic, natural and moral philosophy, metaphysics, scholastic and positive theology, and Sacred Scripture, these are the subjects which those who are sent to the colleges should study.[16]

Here, specific contents and the reason for them are given straightforwardly. The RS organized the material into three stages or "courses of study" that became canonical in the tradition: "Letters" (that is, grammar, language, composition, humanistic studies, rhetoric), philosophy, and theology.

Before the *Ratio studiorum* of 1599

Expression of the basic idea of the *studia Societatis* goes back to the early generations of the Society, when it was engaged in working out the details of many different academic plans and related educational documents. A large number of these are now critically edited and available in the Monumenta Paedagogica.[17] The story of the long road to the final version of the *Ratio studiorum* of 1599 is given by László Lukács (1910–98) in his introduction to the MHSI volume containing the critical editions of the rationes of 1586, 1591, and 1599.[18] A few early documents will demonstrate how the historiography of Jesuit pedagogy began small and occasional, with Jesuits' own short summary presentations, sometimes in quest of external support or permission to operate within a given domain. There are also rules and reports about the educational work to the Society's curia, formational reflections (as with Bonifacio, below), and large-scale systematic overviews (see Possevino, below).

Ignatius of Loyola and Juan Alfonso de Polanco (1517–76) gave a famous summary of the Jesuit educational project in a letter of December 1, 1551 to the provincial of Spain, Antonio Araoz (1515–73). It outlined the methods used to

16 Ibid., no. 351.

17 The Monumenta Paedagogica (abbrev. MP) are a subset of volumes in the Monumenta Historica Societatis Iesu (abbrev. MHSI), 157 vols. (Madrid; Rome: 1894–). Some of the items of the MP have been translated in Cristiano Casalini and Claude Pavur, eds., *Jesuit Pedagogy, 1540–1616: A Reader*, Sources for the History of Jesuit Pedagogy 1 (Chestnut Hill, MA: Institute of Jesuit Sources, 2016).

18 *Ratio atque institutio studiorum Societatis Iesu, 1586 1591 1599*, MHSI, nova editio, 129 (Rome: Institutum Historicum Societatis Iesu, 1986).

establish schools, and then it listed the major advantages for Jesuits (teachers and scholastics), for non-Jesuits studying there, and for the populace of the region served by the school.[19]

Jerónimo Nadal (1507–80) unwittingly created a "kernel" of Jesuit education when he composed the first rules for the Jesuit college at Messina in 1548. The document primarily covered (1) morals and (2) the structure and contents of the studies. Even mathematics, Greek, and Hebrew were represented in the largely Latin curriculum. We also have Nadal's conferences on Jesuit studies, given to the scholastics in Coimbra in 1551. In the eleventh conference, he made clear that studies are essential to the Society: without the academic dimension, "it [that is, the Society] would not be able to go on" (*no podría proceder*), and without learning, "we would not be able to help our neighbor" (*sin letras no podríamos ayudar al prójimo*).[20] Studies are understood as integral to the Institute of the Society of Jesus.

Pedro de Ribadeneyra (1526–1611) published a life of Ignatius in several Latin and Spanish editions between 1571 and 1605. He not only surveyed the many schools that had sprung up with the help of benefactors but he also explained the Society's rationale for undertaking this kind of work, replying to those who did not consider teaching boys to be a fitting use of the energies of a religious order.[21] Ribadeneyra prescinded from details of the education to stress his understanding of the main reason for the Society's involvement: "The proper calling and present state of the Church."[22] That is, education is a worthy enterprise that the Christian community has always valued and promoted, and it is a most effective means of achieving authentic reform in the face of the religious, ecclesial, and moral confusions of Ribadeneyra's day.

Juan de Bonifacio (1538–1606) published in 1575 the first full Jesuit educational tract, *Christiani pueri institutio adolescentiaeque perfugium* (The education of the Christian boy and a shelter for his adolescent years).[23] The third edition added a major section (book 4) on manners.[24] It presented a classically based Christian humanistic approach, with the core idea being the inseparability of virtue and "Letters" in a good education: "I do not see how virtue can be guaranteed without learning or learning without virtue."[25]

19 Casalini and Pavur, *Jesuit Pedagogy*, 55–59.

20 Miguel Nicolau, ed., *Pláticas espirituales del P. Jerónimo Nadal, S.I., en Coimbra* (1561) (Granada: Facultad Teológica de la Compañía de Jesús, 1945), 124.

21 Pedro de Ribadeneyra, *The Life of Ignatius of Loyola*, trans. Claude Pavur (St. Louis, MO: Institute of Jesuit Sources, 2014), nos. 351–87.

22 Ibid., no. 353.

23 (Salamanca: Matías Gastias, 1575).

24 (Burgos: Philip de Junta, 1586).

25 Ibid., 112, cited in Javier Vergara Ciordia, "La edición de Burgos de 1588 del *Christiani pueri institutio adolescentiaeque perfugium*, obra clave del humanismo jesuítico hispano," *Historia de la educación* 31 (2012): 81–103, here 91.

Antonio Possevino (1533–1611) in 1593 published *Bibliotheca selecta de ratione studiorum in historia, in disciplinis, in salute omnium procuranda* (A selected library concerning the plan of studies in history, in the disciplines, in procuring the salvation of everyone), a large encyclopedic bibliography and comprehensive overview of orthodox Catholic education.[26] It covered many areas of learning (for example, law, medicine, poetry, painting, rhetoric, architecture, geography). The first part, entitled *Cultura ingeniorum* (The cultivation of talents), discusses the pedagogical principles of Jesuit humanism.

Some Leading Works on Jesuit Education after the *Ratio studiorum* up to 1965

The complete program or "idea" of Jesuit education has very rarely been the subject of a unified investigation, perhaps precisely because of the very large scope of the full plan. The official documents seemed adequate for the purposes of realizing the educational project. The relevant details were interpreted and handed on in given locations to those who needed to know them for particular professional purposes. Francesco Sacchini (1570–1625) wrote *Paraenesis ad magistros scholarum inferiorum Societatis Iesu* [Exhortation to the teachers of the lower classes of the Society of Jesus] and *Protrepticon ad magistros scholarum inferiorum Societatis Iesu* (Advice for the teachers of the lower classes of the Society of Jesus), but these did not address the philosophical or theological years that were structurally integral to the larger idea of "Jesuit pedagogy."[27] When someone says that the goal of Jesuit education is *eloquentia perfecta*, for example, we must realize that the speaker is looking only at the first stage, the literary part of the *studia*, and not at the entire plan. Of course, one might argue that Jesuit schools had their widest cultural impact in the literary course (roughly, the high school years plus two years of what is presently called college in the United States), so that for most people outside the order's own formational program, Jesuit education was essentially the literary and "cultural" part of the scheme.

Even official initiatives could be of restricted scope, as, for example, the tenth decree of Congregation 14 (1696), which directed that "teachers of humane letters, over and above the rules guiding their teaching, are to have an instruction and a systematized method of learning, in accord with which they should conduct their own private studies, even as they were devoting their efforts to teaching others."[28] The congregation asked Joseph de Jouvancy (1643–1719) to adapt for this purpose a handbook he had published as *Christianis litterarum magistris de ratione discendi et docendi* (For Christian teachers of literature, on the method of learning and teaching).[29] The result was a widely popular and much reprinted booklet known as *Magistris scholarum inferiorum Societatis Iesu*

26 Rome, from the Typographica Apostolica Vaticana: Domenico Basa.

27 (Rome: Giacomo Mascardi, 1625).

28 Padberg, *Matters of Greater Moment*, 364.

29 (Paris: n.p., 1691).

de ratione discendi et docendi (For Jesuit teachers of the lower classes, on the method of learning and teaching).[30] This guide used and expanded upon what Sacchini had written. It is often cited in later studies of Jesuit education.

I will survey here a few notable works that have been particularly indicative or influential in presenting this Society's educational tradition, beginning with those by Robert Schwickerath (1903), Allan Farrell (1937), François Charmot (1943), George Ganss (1954), and John W. Donohue (1963), all Jesuits (as are most of the scholars mentioned in this essay). These writers were able to rely on the publications of the Society's Institutum Historicum (Historical Institute).[31] However, they wrote before the larger collection of volumes in the MHSI, particularly the seven edited by Lukács that appeared between 1965 and 1992. Of course, these scholars still had access to the Society's archives and all published work dependent upon such materials, as, for example, the large collection of pedagogical documents gathered by Georg Michael Pachtler (1825–89) in four volumes.[32]

At the start of the twentieth century, an American Jesuit scholar, Robert Schwickerath (1869–1948), making use of Pachtler's collection as well as other original documentation, composed *Jesuit Education: Its History and Principles Viewed in the Light of Modern Educational Principles.*[33] This large-scale study aimed to correct many of the misconceptions and faulty presentations that were popular at that time, particularly with authors from outside Catholic traditions. Schwickerath was well versed in the literature, as his bibliography sufficiently illustrates.[34] He heaped special praise upon de Jouvancy, noting that in 1752 Superior General Ignazio Visconti (1682–1755, in office 1751–55) wanted all Jesuit teachers to have a copy of his handbook; it was considered by some "a pedagogical gem" that had been "highly praised by Rollin and Voltaire."[35] Apologizing for his sometimes polemical tone, the author directly countered several popular historians of education, such as Gabriel Compayré (1843–1913), Franklin V. N. Painter (1852–1931), Levi Seeley (1847–1928), and others who seemed to have gone astray in numerous respects, especially because of their distance from the

30 (Florence: Michele Nestenius, 1703).

31 MHSI 19, published in 1901, gathered educationally related documents under the title Monumenta Paedagogica. It is entirely separate from the new MP series mentioned above.

32 *Ratio studiorum et institutiones scholasticae Societatis Jesu per Germaniam olim vigentes* (Berlin: Hofmann, 1887–94); vols. 2, 5, 9, and 16 of Monumenta Germaniae Paedagogica, 62 vols., ed. Karl Kehrbach et al. (Berlin: A. Hofmann & Company, 1886–1938).

33 *Jesuit Education: Its History and Principles Viewed in the Light of Modern Educational Problems*, 2nd ed. (St. Louis, MO: B. Herder, 1903).

34 Schwickerath also helped produce German translations from the Latin of some early Jesuit educational documents: Robert Schwickerath, Josef Stier, and Franz Zorell, eds., *Der Jesuiten Sacchini, Juvencius und Kropf: Erlaüterungsschriften zur Studienordnung der Gesellschaft Jesu*, Bibliothek der Katholischen Pädagogik 10 (Freiburg im Breisgau: Herder, 1898).

35 Schwickerath, *Jesuit Education*, 434–35.

primary source material. For example, Schwickerath dissolves Compayré's assertion that Jesuit education was preoccupied with "purely formal studies" to the nearly complete neglect of history.[36] Since educational theory was in ferment around him, Schwickerath found it important to take up certain issues in particular: the elective system, classical education based on Latin and Greek, the place of colleges relative to high schools and universities, and questions relating to moral and religious formation.[37] He was quite aware of the debate that had been going on between the presidents of Harvard University and Boston College. Charles W. Eliot (1834–1926) of Harvard had been arguing for electivism and attacking an education that in his opinion was a fossilized and stultifying.[38] But with Timothy Brosnahan (1856–1915), the Jesuit president of Boston College, Schwickerath ardently defended the vision of the RS and many of its methods, as, for example, the prelection. Furthermore, he proposed that some of the educational practices being promoted in his time were actually well supported in the RS.[39] The book is divided into two large parts, the first covering the history of the Jesuits' educational system up through the nineteenth century, and the second presenting the principles of the RS and evaluating them in relation to contemporary educational controversies. Schwickerath's study is an important one historiographically because of the author's wide knowledge both of the Jesuit sources and of the body of mainstream modern historical criticism that call for so much revision. Reading Schwickerath helps us realize that (1) Jesuit education and the approach of the RS were subjected to much faulty criticism; (2) the RS still had able apologists at the beginning of the twentieth century; (3) there needed to be a turn in the twentieth century to a more careful study of the historical sources in order to attain a balanced historical judgment; and (4) the positive achievements of Jesuit education were considerable, not infrequently appreciated even from outside the order, partly because the work had been based upon sound pedagogy.

Another landmark study appeared in 1938: *The Jesuit Code of Liberal Education: Development and Scope of the* Ratio studiorum by Allan P. Farrell (1896–1976).[40] Whereas Schwickerath had largely surveyed the post-RS traditions of Jesuit education, Farrell looked carefully into the pre-RS history and

---

36 Ibid., 125, citing Gabriel Compayré, *The History of Pedagogy*, trans. W. H. [William Harold] Payne (Boston: D. C. Heath & Co., 1889), 144–45.

37 Ibid., preface, iii–iv.

38 See Kathleen A. Mahoney, *Catholic Higher Education in Protestant America: The Jesuits and Harvard in the Age of the University* (Baltimore: Johns Hopkins University Press, 2003), especially chapter 2, "Time: The Harvard Law School Controversy and the Modern Imperative," 60–98.

39 See, for example, Schwickerath, *Jesuit Education*, 509–10, where he talks about an experiment in the teaching of Latin in Germany that had to be reversed because of the bad results with student learning. Speaking of the principles involved, Schwickerath says: "These are the principles on which the *Ratio* and Jouvancy had insisted centuries ago."

40 (Milwaukee, WI: Bruce Publishing Company, 1938).

documentation from the life of Ignatius, through the early schools and Diego Ledesma's (1519–75) first attempts to create a *ratio studiorum*, to the three great educational plans of 1586, 1591, and 1599. And like Schwickerath, he was not only a *Ratio*-enthusiast but also a true believer in the perduring relevance of the thinking behind that document and hence its power to remedy some of the major educational problems of his day. The major portion of this very thoroughly researched and detailed volume was devoted to the step-by-step historical evolution of the RS in the sixteenth century, but the last chapter, "The *Ratio Studiorum* and Contemporary Education," presented as strongly stated a pro-RS position as one might imagine being composed in the mid-twentieth century.[41] In Farrell's view, the Jesuit educational tradition had suffered great diminishment in the face of growing electivism, departmentalism, specialization, the scheme of credit-hours, curricular proliferation, and the loss of the required collegiate study of the classical languages. All too optimistically, Farrell predicted the imminent end of electivism in American education, and all too idealistically he supported the feasibility of a required classical course that would develop rhetorical abilities more than skills of translation or comprehension. Farrell stressed the importance of the formation of the will as well as the intellect in Jesuit education, the value of Latin and Greek classics and Scholastic philosophy, and the theological dimensions that lift the enterprise to a higher level: "Humanism that does not reach upward to God and find its completeness in Him is not genuine humanism at all."[42] Beyond the "fundamental methodology" of the RS that is "adaptable to the teaching of any branch in the curriculum [and] extensively used in modern pedagogy," he listed eight still-significant principles lying deep in the RS. These had been made explicit only in the *Ratio* of 1586, but they were presumed in what was written thereafter. Farrell expresses them as follows:

> 1. Subordination of subjects of secondary importance to those of prime importance. 2. Clear-cut organization of successive objectives to be attained by the student. 3. Ample opportunity afforded the student by way of repetition to organize in his own mind the knowledge he has thus far gained. 4. The use of objection and discussion and, within proper limits, of emulation, as essential parts of the teaching technique, in order to guard against an attitude of passivity or mere absorption of classified information. 5. Making provision for a variety of class exercises, written and oral, to keep interest aroused and to demand of the student evidence of mastery. 6. Stimulating at every stage development of the power of written and oral expression in accordance with the highest ideals in the intellectual and moral order. 7. Personal interest in and contact with the student for the purpose of inspiring and encouraging him to achieve distinction in

41 Ibid., 401–28.

42 Ibid., 422.

> both learning and virtue. 8. Measuring the academic achievement of the student, not by time, but by achievement.[43]

Such a study shows us that, although the RS was no longer the cultural force that it had once been, there still remained, at least in some quarters in 1938, a very lively, even passionate, commitment to what some regarded as perennial values of traditional Jesuit education. This impression is confirmed in Morton A. Hill's (1917–85) very brief survey of Anglophone writing on the RS during the first half of the twentieth century.[44] This paper indicates that the RS was a topic of lively discussion in the pages of the *Jesuit Educational Quarterly* and elsewhere during that time and that the material sometimes merges with considerations of educational history or broader contemporary issues in Catholic education.[45] Hill included in his survey four master's theses done at Fordham University on the RS between 1942 and 1950.[46]

Two more books from the first half of the twentieth century also deserve mention. The first is William J. McGucken's (1889–1943) *The Jesuits and Education: The Society's Teaching Principles and Practice, Especially in Secondary Education in the United States*, which makes a contribution by describing the American adaptations of the principles and practices of the RS.[47] In tracing the development of the modern American Jesuit high school, he showed how circumstances might force a change in the details of the RS while the primary purpose of "the formation of Catholic youth" might be retained.[48] The second book of note is Francis P. Donnelly's (1869–1959) *Principles of Jesuit Education in Practice*, which is almost entirely devoted to the study of language, literature, and composition as it should be practiced in the tradition of the RS.[49] Donnelly saw the overall educational scheme this way: "The art of composition should be the primary objective of the high-school course in literature; criticism the primary objective

---

43 Ibid., 403–4.

44 Morton A. Hill, "Twentieth-Century Thought on the *Ratio studiorum*," *Jesuit Educational Quarterly* 14, no. 4 (1952): 225–39. This article briefly scans some RS-related reviews and studies from 1900 to 1950.

45 Hill mentions T. [Timothy] Corcoran, *Studies in the History of Classical Teaching: Irish and Continental, 1500–1700* (London: Longman's, 1911), which is primarily about the innovative language methodology of the Irish Jesuit William Bathe (1564–1614); the book devotes its second half to a study of the practice of classical teaching after the Renaissance, carefully depicting the working of a Jesuit college classroom in the seventeenth century. Educational books written by Jesuits but with a wider scope than the RS are William McGucken, *The Catholic Way in Education* (Milwaukee, WI: Bruce, 1934), and Jaime Castiello, *A Humane Psychology of Education* (New York: Sheed & Ward, 1936). See Hill, "Twentieth Century Thought," 229, 231.

46 Ibid., 234–36.

47 (Milwaukee, WI: Bruce, 1932). See Hill, "Twentieth Century Thought," 228.

48 McGucken, *Jesuits and Education*, 169.

49 (New York: P. J. Kenedy & Sons, 1934).

of the early college course, and science the primary objective of the later college and university."[50] Noting that the Society's *Epitome* directs its members to follow the "principles of sound training which are found in the *Constitution* of St. Ignatius and in the *Ratio*," Donnelly's stated purpose was to "formulate some of these principles of the *Ratio* and to show how they are applied practically to the teaching of the classics and of the vernacular."[51]

For Donnelly, McGucken, Farrell, Schwickerath, and many others, a strong classical course is assumed to be a standing feature of the education, and it is usually praised as something to be retained, "even counter-culturally."[52] Part of the rationale is that the Greek and Latin classics are tools by which one can learn the arts of composition: "Did not Greek literature largely create Latin literature? Was not Cicero, as Newman himself testifies, Newman's master in English? Why then may not Latin and Greek still form writers?"[53]

At the midpoint of the twentieth century, the most comprehensive work on Jesuit education appeared: *La pédagogie des jésuites: Ses principes, son actualité* (The pedagogy of the Jesuits: Its principles, its relevance), by François Charmot (1881–1965).[54] This ambitious and masterly synthesis presented many of the major academic dimensions of Jesuit education, recapitulating many of the most important sources and earlier writers from the times of Ignatius and the founding charters of the Society of Jesus. What distinguishes this work is not only the large range and use of sources but also an unprecedented attention to issues of what we might call spirituality (not specifically the spirituality of Christianity as much as that of the interior personal domain of the intellectual, psychological, and creative, as suggested by the Latin *animus* or German *Geist*).[55] This book was one of the first to develop the implications of a connection between Jesuit teaching methods and those of the *Spiritual Exercises*.[56] It also expands upon

---

50 Ibid., 20.

51 Ibid., 1.

52 For example, McGucken, though he spoke so well about adaptability, wanted a type of Renaissance school ("a Vittorino school") with six years of Latin for boys (Hill, "Twentieth Century Thought," 229); Jaime Castiello (fn45 above) wrote: "For Catholics, a classical tradition is not a matter of luxury, but almost a necessity. If, for others, Latin is a dead language, for Catholics it can never be dead [...]" (Castiello, *Humane Psychology*, 184). Schwickerath devoted chapter 12 to a discussion of classical studies in Jesuit education; see especially *Jesuit Education*, 346–60.

53 Donnelly, *Principles*, 18.

54 (Paris: Aux Éditions Spes, 1943; 2nd ed., 1951).

55 Ibid., 12: Charmot expressly admits limiting his book to the intellectual education of the young, and yet he still reveals something of his primary interest in spirituality. The titles of his books are quite indicative of his range of interests: see the bibliography available at Jesuitica.be; http://www.jesuitica.be/catalogue-author/2502/ (accessed October 1, 2018).

56 Charmot, *Pédagogie des jésuites*, 137: "We need to first insist on the very close relationship that exists between the principles of the *Exercises* of St. Ignatius and the pedagogical principles of the *Ratio*. One might be surprised at first that an ascetical book might also

certain dynamics of increasing reach—individual, interpersonal, and cultural. A brief survey of Charmot's major headings is most revealing. The first part treats education as a mission of the church entrusted to the Society, its formational power, the vocational aspects of the Jesuit undertaking, and all that is required in the formation of the teachers. The second and third parts analyze aspects and elements of the method of teaching, situating both the teachers and students in light of a paradigm suggested by the *Spiritual Exercises*. Leading topics are the importance of authority, adaptation, activity; the need to learn to educate oneself, the place of feeling, of thinking, of deeply appropriating; and the arts of writing and speaking. The fourth part attends to psychological dynamics at play: enthusiasm, honor, interest, appetite, emulation, and contest. And, finally, Charmot turns to Christian humanism, discussing collaboration with God, the example of the teachers, the union of the members of the faculty (who would likely all be Jesuits at the time of his writing), the spirit of the college, Christian life, and lastly integral Christian culture.

Charmot's scope was broad as well as deep, perhaps too much so for most of those who were soon finding themselves in situations that were so very different, after cumulative adaptations and variations, even including the steady diminishment of Jesuit faculty after Vatican II (1962–65). The rapidly changing circumstances, in addition to an academic culture increasingly invested in other directions on secularizing lines, may have led to the relative neglect of *La pédagogie des jésuites*. There seems little record of any extensive reception of Charmot's text in Anglophone writings on Jesuit education, except that he is credited as a significant source for the composition of the "Ignatian Pedagogical Paradigm" of 1993.[57] But even with the seismic transformations of culture in the mid-twentieth century and later, it is hard to understand how Charmot's work has escaped translation into English for the last seven decades: cultural changes could not negate either the historical value or the perennial educational insights

---

be a pedagogical one. This surprise quickly vanishes upon reflection" (translation mine). Charmot finds support for this position in Ernst Böminghaus's (1882–1942) *Geist der Gesellschaft Jesu und ihr pädagogisches Werk: 75 Jahre Mare Stella Matutina*, Festschrift Band 1 (Feldkirch, Austria: Selbstverlag der Stella Matutina, 1931), 24–42. He also directs the reader generally to what Nadal says on the topic in the appendix to his book, perhaps thinking of this passage: "Our scholastics might draw a greater profit from their studies and their course if they dispose themselves according to the method of the *Spiritual Exercises*." See Charmot, *Pédagogie des jésuites*, 534–35 (citing from Jéronimo Nadal, *Orationis observationes*, no. 117–74 and 202, in *Epistolae P. Hieronymi Nadal Societatis Jesu ab anno 1546 ad 1577: Selecta Natalis monumenta in ejus epistolis commemorata*, Monumenta Natalis IV, MHSI 47 [Madrid: Institutum Historicum Societatis Iesu, 1898–1964]).

57 See Richard LaBelle, *Rich Enough: What the Jesuits Have Written about Education* (self-published, 2014), 165–66. LaBelle points out here that most of the influence of Charmot derives from the sixth chapter of *La pédagogie des jésuites*, which comprises twenty-nine chapters.

that he surveyed. Indeed, in times of change, educators had all the greater need of the best lights that they could find, and this study was certainly one of those.

But something was also new here. Charmot was heavily and explicitly indebted to a long line of authors writing within the ambit of the RS, and so his text is quite continuous with the insights of earlier ages. Real progress, he says, requires looking back: "The sap of the past needs to rise up into the branches."[58] Yet there is a noticeable shift in the treatment of Jesuit education, one that would increase steadily over the next fifty years. Charmot directly engaged the reality of the RS in his preface, making it quite clear that indeed the letter of the *Ratio* was at that time in part outdated or worn out (*usée*), but "the *Ratio* is above all a spirit. The 'letter' can be corrected, filled out, organized on a new plan."[59] Such a turn was being made in the institutions as well. Thus the RS, whose "letter" was full of concrete details, does not seem as pointedly present here as it was for Schwickerath or Farrell or Donnelly. But the further the details of the RS receded from view, the more difficult became the question of how to perceive, grasp, and retain its spirit in order to produce the results that should be expected. Would the new purveyors know the old manuals—or even the summaries of them in Charmot's very new book—well enough to share, even analogically, in the essential educational genius that was to stand behind all adaptations? Would the new educators have the necessary grounding to make the appropriate judgments and keep the system "in character" in changed conditions?

Even before Charmot's study, the historiography of Jesuit pedagogy had begun to enter a new stage, one marked by an increasing distance from its long attachment to the RS. The emphatic title of a short and sketchy article published in 1940 by Hugh McCarron (1893–1952) was "Not the *Ratio*."[60] It began with the blunt statement: "The chief guide of the Jesuit system of education is not the *Ratio Studiorum* but the *Spiritual Exercises*."[61] Part of the argument was that the prior Jesuit interest was in the life of the person, and Jesuit involvement in education was derivative of that. The *Spiritual Exercises* was "the notebook which created the spirit that animates Jesuit education."[62]

The deepening eclipse of the RS as the most proximately relevant guide for Jesuit education is noticeable in the important study that appeared in 1954, *Saint Ignatius' Idea of a Jesuit University* (second edition, 1956).[63] But for the author, George Ganss (1905–2000), the key to the spirit of the RS was to be found not

58 Charmot, *Pédagogie des jésuites*, 12.

59 Ibid., 10.

60 Hugh McCarron, "Not the Ratio," *Jesuit Educational Quarterly* 3, no. 2 (September 1940): 79–81.

61 Ibid., 79.

62 Ibid., 81.

63 *Saint Ignatius' Idea of a Jesuit University: A Study in the History of Catholic Education*, 2nd ed. (Milwaukee, WI: Marquette University Press, 1956 [1954]).

so much in the *Spiritual Exercises* as in the *Constitutions*, particularly its fourth part. The RS was like a school bulletin, full of variable (and disposable) specifics; the larger principles had to be found in the *Constitutions*.[64] And the difference between the two was decidedly a grand one: "The *Constitutions* are related to the *Ratio Studiorum* as the sun is to the moon."[65] Ganss summarized the main Ignatian educational principles under these headings:

> (1) An awareness that education is a means to the end of his Society (that end being the salvation and perfection of the students, who would promote the same for others and thus transform the world); (2) a care to impart a scientifically reasoned Catholic outlook on life; (3) a training of the whole person to the excellence of all his faculties; (3) a conscious effort to make education both intellectual and moral; (4) a preservation of the preeminence of theology supported by philosophy; (5) abundant self-activity of the students; (6) personal interest of the professors in the students; (7) a transmitting of old truths and a discovering of new ones; (8) a care to have the training psychologically fitted to the ages of the students; (9) a devising of means truly adequate to achieve the ends envisaged; (10) a care for timeliness, through adaptation of procedures to places and times; (11) an alertness to gather the best elements emerging in the educational systems of the day; (12) a care to preserve, discard, and add according to contemporary needs; (13) a courageous yet prudent spirit of experimentation and discussion; (14) a care to have a complete code of a liberal education; (15) a care to educate the complete person towards both wisdom and charity.[66]

Ganss concluded the body of his book with a reiteration of the need for adaptability and change; implicit was the need for a readiness to abandon any details that did not seem likely to be effective in present circumstances.[67] The implication was clear: set aside the RS and look to these larger principles; go back to the *Constitutions*.[68]

It should be noted that there still existed some exponents of the tradition of the RS, for example Matthew J. Fitzsimons (1899–1975), who criticized Ganss for failing to mention "the most significant and progressive development in American Jesuit education, and unique, perhaps, in the entire Society," namely the 1948 *Instructio*.[69] Fitzsimons thought that the spirit of the *Constitutions* might well be

---

64 Ibid., 206.

65 Ibid., 211.

66 Ibid., 191–200. These words are drawn almost verbatim from Ganss's text.

67 Ibid., 201.

68 Ganss included his own fresh translation of part 4 of the *Constitutions*, significantly entitling the section "The Principal Document." Ibid., 281–345.

69 Matthew J. Fitzsimons, "The Spirit and the Letter," *Jesuit Educational Quarterly* 17, no. 4 (March 1955): 213–24, here 223, referring to the *Instructio pro assistentia Americae de ordinandis universitatibus, collegiis, ac scholis altis et de praeparandis eorundem magistris*

found here.[70] Writing from the Ateneo de Manila University, Miguel A. Bernad (1917–2009) also expressed both praise for and deep reservations about Ganss's study.[71] He allowed the characterization of the early Society's "eagerness to experiment," but he claimed the full picture must also include "Ignatius's certainty of the goal to be aimed at."[72] By the time of his review, Bernad had published a summative article listing what he saw as ten essential Jesuit educational principles:

> (1) Great respect for the value inherent in scholarship; (2) study as a means to a higher end; (3) the importance of solid comprehension of what is studied; (4) the need for method and systematic progress; (5) focus or the removal of obstacles that hinder mastery; (6) care of one's health in studies; (7) the need for a general education and the subordination of lesser subjects to more important ones; (8) abstaining from pomp in winning academic credentials; (9) need for mastery of oral and written expression; (10) following the doctrine most approved and the best scholars available, learning a little well rather than many things less well.[73]

Such listings by Bernad here and Ganss above indicate the desire to seize upon the essential and lasting principles, particularly for the sake of authenticity and effectiveness in the face of accommodation. Something important was at stake for the order; the historiography of Jesuit pedagogy from within the Society tended to be an apostolically interested one, just as non-Jesuit (secular or non-Catholic) writings of the nineteenth century tended toward the critical or polemical.

The reactions of Bernad and Fitzsimons to Ganss's book suggest an awareness that more still needed to be done on the topic. In 1959, in an effort to articulate more clearly the perduring core of the tradition, the US Jesuit Educational Association commissioned a professor in the Graduate School of Education at Fordham University, John W. Donohue (1917–2010), to write a thorough study; it was published in 1963 as *Jesuit Education: An Essay on the Foundations of Its Idea*.[74] As the subtitle indicates, the focus was on educational theory, explicit or implicit in the origins and developments of the Jesuit tradition. Donohue did

---

(New York: Jesuit Educational Association, 1948). Fitzsimons studied the history of this document in "The Instructio: 1934–1949," *Jesuit Educational Quarterly* 12, no. 2 (October 1949): 69–78.

70 It "provides for the organization of our education on a national basis, for the Jesuit Educational Association with National Secretary and Regional Directors of Studies, for efficient and modern administration of our high schools and colleges and universities, and the preparation of teachers for them." Fitzsimons, "Spirit and the Letter," 224. Fitzsimons explicitly favors the RS, a careful study of which, he says, "will reveal it as a very great document." Ibid., 223.

71 "The Idea of a Jesuit University," *Philippine Studies* 6, no. 1 (March 1958): 123–28.

72 Ibid., 128.

73 Miguel A. Bernad, "The Ignatian Way in Education," *Philippine Studies* 4, no. 2 (1956): 195–214.

74 (New York: Fordham University Press, 1963).

acknowledge three major sources: the *Spiritual Exercises*, the *Constitutions*, and the legislative tradition, particularly the RS.[75] But he took a philosophical tack, entitling the first part of the book "The Context of the Idea," and the second, "The Content of the Idea." That idea transcended all the concrete details of that Renaissance program of learning in terms of which the early Society had done its pedagogical thinking. Donohue did name a historical innovation in early Jesuit education: its distinctive arrangement of elements, namely "a certain originality in the school program itself, a firm belief in the value of order, graduated curricula and tested methods and finally, a staff of teachers devoted to their work and professionally well prepared."[76] But for Donohue, as for Charmot, the important reality was rather what grounded the various historical manifestations. The "true source of vitality in Jesuit education is indicated by the answer to a why rather than a what," and this factor, "the Society's enduring purposes and motives," is what has given continuity to the Jesuit educational work across space and time.[77] This turn away from specific contents, methods, and curricula marked a decisive step further away from the RS as the authoritative embodiment of or guide for Jesuit education.[78] The stress was put on greater freedom: that is, on flexibility, adaptability, and creativity, all operating in terms of certain larger purposes and perduring wider contexts (of church, society, and culture), and on the basis of fundamental anthropological realities, like the universal dynamics of cognition and volition. Jesuit education aims above all at nurturing intellectual, moral, and social maturity, with the moral sphere being given primacy. These are to lead the student to the love of God that promotes service and ultimately spreads the graces of salvation.[79]

After 1965: Losing the *Ratio studiorum*

In that very period during which Lukács was publishing his seven volumes of definitive critical editions of the early Society's pedagogical documents, the RS seems to have been fully retired, deprecated, and largely forgotten except in name. Most telling are some lines written by Robert J. Henle (1909–2001) in 1967:

> There is no way in which Jesuit education can be defined as a set of specific traits. I myself have made various attempts so to define it, but I finally became convinced that the effort was futile. I think we must say that *Jesuit*

75 Ibid., xiii, xvii.

76 Ibid., 39.

77 Ibid., 9.

78 Donohue's stance comes through in such sentences as "The full philosophy of education subscribed to by a Jesuit School is not to be found wholly or even chiefly in any Jesuit documents." Also: "This unity and continuity will not be detected on the plane of curricula and concrete procedures, for civilizations change and so do their demands on the school." Ibid., 82, 83.

79 Ibid., 130.

> *education is education given by Jesuits.* Jesuit education cannot be described in a set of specific educational traits, specific subjects, procedures or methods; it can be described in terms of Jesuits, in terms of Jesuit character.[80]

Donohue quoted these words approvingly in *America* magazine in 1985 with the comment, "Certainly Jesuit education cannot be defined in terms of the *Ratio*. That was only one of many Renaissance school plans, Protestant as well as Catholic, all of which looked alike on paper."[81] Such sentiments would have been utterly incomprehensible to a Schwickerath, a Farrell, or a Donnelly earlier in the same century.[82] This attitude made it hard to imagine any large-scale study of the "idea of Jesuit education" that might improve very much on Donohue's study from 1963.

Indeed, there had been seismic historic changes coming in and around Vatican II that helped power the prevailing direction away from the RS. The year Henle's article appeared was also the year that marked the first "separate incorporation" of an American Jesuit institution of higher learning, Saint Louis University: final responsibility for the school was put into the hands of a predominantly lay board.[83] The Land O' Lakes statement also appeared in 1967, declaring "true autonomy and academic freedom" for Catholic universities *qua* universities, operating within the standing secular paradigm for universities.[84]

---

80 Robert J. Henle, "Jesuit Aims in Higher Education," *Jesuit Educational Quarterly* 29, no. 4 (March 1967): 213–29, here 219. The emphasis is original.

81 John W. Donohue, "Notes on Jesuit Education," *America* 153, no. 11 (October 26, 1985): 252–58, here 255. See http://americamagazine.org/issue/100/notes-jesuit-education (accessed October 1, 2018).

82 Just two years before Henle's article, a very different stance had been taken by William D. Ryan, "Is There Anything Distinctive about Jesuit Education?," *Jesuit Educational Quarterly* 28, no. 1 (June 1965): 58–60. The distinctiveness consisted in a "combination of elements," notably: elements of government, commonalities of culture and motivations, spirituality, and a heritage of instrumentalities traditionally associated with Jesuit education.

83 "A Louder Voice for Laymen," *Time*, 89, no. 5 (Friday, February 3, 1967). Henle was already a widely known personality. He had been the author of a series of Latin textbooks and a Latin grammar popular in American Jesuit high schools in the 1950s and 1960s. In 1967, at the time of the separate incorporation, he was the academic vice-president at St. Louis University, and in July of that same year he became a signer of the Land O' Lakes statement.

84 "The Idea of the Catholic University"; http://archives.nd.edu/episodes/visitors/lol/idea.htm (accessed October 1, 2018). The first paragraph of the document is pointed: "The Catholic University today must be a university in the full modern sense of the word, with a strong commitment to and concern for academic excellence. To perform its teaching and research functions effectively the Catholic university must have a true autonomy and academic freedom in the face of authority of whatever kind, lay or clerical, external to the academic community itself. To say this is simply to assert that institutional autonomy and academic freedom are essential conditions of life and growth and indeed of survival for Catholic universities as for all universities."

Furthermore, a perhaps equally momentous change was taking place in Jesuit formation: a major stage of the traditional academic preparation was virtually suppressed. Almost every US province lost the entire juniorate period (a two-year period after the two-year novitiate, usually conducted in a separate institutional space and mostly focused on Latin, Greek, and English language and literary study). Jesuit formation for scholastics therefore no longer followed that perduring stadial scheme of the RS: Letters–philosophy–theology. This pattern had had its origins in the biography of Ignatius of Loyola himself, and it had been the recognized standard for all of the Society's existence up to that point.[85] This change entailed another major loss of particular content and therefore of Jesuit investments and competencies in the classroom: Latin and, for the Society, Greek language and cultural studies, though mandated by the new *Code of Canon Law* (1983) and later by the Society's own *Complementary Norms* (1995), *de facto* disappeared entirely from the common scholastic program.[86]

Donohue's and Henle's philosophically framed approaches to Jesuit education were representative of a generational shift in attitude that continued on for decades. In 1989, another leading Jesuit educator, William McInnis (1923–2009), questioned and opined as follows:

> Obviously Jesuit education is one form of Catholic education. But is there something distinctive (though not articulated) that sets it apart from Dominican, Franciscan, or diocesan educational systems? [...] Our problem is not that we do not have one clear answer, but that we have not engaged in systematic, serious thought. [...] The search for the uniqueness of Jesuit education has always ended in frustration.[87]

Here, the idea of that distinctive tradition established by the fourth part of the *Constitutions* and the RS and hundreds of years of Jesuit institutional practices seems utterly lost, perhaps because different philosophical approaches and new apostolic-cultural imperatives were overriding a particular sense of the history.

---

85 Ignatius began his study of language and literature in Barcelona in 1524, and he reviewed these studies at the Collège de Montaigu in Paris in 1528–29. He always insisted on the value of this study for the scholastics.

86 Canon 249, available in English at http://www.vatican.va/archive/ENG1104/__PW.HTM and in Latin at http://www.vatican.va/archive/cod-iuris-canonici/latin/documents/cic_liberII_lt.html#TITULUS_III (accessed October 1, 2018). The Society's *Complementary Norms* of 1995 are published with the *Constitutions*, ed. Padberg. The relevant number is part 4, no. 86, 153.

87 William McInnis, "The Current State of the Jesuit Philosophy of Education," in *Jesuit Higher Education: Essays on an American Tradition of Excellence*, ed. Rolando E. Bonachea (Pittsburgh: Duquesne University Press, 1989), 26–45, here 182nn22, 28. McInnis, like Henle, was a well-known figure in Jesuit education: he was president of Fairfield (1964–73), the University of San Francisco (1972–77), and then the Association of Jesuit Colleges and Universities (1977–89).

The new generation was standing on the other side of an epochal cultural break that made the past harder to evaluate. Even a leading historian of the Society, John W. O'Malley (1931–), followed this trend, writing in 2015 of the RS as being merely an "in-house document" that had clearly been useless for a very long time.[88] This understanding of the RS is quite far from that foundational document and perennial guide celebrated in the first half of the twentieth century and praised as a living reality and standard by the thirtieth general congregation in 1957.[89]

Revaluation

The new "post-Ratio" stance contributed to and was accompanied by changes in the historiography of Jesuit pedagogy: (1) particularly as Lukács's critical editions became available in the Monumenta Paedagogica, the presentation of the idea of Jesuit education could be treated by scholars in more purely historical terms (that is, rather than as part of an "apostolically engaged" or apologetic kind of representation); (2) non-Jesuit scholars indeed began to do more work in this field (e.g., Aldo Scaglione [1924–2013], Paul Grendler [1936–]), as has been true of Jesuit studies more generally;[90] (3) without the dominance of the RS as the educational charter, thinking on "Jesuit education" (which remained a quite relevant topic in Jesuit educational institutions) tended to be more "essayistic" and partial rather than large-scale and comprehensive like the treatises of Schwickerath, Farrell, and Charmot;[91] (4) without the RS as a controlling framework encompassing many particulars, more emphasis could be put on the *Spiritual Exercises* and on "what is Ignatian" as the source of the distinctive principles and

---

88 John W. O'Malley, "Jesuit Schools and the Humanities Yesterday and Today," *Studies in the Spirituality of Jesuits* 47, no. 1 (2015): 1–34, here 2. Of the restored Society's efforts in the United States, O'Malley wrote, "The *Ratio studiorum* of 1599 was hopelessly out of date and impracticable, and all efforts to revise it failed utterly." Ibid., 27. This article is available at https://ejournals.bc.edu/ojs/index.php/jesuit/issue/view/641 (accessed October 1, 2018).

89 See fn7 above.

90 Aldo Scaglione, *The Liberal Arts and the Jesuit College System* (Philadelphia: John Benjamins, 1986); Paul Grendler is a well-known Renaissance scholar who has written many items about Jesuit education; see, for example, "Jesuit Schools in Europe: A Historiographical Essay," *Journal of Jesuit Studies* 1, no. 1 (2014): 7–25; doi: 10:116/22141332-00101002.

91 For some examples of collections of essays and short pieces on Jesuit education, see Bonachea, *Jesuit Higher Education*; Duminuco, *Jesuit* Ratio studiorum; Martin R. Tripole, ed., *Jesuit Education 21: Conference Proceedings on the Future of Jesuit Higher Education* (Philadelphia: Saint Joseph's University Press, 2000); George W. Traub, ed., *A Jesuit Education Reader* (Chicago: Loyola Press, 2008); Edmund P. Cueva, Shannon N. Byrne, and Frederick Benda, eds., *Jesuit Education and the Classics* (Newcastle upon Tyne: Cambridge Scholars Publishing, 2009); and the magazine *Conversations on Jesuit Higher Education*, available at http://www.conversationsmagazine.org/ (accessed October 1, 2018).

character of Jesuit education, particularly in the apostolically engaged writing that looked to serviceable norms for operation or evaluation.[92]

It was probably the lack of the RS's perceived apostolic usefulness that led the Society's educators to shelve it in the first place. Since the fourth part of the *Constitutions* was closely linked to it, to what other authoritative source could practitioners go, then, other than the *Spiritual Exercises* and the broader concept of what is "Ignatian"? Charmot and others had already indicated the importance of the spirituality for Jesuit schools. For Robert Newton, the *Exercises* are the "original source of the Jesuit educational tradition."[93] And yet the *Exercises* had not been written with formal schooling in mind at all. The *Constitutions* did not explicitly make them any kind of operational guide. Ignatius's spiritual notes from Manresa (1522) had been written years away from his exposure to university life in Paris (1528). Moreover, the academic exercises and structures of the university that were going to impress the early Jesuits were already in operation at Paris and elsewhere even as Ignatius was sketching out his spiritual handbook, so there seems no easy way to derive very much of a distinctive idea of Jesuit education from this ascetical manual.[94] The proximate guide for Jesuit schools could only be something like the RS, which was composed for the particular sphere and intentionalities of the *studia Societatis*.

But progressive secularization along with other cultural and societal upheavals so greatly challenged the Society's rethinking of Jesuit education that

92 See, for example, the use of the phrase "Ignatian pedagogy" (Sharon J. Korth, "Precis of Ignatian Pedagogy: A Practical Approach," in Traub, *Jesuit Education Reader*, 280–84). An example of a widespread appropriation from Ignatian spirituality is "magis" (see Barton T. Geger, "What Magis Really Means and Why It Matters," *Jesuit Higher Education* 2, no. 16 [2012]: 16–31). See especially Robert R. Newton, "Reflections on the Educational Principles of the *Spiritual Exercises*: Summary Conclusions and Questions for Teachers," in Traub, *Jesuit Education Reader*, 274–79; originally published in 1977 by the Jesuit Secondary Education Association (Washington, DC). Newton explains the underlying assumption that "since the *Spiritual Exercises* provided the experience that formed the Jesuit spirit and gave it method and direction, an analysis of the *Spiritual Exercises* as an educational treatise would shed light on the fundamental principles of Jesuit education." Ibid., 274.

93 "This exploration is given added impetus by the realization that the contemporary rediscovery of the original method of the *Spiritual Exercises* has led to a renewal and rearticulation of the authentic Jesuit charism and vocation. A return to the *Spiritual Exercises* as the original source of the Jesuit educational tradition could be expected to generate analogous benefits." Newton, "Reflections on the Educational Principles," 274.

94 Peter Schineller (1939–) has in fact shown the differences between the spirituality of the Exercises and that of the *Constitutions* in his "From an Ascetical Spirituality of the Exercises to the Apostolic Spirituality of the *Constitutions*: Laborers in the Lord's Vineyard," in Ite inflammate omnia: *Selected Historical Papers from Conferences Held at Loyola and Rome in 2006*, ed. Thomas M. McCoog (Rome: Institutum Historicum Societatis Iesu, 2010), 85–108. The spirituality of the RS would be an even further step in the direction taken by the *Constitutions*.

even at the most general level of the old structure of "Letters–philosophy–theology" there was a great difficulty: trends in the curriculum over the twentieth century showed a massive universal devaluation of precisely these areas in higher education, the very ones in which Jesuit education was most heavily invested for centuries.[95] The principle of adaptability is overtaxed if essential structures and contents must be jettisoned or minimized. It is one thing not to read Cicero in Latin, and quite another to have one's entire college theology requirement reduced to one or two courses that might not even focus on Christianity. In 1991, William P. Leahy wrote that American Catholic higher education "urgently requires a coherent, convincing theory of education and articulate, persuasive proponents of it."[96]

The quest to refine "the theory" and to identify the primary abiding principles of Jesuit education and then to integrate these with a new set of practices in Jesuit education continues. No single model or document or understanding has proven "authoritative." In fact, given the largely decentralized structure in the Society today, the consensus seems to be that there will be nothing ever again in the line of the RS, so the idea of Jesuit education must look for new modes of thought. In the early 1970s, a serious attempt to make a way forward with the American Jesuit higher educational institutions failed to produce any noticeable winning results.[97] Nevertheless, the long Jesuit history of a distinctive tradition in education has continued to exert pressure, so that essays and documents keep being produced. Five contributions deserve special mention. Most important is Michael J. Buckley's historical and philosophical collection of essays, *The Catholic*

---

95 David John Frank and Jay Gabler, *Reconstructing the University: Worldwide Shifts in Academia in the Twentieth Century* (Stanford: Stanford University Press, 2006). The humanities (now redefined to include philosophy and theology) have lost the most ground in the curriculum: the greatest losses are in classics (down eighty-seven percent), philosophy (down seventy-one percent), and theology (down sixty percent). See the table on 105.

96 *Adapting to America: Catholics, Jesuits, and Higher Education in the Twentieth Century* (Washington, DC: Georgetown University Press, 1991), 156.

97 "Project 1: The Jesuit Apostolate of Education in the United States: Agreements and Decisions: A Step on the Way" (Washington, DC: Jesuit Conference, 1975). This summary report mostly looked to future developments for the assistancy's preference for "a corporate national apostolate." It began by saying that detailed decisions could not be made as they had been for secondary education (no. 1, ibid., 11), and that "there is still need for much more development and clarification in regard to the nature, scope, and objectives of a corporate Jesuit apostolate on the local, provincial, and national levels" (no. 4, ibid., 12). Each local community was to come up with "a concrete plan of action" (no. 5, ibid., 12). There will need to be "further collaborative work on the part of provincials, presidents, rectors, and Board chairmen" (ibid., 29). Project 1 had been a "strategic planning process" conducted from 1973 to 1975, "involving five university-trained men and costing perhaps three-quarters of a million dollars" (Joseph Tetlow, "Intellectual Conversion: Jesuit Spirituality and the American University," in *Spirit, Style, Story: Essays Honoring John W. Padberg, S.J.*, ed. Thomas M. Lucas [Chicago: Loyola Press, 2002], 93–115, here 93).

University as Promise and Project: Reflections in a Jesuit Idiom.[98] A simple summary is impossible, but it is worth noting that Buckley has set a very high standard for understanding the tradition and its possible directions. His very rich collection of essays stands as the most advanced, most comprehensive thinking on the idea of Jesuit education since Donohue's study from 1963. It treats the full range of themes of mission, social justice, humanism, philosophy, and theology.

There have also been at least four official attempts to define Jesuit education more clearly. In 1986, a summary document was issued by the International Commission on the Apostolate of Jesuit Education (established by the Society in 1980 mostly with secondary education in mind). Entitled "Go Forth and Teach: The Characteristics of Jesuit Education," it attempted to provide not a new RS but rather an instrument for establishing a common vision, a common sense of purpose, and a standard against which educators in the tradition might measure themselves.[99] Many of the traditional and recent formulae are listed, along with salient points from the history and literature of Jesuit education. In 2013, American Jesuit higher education composed a much briefer parallel document, "Some Characteristics of Jesuit Colleges and Universities: A Self-evaluation Instrument."[100] Each institution was invited to review itself under whatever it might find to be helpful from a list of seven categories: leadership's commitment to the mission; the academic life; a Catholic, Jesuit campus culture; service; service to the local church; Jesuit presence; and integrity. The third document, "Ignatian Pedagogy: A Practical Approach" (1993), has been put forward as a new *Ratio.*[101] It does not list characteristics but rather attempts to identify a kind of transcendental method, that is, a radical process applicable to all curricula, subjects, and grade-levels. The key elements are context, experience, reflection, action, and evaluation. The scheme as a whole is known as the Ignatian Pedagogical Paradigm or "IPP." It especially looks back to the *Spiritual Exercises* and to certain other strands of social and philosophical thinking far more than it does to the RS, which is partly defined by a concreteness that is very far from the IPP's high abstraction. The most recent document, "Our Way of Proceeding: Standards and Benchmarks for Jesuit Schools in the 21st Century," was issued by the recently

---

98 (Washington, DC: Georgetown University Press, 1998).

99 (Washington, DC: Jesuit Secondary Education Association, 1987). The description given here is based on the words of Superior General Peter-Hans Kolvenbach's accompanying letter of December 8, 1986, 1–3, here 1. This document is reprinted in Duminuco, *Jesuit* Ratio studiorum, 161–230.

100 Published by the American Jesuit Colleges and Universities (Washington, DC, 2013). It is also available at http://www.xavier.edu/mission-identity/programs/documents/CharacteristicsFINALDec2012A.pdf (accessed October 1, 2018).

101 Vincent J. Duminuco, "A New Ratio for a New Millennium," in Duminuco, *Jesuit* Ratio studiorum, 145–60. The text of the document (Rome: International Commission on the Apostolate of Jesuit Education, 1993) is reprinted in this same volume, along with three appendices, ibid., 231–93.

established national office for American Jesuit high schools, the Jesuit School Network (2015).[102] It articulates many standards to help schools think through, measure, and document their Jesuit identity in coordination with a "sponsorship review process." The five domains covered are (1) Jesuit and Catholic Mission and Identity, (2) Governance and Leadership, (3) Spiritual Formation, (4) Educational Excellence, and (5) Faith That Does Justice. The results of these four documents are largely in the hands and judgments of the local communities to which they are addressed. They all point to the ongoing effort to portray the idea of Jesuit education and to carry it on as a living tradition well rooted in older sources.

Final Reflections and Questions

Historians of Jesuit education have much to do, particularly after Lukács's annotated critical editions in the Monumenta Paedagogica. The present essay has sketched out a few major features of one part of the landscape and provided a core narrative, but much more material remains, even for a fully adequate historiographical survey.[103] This rapid overview might nevertheless sufficiently show that the historiography is deeply implicated in a wide range of topics with various levels of relevance both to the historical narrative and to the ongoing self-fashioning in Jesuit educational institutions.

More localized research could ask whether in given situations the tradition of the RS maintained its position as some kind of "perceived" core, even with the inevitable adaptations. Or did the modifications fundamentally alter a particular community's attitude toward the normative core? Did the Society's leadership in various regions and at the central curia in Rome keep aiming for a particular legislated ideal in the restored Society (following Roothaan's lead, mentioned above), or did it have a growing appreciation for creative license?[104] What, in

102 The document, published in late 2015, is available at the JSN's website, https://jesuitschoolsnetwork.org/wp-content/uploads/2017/07/Our-Way-of-Proceeding-Standards-and-Benchmarks-for-Jesuit-Schools-in-the-21st-Century_0.pdf (accessed October 1, 2018). The JSN has replaced the JSEA (Jesuit Secondary Educational Association), which had been founded in 1970, along with the higher educational unit, AJCU (Association of Jesuit Colleges and Universities) out of the earlier JEA (Jesuit Educational Association), which had dealt with Jesuit educational work in the United States from 1937 to 1970. See Paul A. FitzGerald, *The Governance of Jesuit Colleges in the United States, 1920–1970* (Notre Dame: University of Notre Dame Press, 1984).

103 For example: Thomas Hughes, *Loyola and the Educational System of the Jesuits* (New York: Charles Scribner's Sons, 1892); J.-B. [Jean-Baptiste] Herman, *La pédagogie des jésuites au XVIe siècle: Ses sources, ses caractéristiques* (Louvain: Bureaux du recueil [UCL], 1914); Bernhard Duhr, *Geschichte der Jesuiten in den Ländern deutscher Zunge* [bis 1773], 4 Bände in 6 Teilbänden (Freiburg im Breisgau: Herder, 1907–28); François de Dainville, *L'éducation des jésuites (XVIe–XVIIIe siècles)* (Paris: Éditions de Minuit, 1978).

104 See fn6 above.

short, was the value of uniformity, and how widely or deeply was it championed? Even the RS explicitly allowed for flexibility, after all. How far was this flexibility in fact taken in various regions around the world?

Historians might well ask too about how informed were those who have been transforming the structures in accord with the demands of late modernity? How great an impact have the major works discussed in this essay had on the active understanding and discourse of the practitioners and revisers? What has been the actual level of absorption both of the official documentation and the major works from Schwickerath (1903) to Buckley (1998)? Also, how well has a knowledge of this tradition informed the new intensity of interest in social issues? What are the guidelines, sources, and authorities being used in dealing with politically and socially controverted topics?

Because the tradition is still alive, part of the historiography will remain "apostolically engaged." That is, it will be rooted in the Society's official self-understanding and its sponsored practices. This emic stream will probably also continue as long as the idea of Jesuit education is a viable concept. For the concept to remain viable, however, the leadership may have to come to terms with the need for more focus, content, and structure than has yet been achieved in the post-*Ratio* period. Can there in fact even be a post-*Ratio* Jesuit education if the RS is best understood as a (or as the) major constitutive document of the tradition? (Consider the prospect of a post-*Spiritual Exercises* Ignatian spirituality: Is it really possible?) Can Jesuit education forgo larger authoritative or legislative guidance of some kind and still claim to be operating in the tradition that was so signally marked by the RS? If not, how is that guidance to be understood?

Jesuit education may itself evolve into a wide range of very different forms. In such an event, the historiography will take into account these new directions, their sources, their motivations, and their expressions. If the concept of Jesuit education becomes so hopelessly broad and diverse as to become largely meaningless, this new situation might at least be well described. What will be said to survive in each of the schools professing allegiance to "the Jesuit tradition"? Some might take the hallmark of Jesuit education as "excellence," or education for rhetorical mastery, or a concern for social justice, or *cura personalis*, or the study of classical languages, or interdisciplinarity, or philosophy and theology requirements, or a vital retreat- and sodality-oriented campus ministry, or some such particular feature, substituting the part for the whole. What then becomes of the concept of Jesuit education?

Particularly for the sake of counter-secularizing interests, the idea of Jesuit education might well continue to merge more and more with spirituality. Such a direction suggests the importance of clarifying the relationship that Jesuit education has historically had to the *Exercises*. Nothing prevents the tradition from taking new turns and making new amalgamations; the question is rather one of how justifiable and coherent and widely accepted will new approaches be. Or will the use of the *Exercises* as a key to Jesuit education finally be judged to be misguided, partly on the basis of historical studies? Perhaps a more relevant kind of spirituality will be found in that other kind that Ignatius himself found available in his day, the spirituality of *docta pietas*.

Another question will have to do with content: for example, the classical course (particularly as grounding for rhetorical abilities) has been eliminated. Should there be no replacement for this long-standing defining feature of the tradition, not even one adapted to a wider, "updated" range of classics and communicative education? Will people informed by the tradition easily cast off the idea of a core high-quality long-approved canon (formerly centered largely but not exclusively on Cicero, Aristotle, Thomas, and scripture), one that not only challenged students by setting for them a very high standard of thought and articulation but also gave them an important "common cultural alphabet" of great educational and communal import?

Studies of Jesuit education have failed to attend sufficiently to the *ad intra* formational dimensions of the RS. This programmatic infrastructure was absolutely necessary for the Society to train the teachers and administrators competent to carry on its vision through particular tasks that functioned within a coherent larger plan. Without any organized formational revision within the Society (or some kind of parallel formation program for non-Jesuit colleagues), will any new self-understanding of Jesuit education tend to be limited, vague, confused, idiosyncratic, or short-lived?[105] Will the same be the case if there is too much practical assimilation to secularizing practices? Historians will be able to use the many mission statements composed by individual institutions to attain some insight into the range of understandings of the tradition at the local levels.

Some will say that any *Ratio*-like "constitutional" type of charter is now either utterly impossible or completely undesirable. On the other hand, an approach that effectively joins many concrete particulars to spirit and goals may fall well within the realm of possibility, particularly if the Society comes to the view that the RS, as a foundational document both for Jesuit education and for the Jesuit order itself, simply cannot be put aside, at the very least as an operational model that can exert a kind of historical-exemplary pressure on contemporary reformulations.[106] To try to capture the "spirit" of the RS without any descent into concrete particulars might prove to be unworkably idealistic (and actually quite foreign to the spirit as well as to the practices of the tradition).

105 One might analyze the needs as involving infrastructure (training teachers by having them learn what they will be giving); structure (the program itself: its contents, its disposition, and its delivery); and superstructure (an authoritative oversight body that keeps the whole picture and the desired ends in mind as adjustments are made).

106 See, for example, the author's "Toward a Revised *Ratio studiorum* for Jesuit Colleges" (2015), chapter 6 in the present volume. For the RS as a foundational document, see chapter 5, "The *Ratio studiorum* of 1599: Inescapably Foundational."

Most likely, the idea of Jesuit education will (1) continue to evolve and sharpen into a new form or into many different local forms; (2) remain somewhat eclectic, unfocused, secularized, or diverse; or (3) all but disappear as a living reality. In any case, historians will have ample material for relevant and valuable research and reflection.

5. The *Ratio studiorum* of 1599: Inescapably Foundational

> Thus says the Lord: Stand at the crossroads, and look, and ask for the ancient paths, where the good way lies; and walk in it, and find rest for your souls. But they said, "We will not walk in it."
>
> —*Jeremiah 6:16*

> History may be servitude, History may be freedom.
>
> —*T. S. Eliot,* Four Quartets, *Little Gidding III*

> There are assuredly two things that constitute our Society's bulwark and mainstay: the burning zeal of devotion and a surpassing knowledge of reality.
>
> —*Acta Congregationis Societatis Iesu, 1584*

Retelling a community's story can stabilize it, guide it, and give it a greater cohesive vitality.[1] At the present moment, the Society of Jesus can profit greatly from a searching review of this type, particularly because recent changes have been numerous, profound, rapid, and ubiquitous. Of course, many stories can be told, and they can all be told in many ways. I am proposing here that *however* the Society tells its story, it must never leave out one particular part, a part that has unfortunately been all but forgotten for at least half a century. The proposal is already given in the title: the Jesuit plan of studies known as the *Ratio studiorum* is "inescapably foundational." Failing to attend intelligently to this essential part of the story of the Society does not help it or its allies or the work to which they are dedicating their efforts; in fact, such failure rather produces the opposite of help. In this essay, I will first show how the boundaries of the foundational period are not necessarily what most people think they are; then I will present seven arguments for understanding the *Ratio studiorum* as foundational; and finally I will explain what difference the thesis makes, why it stands strong against some leading counterarguments, and what other relevant implications it might have. It will become apparent that what is at stake is much, much more than a good story.

1 For more on the value of the "larger stories" that highlight such moments, see Claude Pavur, "Restoring Cultural History: Beyond Gombrich," *Clio* 20, no. 2 (1991): 157–67. Also available at https://www.academia.edu/897964/ (accessed October 1, 2018).

The Society's First Founding Moments

First, how we should identify the Society of Jesus's founding moment? Some might well say that the Jesuit order had its most meaningful moment of inception in Montmartre on August 15, 1534, at a chapel dedicated to Saint Denis. There, seven students at the University of Paris professed vows, firmly constituting a perduring fellowship of religious service in the Lord. All subsequent Jesuit history depends on the bond created at that moment. More frequently, however, the foundation of the Society of Jesus is simply linked, legally and institutionally, with September 27, 1540, the date of the first written papal approval, *Regimini militantis ecclesiae*, issued by Paul III (1468–1549, r.1534–49). It contained the *Formula of the Institute*, which sketched out the basic idea and scope of the Society. But as yet there were no particular superior generals, no *Constitutions*, no provinces, no institutions for Jesuit formation, no temporal coadjutors (that is, "lay brothers," non-clerical religious with vows); and the membership was limited to sixty. Ignatius of Loyola (*c.*1491–1556) was not elected the first general of the Society until April 7, 1541; and on April 22, the first companions made their vows in the newly established order at the church of Saint Paul's Outside the Walls near Rome.

On July 23, 1550, the *Formula of the Institute* re-appeared, noticeably revised, as part of the next papal bull of approval, *Exposcit debitum*, issued by Pope Julius III (1487–1555, r.1550–55). The limitation to sixty members was removed; brothers introduced; the purpose of the Society stretched to include, in addition to the progress of souls in Christian life and doctrine, not just the propagation of the faith but its defense as well; and the listing of the possible apostolic involvements of the Society expanded. The very fact that the *Formula* came to be rewritten ten years after its first appearance strongly suggests that the idea of the Society was still taking shape. In fact, there is some specific, rather striking proof of how some of the basic lines of the Society's self-concept were evolving: we can point to change in the founder's own thinking.

Morphing the Society: Traveling, Teaching, and the Jesuit Vocation

At first, the Society was to be a group of members on the move "without fixed abode" (1 Cor. 4:11, Douay–Rheims version). When one of the founders, Claude le Jay (1504–52), was being promoted for episcopal office in Trieste, Ignatius wrote to the king of the Romans, Ferdinand I (1503–64, r.1558–64), giving the following as his first reason why this was an unacceptably bad idea:

> This Society and its members have been joined together in one and the same spirit; namely, to travel to various places in the world, among the faithful and the infidel, as we are sent by the supreme pontiff. Indeed, *it is the spirit of the Society to go in all humility and simplicity from city to city and place to place, without taking root anywhere.* [...] To abandon this simplicity of Ours

> *would be the undoing of our spirit, of our profession*; and this done, *the Society would be utterly destroyed. So we see that doing good in a particular place would involve greater harm to the whole body.*[2]

These words date to December of 1546. By the time Ignatius died less than a decade later, we see that he had enshrined in the *Constitutions* a notably different approach:

> Whether they carry on their labor *not by traveling but by residing steadily and continually in certain places* where much fruit of glory and service to God is expected. [...] Since the Society endeavors to aid its neighbors *not only by traveling through various parts of the world but also by residing continually in certain places, as is the case with the houses and colleges*, it is important to have a clear idea of the ways in which souls can be helped in those places, so as to put into practice those of them which are possible for the glory of God our Lord.[3]

The early model of ever-in-motion Francis Xavier (1506–52) was still and would long remain a powerful example of the missionary mode of existence. A summary of the *Constitutions* says this: "It is according to our vocation to travel to [and live in] any part of the world where there is hope of God's greater service and the help of souls."[4]

This descriptive sentence has become an influential part of many "thumbnail sketches" of the Society: Jesuits are travelers. But we should be aware that this part of the *Constitutions*, no. 304, is primarily about the sick who must restrict the scope of their activities:

> Moreover *although* our vocation is to travel through the world and to live in any part of it where there is hope of greater service to God and of help of souls, nevertheless, if experience shows that a person cannot stand the climate of a particular region [...] [the superior will have to decide whether a re-assignment is best].[5]

---

2 William John Young, ed., *Letters of St. Ignatius of Loyola* (Chicago: Loyola Press, 1959), 112, emphasis added.

3 *Constitutions*, nos. 603 and 636, emphasis added. The edition used in this essay will be John W. Padberg, ed., *The Constitutions of the Society of Jesus and Their Complementary Norms: A Complete English Translation of the Latin Text* (St. Louis, MO: Institute of Jesuit Sources, 1996).

4 "Nostrae vocationis est diversa loca peragrare et vitam agere in quavis mundi plaga ubi maius Dei obsequium et animarum auxilium speratur." Rule 3, *Summary of the Constitutions*, 1590, excerpted from *Constitutions of the Society of Jesus* [304]. Cited in John W. O'Malley, "To Travel to Any Part of the World: Jerónimo Nadal and the Jesuit Vocation," *Studies in the Spirituality of Jesuits* 16, no. 2 (1984): 1–20, here iv. The bracketed words were not given as part of the translation in O'Malley's text.

5 *Constitutions*, no. 304, emphasis added.

The current standard English edition of the *Constitutions* uses this phrasing, "our vocation is to travel," although the one given above is closer: "It is *according to* our vocation [...]." The Latin has a characteristic genitive (*Nostrae vocationis est*) : "It is *characteristic* of our vocation."[6] This is quite different from saying that it simply *is* our vocation. The original Spanish reads *Y aunque nuestra vocación* es para discurrir *y hacer vida en qualquiera parte del mundo [...].*[7] The addition of *para* qualifies the statement a bit ("though our vocation involves moving about"), and it is followed by a phrase that in itself suggests a stable presence (*hacer vida*; Latin: *vitam agere*, to spend [one's] life).

Why the change from Ignatius's insistently expressed mindset in 1546, when he had been passionately pleading that *the very existence of the Society* depended on this principle of constant motion from place to place, with no fixed abodes? It is easy to suspect that the critical factors were the adoption, appeal, success, and steady proliferation of schools. This decisive new direction made stable community life in the Society a more widely appreciated apostolic desideratum, even a necessity, while individual Jesuits might still be expected to cultivate a spiritual readiness for any new mission assignments, near or far. We see both sides of this polarity represented in a letter from Ignatius to Gian Andrea Schenaldo (February 24, 1554). Late in his life, Ignatius is resisting the idea that the Society should commit itself long term to the responsibilities of parish life. Certainly, the Society wants to help souls wherever there is need, he says, and yet—

> It is not this which our Constitutions forbid us, but rather the obligations customarily attached to a cure of souls or pastorate. The members of this Society need to be free and unencumbered, so that they can fly off to any place on earth where greater hope of God's glory and the salvation of souls beckons us, not settling in any particular place (*unless we happen to have a college or house there*), but working for different people over limited periods of time, gratis and without being bound.[8]

The very fact that standing educational works suddenly began to loom ever larger in Ignatius's own thinking can certainly be added as yet another clear proof that the *Gestalt* of the Society's particular self-concept was evolving in significant ways. Though an early note written in 1541 sketching out content for the anticipated *Constitutions* read "neither studies nor classes in the Society," Ignatius very soon became enthusiastic for both when he saw the apostolic promise

---

6 For the Latin version of the *Constitutions*, see *Constitutiones Societatis Iesu et Normae complementariae* (Rome: Curia of the Father General of the Society of Jesus, 1995).

7 MHSI 64:378 (Textus A, *c.*1550). MHSI = Sancti Ignatii de Loyola, *Constitutiones Societatis Jesus*, tomus secundus, textus Hispanus (Rome: Institutum Historicum Societatis Iesu, 1936).

8 Ignatius of Loyola, *Letters and Instructions*, trans. Martin E. Palmer, John W. Padberg, and John L. McCarthy (St. Louis, MO: Institute of Jesuit Sources, 2006), 472. Emphasis added.

of the schools.[9] Nor did it take long for him to show his great desire to upgrade the Roman College to exemplary status for all other Jesuit schools, far beyond the very modest aims stated in its first advertising display: "School of grammar, humanities and Christian doctrine, free." Within three years, Ignatius was waxing eloquent about the institution's great potential.[10] It is interesting that the very last bit of business Ignatius conducted the night before he died concerned the Roman College.[11] By that moment, at least thirty-nine schools had either already been opened or were scheduled for approval, in striking contrast to professed houses (of which there were only two when Ignatius died).[12] A mere eight years had passed since the opening of the first Jesuit college in Messina. The Society was beginning to fill out a particular shape that would perdure for centuries.

The Ultimate Foundational Moment of the Society

The point for our immediate purposes does not so much concern the *reason* for these changes as much as the *fact* of their occurrence, for major changes early on raise the question about the first "full" form of the Society: *When were all the essential pieces in place, known, and accepted as such*? Since Ignatius's own understanding was evolving during the nearly sixteen years that he spent in the papally approved association, it seems quite fair to ask: When did the "major changes" come to an end? Or to pose it in another way: When was the Society "fully founded"?

---

9 *No estudios ni lectiones en la Compañía*. This is a single line without further explication. It follows a mention of the text written on the founding of (residential) colleges (the text discussed in notes 18 and 19 below), and it is followed by a directive on begging door-to-door: *Hacer colleggios en huniversidades léase en la fundación. No estudios ni lectiones en la Compañía. Quando al perlado pareciere, pidan ostiatin [...]*. The statement must have meant that there would be no schooling formally delivered by members of the Society, since the scholastics were indeed going to classes (*lectiones*) and engaging in studies (*estudios*). See MHSI 63:47.

10 See his letter of November 6, 1553 to Carlos Borja and Diego Hurtado de Mendoza, in Cristiano Casalini and Claude Pavur, eds., *Jesuit Pedagogy, 1540–1616: A Reader*, Sources for the History of Jesuit Pedagogy 1 (Chestnut Hill, MA: Institute of Jesuit Sources, 2016), 65–68, here 66, emphasis added: "The reason for establishing this college was the importance for both the service of God and the common good of the Society, to the greater glory of God Our Lord, that colleges of the Society, as well as professed houses, would take shape here at the seat of the Apostolic See, under the eyes of the vicar of Christ and of all Christianity. And not only do we never have occasion to regret what was begun but every day we take more satisfaction, because we can see in an ever better way the importance of this work in the service of God. *And so we have decided to develop it as much as we can, with the grace of Our Lord*."

11 See Pedro de Ribadeneyra, *The Life of Ignatius of Loyola*, trans. Claude Pavur (St. Louis, MO: Institute of Jesuit Sources, 2014), no. 479fn.

12 Ignatius had thought that the professed houses would be predominant. See, for example, Maurice Whitehead, *English Jesuit Education: Expulsion, Suppression, Survival and Restoration, 1762–1803* (Burlington, VT: Ashgate, 2013), 9–10.

One might be tempted to say that the approved publication of the *Constitutions* (1558) marked that moment at which the Society's idea was finally complete. For years, Ignatius had assiduously spent himself in the task of composing this document. So important was this achievement deemed that it is the book of the *Constitutions*, not the *Spiritual Exercises*, that is the one typically depicted in his iconography. And yet, years after this document was approved, in the perspective of the fourth general, Everard Mercurian (1514–80, in office 1573–80), the form of the Society was not considered finished, even if it had a schema or core idea ("the Institute") in place: "The Society is working more at its form than at its reform, since it has not yet been brought out to the fullest actuality of its Institute."[13]

If the form of the Society had not yet been fully finished by the time of the fourth generalate, then perhaps the fifth one, that of Claudio Acquaviva (1543–1615, in office 1581–1615), ought to be considered as the most likely answer, particularly in light of his monumental institutional organization. Quite pertinently here, Acquaviva has been called "the second founder" of the Society of Jesus.[14] Partial justification for such a title can be found in that major document promulgated in 1599 as the *Ratio studiorum*, or "Plan of Studies." The formal title, *Ratio ac Institutio Studiorum Societatis Iesu* might be translated as *The Official Plan for Jesuit Education.*[15] Based on extensive reviews and discussions that stretched from expert teachers to the highest levels of administration, this text formally organized the Society's studies in an authoritative way with universal scope. It was comprehensive, stretching from "Letters" (covering grammar, Latin and Greek language, composition in prose and poetry, rhetoric, literature) to

13 Statement attributed to Everard Mercurian. See Thomas McCoog, ed., *The Mercurian Project: Forming Jesuit Culture (1573–1580)* (St. Louis, MO: Institute of Jesuit Sources, 2004), epigraph, emphasis added, taken from unpublished material at ARSI, the Archivum Romanum Societatis Iesu.

14 It is hard to find the exact origin of this often-used phrase, "the second founder of the Society." It dates at least as far back as 1854, when it appears in the anti-Jesuit work by Giovanni Battista Niccolini, *History of the Jesuits: Their Origins, Progress, Doctrines, and Designs* (London: Henry G. Bohn, 1854), 255. Ninety years earlier, an anti-Jesuit tract written by Bernardo Tanucci (1698–1783), secretary of state for King Ferdinand (1751–1825, known as Ferdinand I of the Two Sicilies and as Ferdinand IV, king of Naples [r.1759–1816]), had already presented Diego Laínez (1512–65) and Claudio Acquaviva (1543–1615) as the "true founders of the Society as it has existed for a long while in the world." See Bernardo Tanucci, *Inquietudini de gesuiti* [Worries about the Jesuits], 4 vols. (Naples: The King's Press [Stampa Reale], 1764–69), here 1:9. Some scholarship prefers to describe Acquaviva as "the second *legislator* of the Society." See Mario Fois, "Aquaviva, Claudio," s.v. "*Generales*," in *Diccionario histórico de la Compañía de Jesús*, ed. Charles E. O'Neill and Joaquín M. Domínguez, 4 vols. (Rome: Universidad Pontificia Comillas, 2001), 2:1614–21, here 1621.

15 The Latin–English edition of the *Ratio studiorum* used here will be Claude Pavur, ed., *The* Ratio studiorum: *The Official Plan for Jesuit Education* (St. Louis, MO: Institute of Jesuit Sources, 2005).

philosophy (the "arts course") to theology, over a range roughly paralleling high school, college, and graduate-level courses. The content of this book was practical and specific rather than theoretical or general: it consisted of lists of rules for all associated personnel, from the provincial to the beadle (student assistant), as well as for particular procedures and institutions in the school (e.g., admissions, exams, promotions, academic performances, prizes, study clubs).

The Case for the *Ratio studiorum* as a Foundational Document

Other ages saw what we generally do not, namely that only with the *Ratio studiorum* of 1599 (hereafter abbreviated as RS) was the founding of the Society of Jesus complete. This educational charter that had been so long in the making, that had been so long an important part of the Society's concerns and practices, finally gave the order a formally expressed, well-tested, official, universally promulgated way of replicating itself. It now had its fully functioning "genetic code." Some now see in the RS only an "in-house" low-status administrative document, one that was out of date not long after its publication: they might claim that it was designed to run Renaissance schools, and with the passing of the Renaissance, it lost any force it had.[16] From such a perspective, the RS could not be something that capped and distinguished the order's special character or paralleled in any significant way the Society's *Spiritual Exercises and Constitutions.* Nevertheless, an awareness of Jesuit educational activity suggests that one might make a case for the high status and long continuing relevance of the RS—and perhaps even a case for its perennial importance. At least the argument for the full living value of the RS should be weighed carefully, not dismissed offhandedly. In fact, there are several grounds on which to argue that the document was not just significant but *foundational* (and therefore essential) for the Society of Jesus. I offer here seven arguments in support of this understanding.

1. Institutional genealogy. Origins are telling. The RS was genealogically rooted in that prime foundational document known as the *Constitutions*, which says:

> Concerning the hours of the lectures, their order, and their method, and concerning the exercises both in compositions (which ought to be corrected by the teachers) and in disputations within all the faculties, and in delivering orations and reading verses in public—all this will be treated in detail in a separate treatise [approved by the general]. This present constitution refers the reader to it, with the remark that it ought to be adapted to places, times, and persons, even though it would be desirable to reach that order as far as this is possible.[17]

16 See Chapter 4, "The Historiography of Jesuit Pedagogy," particularly the section entitled "After 1965: Losing the *Ratio studiorum*."

17 *Constitutions*, no. 455 (part 4, chapter 13, no. 2 [A]).

One might read in this declaration the understanding that the *Constitutions* were to be fleshed out by the document that was being called for. It was to be "a separate treatise." Yet nowhere is it indicated that this document would be an optional or minor one. The more natural conclusion would be that it was so important that it deserved special focused attention, that is, a full development outside the text of the *Constitutions*, though thoroughly coherent with it. Variability of situations is expected, but presupposed is the desire to reach a common norm clearly stated: *The norm must always be considered whatever the adaptation.* Interestingly, the Latin version does not read: "This present constitution refers the reader to it [that is, the "separate treatise" to be known later as the *Ratio studiorum*], but rather "and to it this Constitution *refers us*" (*ad quem haec Constitutio nos remittit*), pointing to its universal corporate relevance. It is not simply a matter for just any particular reader who happens to come across this passage.

Significant also is the fact that, even though there is to be this separate document setting out the academic details, Ignatius nevertheless found it important to devote to these very issues *the entire fourth part* (of the ten parts) of the *Constitutions*. This is a part that on its own makes up an impressively large portion of the totality, *nearly a quarter of the entire work.*[18] Such extensive presence in the *Constitutions* loudly proclaims that the *studia* were indeed considered to be integral to the Institute. They were not treated sketchily nor were they merely relegated to some subsidiary document of far lesser consequence.

In fact, the connection is closer than may appear at first. Even this prime foundational document, the *Constitutions*, attends to very particular details, as we discover, for example, in no. 312, with its description of when and what kind of waxed candle should be presented yearly to the founder, and in no. 376, where superiors are told to determine whether students should have notebooks. Such details are not too small to stand in this primary regulative text. In addition, there is noticeable overlap between many considerations in the *Constitutions* and those of the RS. For example, the *Constitutions* states that "the doctrine of Aristotle should be followed" (*Constitutions*, no. 470), and the RS states that the professor of philosophy "should not depart from Aristotle," except in certain specific cases (RS, no. 208). A full study of textual and thematic parallels would be most revealing. One might well wonder if the first intention was actually to have the *Constitutions* include a detailed plan of studies, in effect, the core of a workable RS. Perhaps such an idea had to be abandoned when it became clear that the complexity and length of the section would not only cause a delay in publication but also a displeasing disproportion in the text as a whole.

---

18 The fourth part has seventeen chapters; the average number for the other parts is about five, with the second highest number of chapters being seven, for the eighth part. In George Ganss's edition (St. Louis, MO: Institute of Jesuit Sources, 1970), the eighth part covers twenty-two pages (nos. 655–718), over against fifty-nine pages for the fourth part (nos. 307–509, over two hundred out of a total of 827 total paragraphs).

What can be said here is that more than a few echoes of the *Constitutions* are found in the RS and that there are material interconnections suggestive of an organic integrity between the two documents. And no one can justifiably doubt that the *Constitutions* is foundational or the idea that part 4 genuinely represents the thought of the primary founder, even if the words on the page derive most proximately from Juan Alfonso de Polanco (1517–76) or others: Ignatius examined and approved what appeared there. The RS can therefore fairly be judged to be essential to the Society's Institute—at least for anyone who takes the *Constitutions* seriously: with the *Constitutions*, the RS substantively coheres, and in the *Constitutions*, the RS finds its beginning and lasting establishment.

2. Investment. From the very beginning, the Society manifested widespread, continuous, and deep interest in the *studia Societatis* (Jesuit education). This line of development culminated in the RS, which is not just a concrete documentary result but also a kind of dynamic *symbol* representing all of the preliminary work, experiences, prayers, hopes, reflections, and discussions that lie behind it as well as all the practical implementations, refinements, and adaptations that were instituted in its wake.[19] In such a perspective, the RS can more easily be understood as foundational to the order from the beginning, as in fact an integral dimension of the Society.

And some sixteenth-century Jesuits said as much. While many of them showed by their investment of time and effort that what was done in the *studia* was of the essence for Institute, Jerónimo Nadal (1507–80) left a more direct testimony, putting it simply and directly: without the right academic preparation, the Society "would not be able to go on" *(no podría proceder)*, without learning, "we would not be able to help our neighbor" (*sin letras no podríamos ayudar al prójimo*).[20] This was not some late idea that arose after schools began to be founded. Ignatius was sending young Jesuit aspirants to the University of Paris as early as 1540. They could not be Jesuits without the studies. The Society's right to run residential colleges that had the power to oversee and to direct programs of study is stated even in the 1540 *Formula of the Institute*.[21] And in 1541, one of the

---

19 For a very detailed account of the Jesuit investment, see especially Allan P. Farrell, *The Jesuit Code of Liberal Education: Development and Scope of the* Ratio studiorum (Milwaukee, WI: Bruce Publishing Company, 1938), and also the introduction to Casalini and Pavur, *Jesuit Pedagogy*, 1–33.

20 Miguel Nicolau, ed., *Pláticas espirituales del P. Jerónimo Nadal, S.I., en Coimbra (1561)* (Granada: Facultad Teológica de la Compañía de Jesús, 1945), 124.

21 This arch-foundational document (included in the papal charter *Regimini militantis ecclesiae* of 1540) pointed clearly toward *superintended* courses of studies for Jesuit scholastics in residential colleges. See Casalini and Pavur, *Jesuit Pedagogy*, 7. Note that "college" had different and evolving meanings in Ignatius's day. For the best concise overview, see George Ganss's note in his edition of the *Constitutions* (Saint Ignatius of Loyola, *The Constitutions of the Society of Jesus*, ed. George Ganss [St. Louis, MO: Institute of Jesuit Sources, 1970], 174n1).

earliest documents of the young Society outlines how the college is to be founded (*Fundación de collegio*).[22] It makes the nascent idea of the novitiate (as a series of probations to test the intentions and character of the candidates) seem merely a gateway to studies under the auspices of the Society. When the *Fundación* was revised in 1544 or 1545, it used a plural form in its title along with a different phrasing, *Para fundar colegios*. It looked forward to the definitive establishment of all the details in the context of a certain essential frame that had already been established.[23] The concentrated interest in and high valuation of *studia* continued all the way through the period of the founding of the schools, as the seven volumes of the Monumenta Paedagogica massively illustrate.[24] The thinking about the *studia*, in both their externally and their internally oriented dimensions, culminated in the RS. But that "late" document of 1599 rested upon a very long-labored, generally cumulative series of efforts, including many moments: the documents produced in Messina (1548, 1551) by Frs. Hannibal du Coudret (1525–99) and Nadal; the rules for the rector of the Roman College (1551), written by Alfonso de Polanco; the work of Diego de Ledesma (1519–75), including the *Ratio Borgiana* (1569), which was used until the final version of the *Ratio*

22 MHSI 63:48–67.

23 The 1541 version of the *Fundación de collegio* had already laid out the areas of study in Letters, philosophy, and theology, and it spoke of the other details of each school as not being necessary to arrange at that moment (1541) since "God our Lord through some good instrument of his" (*por algún su buen instrumento*) is beginning to make a start in this (*comience a poner principio en ello*). The later version of 1544/45 lists even more of the details awaiting a later specification, one that will respect the essentials (*las partes essentiales*) that had already been stated (*De otras particularidades, es a saber, de horas y oraciones ordinarias, en mesa y fuera della, de oyr missa, sermones y lectiones, de ordenar preçeptores, escolares y officiales, de orden de comer y modo de vestir y dormir, y de otras cosa símiles, por la variedad de las tierras, y diuersas condiçiones, y devoçión de los fundadores y de otros bienheçhores, para complazer y seruir a todos los que en el Señor nuestro pudiéremos, quedará para después dar orden a cada collegio, según y donde se fundaren, guardando siempre las partes "essentiales" según que están diçhas y declaradas y las otras que inmediate se siguen*). For a presentation of this section in the 1541 and 1545 versions, see MHSI 63:58–59. The language foreshadows the passage on the RS in the *Constitutions* (no. 455).

24 The Monumenta Paedagogica (often abbreviated as MP or Mon. Paed. or MPSI) are a subset of seven volumes within the 157 volumes of the Monumenta Historica Societatis Iesu (MHSI). Though there is an early volume from 1901 entitled Monumenta Paedagogica (= MHSI 19), these later volumes are part of a new series edited by László Lukács, S.J. (1910–98) and published in Rome by the Institutum Historicum Societatis Iesu, Via dei Penitenzieri, 20. They include the following: MP 1 (1540–56) = MHSI 92 [published 1965]. MP 2 (1557–72) = MHSI 107 [1974]. MP 3 (1557–72) = MHSI 108 [1974]. MP 4 (1573–80) = MHSI 124 [1981]. MP 5 Ratio atque institutio studiorum Societatis Iesu (1586, 1591, 1599) = MHSI 129 [1986]. MP 6 (Collectanea de ratione studiorum Societas Iesu: 1582–87) = MHSI 140 [1992]. MP 7 (Collectanea de ratione studiorum Societas Iesu: 1588–1616) = MHSI 141 [1992].

studiorum (1599) had been carefully worked out through two full preliminary documents, one for review (1586) and one for a three-year trial (1591).[25]

We should insert into this list what has become known as the *Constitutiones collegiorum*, a document written out by Polanco around the year 1549, but quite possibly "authored" in some significant sense by Ignatius himself.[26] Its full title is *Constitutiones que en los collegios de la Compañía de Jesú se deven observar para el bien proceder dellos a honor y gloria divina* (Constitutions that ought to be observed in the colleges of the Society of Jesus for their good functioning in service of God's honor and glory).[27] The work has an important relationship to part 4 of the Society's *Constitutions*, and though it focuses more on what would have been Ignatius's experience (that is, more on the learning and not at all on the teaching), Miguel Bernad (1917–2009) calls it "the first Jesuit *Ratio Studiorum*—at least the first of a universal character intended to bind all colleges."[28] If one seeks a direct documentary link between Ignatius and the RS, this may be the best example outside of the order's *Constitutions*. Bernad asserts a stable continuity between the RS's principles of Jesuit pedagogy and the writings of Ignatius himself as found here.[29] The *Constitutiones collegiorum* seems to have been set aside early in favor of the fuller constitutional legislation, but at some point this shorter document must have been expected to carry quite a high status: its last directive, written in upper case, instructs that it be read every fifteen days.[30]

The fathers convened by Superior General Claudio Acquaviva in 1584 to consider the definitive plan of studies were quite aware of the nature of the project. After citing two sections from the *Constitutions*, they write:

> This treatise recommended by those constitutions, one that might structure and govern both the method to be followed in the studies and the selection of contents respecting authorities and solid doctrine, just as we ought to have—this treatise was something that all our fathers [*nostrum omnium patrum*] deeply desired and sought already from the very rise and origin of the Society [*ab ortu ac primordio Societatis*]. Although those in positions of authority are endeavoring mightily to refine the other parts of our Institute [*caeteras Instituti nostri partes*], the part that is contained in correctly establishing and regulating the academic course of studies seems not yet fully

25 See the timelines in Casalini and Pavur, *Jesuit Pedagogy*, xiii–xix, and in the first appendix in this volume.

26 See Miguel Bernad, "The Ignatian Way," *Philippine Studies* 4, no. 2 (1956): 195–214, here 203.

27 For the edition of the entire document, see MHSI 71 (Regulae Societatis Iesu 1540–1556): 212–45. The second part is re-edited and reprinted by László Lukács in MHSI 92:37–45.

28 Bernad, "Ignatian Way," 204.

29 Ibid., 196.

30 MHSI 71:245.

> perfected nor brought home to that splendid form that properly meets the expectations of all the most learned individuals.[31]

Here is an explicit statement that what was to become the RS was indeed "a part" of the Institute and something desired from the Society's earliest beginnings, on the part of "*all* our fathers."

It would be hard to imagine the early career of the Society or the growing expression of its self-concept without this robust academic vision, practice, reflection, and eventually legislation. The Society seemed to know from the beginning that it was "making itself" under the favor and inspirations received by God and that *studia* were an important part of the idea. This was later amply confirmed by the continuous additions of schools and membership to the Society. Inseparable from the thinking and workings of the Institute from the beginning, the entire enterprise that culminated in the RS can therefore fairly be understood as foundational.

3. Primordiality. The beginnings of the RS reach back beyond the *Constitutions* and even beyond the first form of the Society. They lie deep in Ignatius's early biography, with two moments standing out: (1) Ignatius's realization (from his time in Barcelona, 1524–26) of the importance of studies for helping souls (a realization developed by the church from its earliest centuries), and (2) his discovery that the Parisian pedagogy seemed far more effective than others he had known.[32] The structure, method, and content that Ignatius found in his academic program at the University of Paris lie at the core of what would later become the RS. These elements and their later historical development cannot be derived from the *Spiritual Exercises*. It is a separate aspect of the Society's foundation, and a crucial one.

This argument from primordiality might also include the quality of personal commitment to studies that Ignatius had early and maintained throughout his life. At least from his conversion bed in 1521, he had shown that he could take

---

31 *Hic tractatus iis constitutionibus commendatus, qui et studiorum praxim, et doctrinae solidioris, authorumque delectum, sicut oportet, informet ac moderetur, nostrorum omnium patrum votis iam inde ab ortu ac primordio Societatis expetitus est, quod cum in caeteras Instituti nostri partes excolendas strenue ab iis, qui praesunt, incumbatur; pars ista tamen, quae literariis studiis recte instituendis temperandisque continetur, nondum plane exculta, nec ad eam speciem ac splendorem, quem in optatis esse doctissimo cuique par est, perducta videretur.* MHSI 129:2. The phrase *literariis studiis* is translated here as "academic course of studies" because in this context the subject matter is not limited to the literary or humanistic part of the program but covers the range of letters, philosophy, and theology; all of these are "literary" in the sense that they all involve an understanding of texts.

32 For an overview of the nature and impact of the Parisian style of education on the Society of Jesus, see Gabriel Codina, "The 'Modus Parisiensis,'" in *The Jesuit* Ratio studiorum: *400th Anniversary Perspectives*, ed. Vincent J. Duminuco (New York: Fordham University Press, 2000), 28–49.

reading seriously, and the books that held his attention during his recovery were not at all lacking in learning.[33] Perhaps his religious conversion also included a new vision of how spiritual good can come through the written word. Though Ignatius himself is rarely if ever given a "scholarly persona," he avidly promoted studies in the Society, and particularly an excellent foundation in Letters. Pedro de Ribadeneyra (1526–1611) recalled that

> [Ignatius] wanted all [Jesuits] to be well grounded in grammar and the humanities, especially when age and inclination made this easier; in the case of those who were less well trained in that way, *even if they already had undergraduate and postgraduate degrees in theology*, he insisted that they should study Latin again in Rome. Otherwise there was no branch of approved learning that he rejected, because he was delighted that the Society should be equipped with all possible arms.[34]

We recognize here the same person who had bent himself to the task of learning Latin in Barcelona and who had repeated his language and literary studies for about a year and a half in Paris at the Collège Montaigu (1528–29) before undertaking his philosophical and theological courses. Ignatius's desire for thoroughness, depth of learning, and cultural foundations deeply shaped the tradition of Jesuit education. And yet it was not a tightly limited vision, as this very citation testifies: Ignatius was a person of great scope: Jesuit education was to be open to all branches "of approved learning." We can compare the programmatic statement in the RS in the first rule for provincials at the beginning of the text proper: "One of the leading ministries of our Society is teaching our neighbors *all the disciplines in keeping with our Institute* [...]" (RS, no. 7, emphasis added). Thus Jesuit education could ambitiously try to include Hebrew or

33 See chapter 2, "In the School of Ignatius: Studies, Spirituality, and Service in the Society of Jesus."

34 Pedro de Ribadeneyra, *Treatise on the Governance of St. Ignatius of Loyola*, trans. and with introduction by Joseph A. Munitiz, afterword by Mark Rotsaert (Oxford: Way Books, 2016), 2.6 (9–10, emphasis added). Munitiz cross-references a corroborating passage in Luís Gonçalves da Câmara's (*c.*1519–75) *Memoriale* (*Remembering Iñigo: Glimpses of the Life of Saint Ignatius of Loyola; The* Memoriale *of Luís Gonçalves da Câmara* [Leominster: Gracewing, 2004], 153 [no. 262.2]): "In the matter of studies our Father is very precise; he always wants to build on a firm foundation, and above all that students should know Latin and the humanities well, as he did in the cases of Neyra and Benedetto. These two had been preaching for many years and everyone thought they were ready to study theology, but the Father never wished it so, but rather that they should begin the course in humanities, while continuing to preach in Rome, the one regularly, the other on certain occasions." Most telling is the letter of March 17, 1554 from Ignatius to Pierre Le Gillon (*c.*1520–*c.*1565), where the founder, very late in his life—in fact, less than eighteen months from his death—takes very seriously a question about how to correct compositions; he even gathers a committee to deal with it. See Casalini and Pavur, *Jesuit Pedagogy*, 241–42.

Aramaic ("Chaldee"), and under the great promotion of Christopher Clavius (1538–1612), it could more successfully incorporate a mathematical program far beyond Ignatius's own investments.[35]

But it was not just the experience of Ignatius: even before the other founders had met one another, they had already decided to pursue master's degrees at the University of Paris. Thus the core fellowship of the order arose in an educational context with individuals seeking academic credentials that would allow them to teach. The common educational background was never absent from what they did later. The first Jesuits always necessarily worked on the basis of this implicit biographical substructure, namely the vision and habits and understandings operative in their common schooling. A "Society of Jesus" founded on the basis of Ignatius's Manresa rather than his Paris would have been a radically different type of organization. The academic cast of the historical actuality is palpable in Ignatius's habit of referring to his degreed companions as "Master": they were *magistri* (teachers). The birettas of Jesuit iconography point in the same direction, as that headwear, likely a development from the scholar's cap, was used extensively in academic circles.[36]

The seeds of the RS are therefore to be found even in the earliest moments of the genesis of the Society. What is more, the RS can even be understood as tightly attached to that most primordial Ignatian apostolic strategy "to help souls." It is true that Ignatius first engaged in prayer, penances, sacramental activities, spiritual conversations, almsgiving and services to the poor, begging, general poverty of lifestyle, and pilgrimage to the Holy Land; but it is also true that quite early on he came to the realization that helping souls required the proper training. That is, he saw as his primary way forward a path that took him through a period of studies, one that lasted more than ten years of his post-conversional adult life. The RS can therefore reasonably be understood as consequence, continuance, and culmination of something original and essential to Ignatius's leading apostolic strategy; as such, it can be understood as an integral part of the core of the Society as well.[37]

---

35 For Clavius's own enthusiastic promotion and vision of mathematical studies, see Casalini and Pavur, *Jesuit Pedagogy*, 281–300. With mathematical studies, Clavius made a new innovative space in Renaissance curricula. See László Lukács and Giuseppe Cosentino, *Church, Culture, and Curriculum: Theology and Mathematics in the Jesuit* Ratio studiorum, trans. and ed. Frederick A. Homann (Philadelphia: Saint Joseph's University Press, 1999).

36 See, for example, the ceremony known as the *birettatio*, mentioned in Hastings Rashdall, *The Universities of Europe in the Middle Ages*, 2 vols. (Oxford: Clarendon Press, 1895), 1:473. The biretta has appeared often in Ignatius's iconography.

37 For an overview of how Ignatius continued to attend to the educational work beyond his "primordial" inspirations, see Farrell, *Jesuit Code*, chapter 6, "Ignatius' Role in Developing the Jesuit Code of Education," 130–52. Farrell summarizes (149): "Thus his role in developing the Society's code of education was fourfold: (1) He drafted its first principles and appointed able teachers and administrators to apply and elaborate them; (2) he not only

4. Constitutive function. The schools run by the Society, even from Messina in 1548, had to have some kind of guiding rules or plan (*ratio*). There was therefore a great practical need, as well as a general desire, to have a uniform model for the best direction and effective functioning of this apostolic work, soon to become a major Society enterprise. Rules were shared across institutions, critiqued, improved upon. These plans or *rationes* culminated in the RS of 1599, which then could be said to define the overall character or concept of Jesuit *studia*. Here too we see an unfolding of Ignatius's vision. The founder was interested both in the details of the educational plans in the schools and in the idea of achieving a *common order* for all the schools of the Society. Writing to André des Freux (*c*.1515–56) on October 31, 1551, he made it clear that he wanted to be told about all the religious and literary exercises, and that he should set up nothing permanent: there should be no fixed pattern "until an order was formally completed in writing, one that was to be followed in all Jesuit schools."[38]

But at the same time this educational plan represented what the Society thought necessary in the formation of all younger Jesuits (excepting the temporal coadjutors). In fact, the schools were a means through which Ignatius could not only "care for the neighbor" but also form the young membership of the Society (and attract new recruits). Young Jesuits were learning and teaching at Jesuit schools; they were supported on the endowments of the schools' founders and benefactors.[39] Under the second general, Diego Laínez (1512–65, in office 1558–65), "regency" was invented: teaching became a permanent and universal part of all scholastics' formation.[40] Since those days up until about 1967, Jesuit scholastics had to pass through an "RS-inspired type of training" via the stages of Letters, philosophy, teaching ("regency"), and theology. After such an academic career, the most competent of the scholastics could be presumed to be capable of passing on the Jesuit educational tradition in the roles of administrators or teachers: they would be repeating (and possibly even improving upon) what they had learned how to do in their classes.

The RS thus played an essential part in "making" and "replicating" the core of the Society. As the essential set of directives *for all Jesuit academic formation*,

approved of the work of educating secular youth, but devoted himself wholeheartedly to its spread; (3) he showed intimate and painstaking concern for the success of each school and for the proper training and development of individual teachers; (4) he set forth in the *Constitutions* a clear definition of his educational policy and epitomized its chief features."

38 These words are taken from the Latin summary of the letter, no. 2163 in MHSI 28:703: *Interea vero nullum firmum ac stabilem inducat morem donec ordo in omnibus Societatis gymnasiis servandus perscribatur.*

39 Ignatius made this support a standard precondition for opening a school. See Casalini and Pavur, *Jesuit Pedagogy*, 11–12. Jesuit formation was therefore interwoven into this apostolate.

40 See Paul Grendler, "Jesuit Schools in Europe: A Historiographical Essay," *Journal of Jesuit Studies* 1, no. 1 (2014): 7–25, here 12.

the RS can rightfully be called constitutive of the Society itself; it was not merely the arch-document for its single greatest and most distinctive apostolate. Furthermore, the distinctive verifiable public success and positive reputation of the entire educational scheme likely played a major role in publicizing the Society and persuading many young men to join the effort that was the source of so many goods—spiritual, intellectual, social, cultural, professional, and religious. The order could simply not have been what it was without its plan of studies, nor would it likely have grown so great so fast with so many benefactions without its successful realization in many locales. How can one image that such expansion would have occurred if individual schools had been largely left to their own devices without being easily able to use the insights and advances of others?

5. Formal declaration. But was there ever some kind of official indication that the RS was understood to be a foundational document? Yes, repeated formal public recognition can be found in all those collections published under a title designating the documents defining the Institute of the Society. The comprehensive editions include at least the following six, which stretch from 1635 to 1893:

1. *Institutum Societatis Jesu* (Antwerp: Apud J. Meursium, 1635).
2. *Corpus institutorum Societatis Iesu.* In duo volumina distinctum: Accedit catalogus provinciarum, domorum, collegiorum etc. eiusdem Societatis; iuxta exemplar excusum (Antwerp: Apud Iohannem Meursium, anno 1702).
3. *Institutum societatis Jesu.* Auctoritate Congregationis generalis XVIII (Prague : Typis universitatis Carolo-Ferdinandeae, 1757).
4. *Nova et accuratissima editio Instituti quondam Societatis Jesu.* Extinctae per Clem. XIV. per ejus brevem 13. Augusti anni 1773 [...] (Petra of Brescia: [s.n.], anno 1784)
5. *Institutum societatis Iesu* (Rome: Typis Civilitatis Catholicae, 1869–70).
6. *Institutum societatis Iesu* (Florence: Ex Typographia A SS. Conceptione, 1892–93).

The *Ratio studiorum* is included in each of these volumes. There does not seem to be a similarly comprehensive official collection that derives from the years anterior to the promulgation of the RS. If this is indeed the case, it could well indicate that only after the RS was finally in place did there arise a conviction that the full range of foundational documents was essentially complete. Since later congregational decrees or papal charters could also become part of such collections, the Institute itself need not have been considered closed, even if the core *original* "foundation" might have been. Later documentary additions could not claim to have been present as the RS had been in all these editions of the *Institutum Societatis Iesu.*

The most recent formal declaration of the *universal normative importance* of the RS can be found in the decrees of the thirtieth general congregation (1957):

"All should know well and greatly esteem the *Ratio Studiorum*; and its method and rules should be carefully observed in the education of our young men."[41]

In effect, the RS was therefore—not just once but many times—declared to be significantly integral to its Institute and part of its core self-defining documentation. Particularly in light of the importance and scope given to its anticipatory elements in the Society's beginnings, we have grounds to believe that the RS was understood to represent something foundational for the Society. The "lateness" of the date of 1599 does not diminish the significance of its roots; rather to the contrary, it points to their very depth and long reach.

6. Content. The text of the RS communicates its own stature by dealing with essential matters in an authoritative way and by addressing the entire leadership of the Society, appealing to the *Constitutions* and the will of the superior general. This point goes beyond the matter of the RS's constitutive function (forming the members who form the Society) to the matter of *the scope and authority that the text apparently claims for itself.* The prefatory letter of promulgation states the RS's ultimate, binding, normative, and universal status over against all other academic plans used in the Society up to that time. It goes on to mention that following the RS is a matter of great personal interest to the general himself and refers to its linkage with the very strong appeal made for such a document in the *Constitutions* (RS, nos. 1–6). The main body of the RS is structured into sections that are mostly lists of rules concerning the various positions or offices, proceeding from those of the provincial, the rector, the prefects, and the teachers all the way to the optional study-groups or "academies." The office that gets the most rules is in fact the provincial. Though technically not even "in" a school office, he is given the chief responsibility for the success of this work: his very first rule says that he "should consider himself obliged to do his utmost to ensure that our diverse and complex educational labor meets with the abundant results that the grace of our calling demands of us" (RS, no. 7). This means that the RS is not just a "school document." It is telling *provincials* what their job includes. They are to have direct personal concern even for the staffing and running of the institutions. In fact, they are being entrusted with one of the chief ministries of the entire Society (RS, no. 7). Not only do the RS's rules for the provincial cover questions concerning which Jesuits may be allowed to take the longer courses of theological studies but they extend even to the matter of *accepting people into the Society* as career teachers: "It will also be advantageous to accept some into the Society only on the condition that they are willing to dedicate their lives under holy obedience to this teaching of language and humanistic literary studies" (RS, no. 48).

41 John W. Padberg, Martin D. O'Keefe, John L. McCarthy, ed. and trans., *For Matters of Greater Moment: The First Thirty Jesuit General Congregations*, Jesuit Primary Sources in English Translations, no. 12. (St. Louis, MO: Institute of Jesuit Sources, 1994), 678.

Clearly, the text of the RS claims a large scope and authority here, going well beyond academic administrative and schoolroom details to some very fundamental issues, like admissibility into the Society and the primary functionality of one important sector of its membership.

7. Reception. Are there any indications that the RS was accepted as foundational? A fuller story of the career of the RS in the practice of the order has been told elsewhere.[42] Here, we can say that the Society never formally replaced the text, although adaptations could be found everywhere (as the original document had anticipated); and when the Society did send out an experimental revision in the early nineteenth century, full recognition and weight was still explicitly given to the earlier document in the cover letter written by Superior General Jan Roothaan (1785–1853, in office 1829–53):

> Whatever else this undertaking was, it was certainly a significant one in which it was important to do nothing nonchalantly or precipitately. But neither was it a matter of having to fashion a new order of studies (as I pointed out in the letter to the provinces that called for fathers to be deputed to draw up what was necessary for this work). Rather, it was a matter of adjusting the very same venerable text to our times, so that people might realize with what great reverence this undertaking had to be handled, and how nothing was to be changed offhandedly or rashly in that work that had been composed by the very best men after a long process of gathering a great body of advice, well tested by the successful experience of almost two centuries and often recommended by the praise even of the very enemies of the Society.[43]

Jesuits were still arguing strongly for the validity and value of the RS in the mid-twentieth century, right up to the affirmation already cited from the thirtieth congregation.[44]

---

42 See Pavur, "Historiography of Jesuit Pedagogy."

43 *Grave sane erat, si quod aliud, negotium, in quo nihil leviter, nihil praepropere actum oportuit. Neque vero, ut in epistola ad Provincias missa, qua Patres deputati ad praeparanda huic operi necessaria vocabantur, monuimus, de nova studiorum Ratione formanda agendum fuit, sed de eadem illa antiqua nostris accommodanda temporibus, quo intelligeretur, quanta cum reverentia hoc negotium tractandum esset, quamque non leviter nec temere quidquam in eo opere mutandum, quod et a summis viris, collatis diu multumque consiliis, redactum et duorum fere saeculorum felici experientia comprobatum, et ab ipsis etiam Societatis hostibus non raro laudibus commendatum fuisset.* This text can be found in G. M. [Georg Michael] Pachtler, S.J., *Ratio studiorum et institutiones scholasticae Societatis Jesu per Germaniam olim vigentes collectae concinnatae dilucidatae*, ed. Karl Kehrbach, tomus 2 Ratio studiorum ann. 1586, 1599, 1832, Monumenta Germaniae Paedagogica 5 (Berlin: A. Hofmann & Company, 1887), 228–33.

44 See Pavur, "Historiography of Jesuit Pedagogy."

Beyond the Society, the reception of the RS is best marked by the spread of schools as a "super-category equivalent to that into which all the other *consueta ministeria* [customary ministries] fell" and by the wide impact of the intellectual apostolates undertaken by Jesuits.[45] It might be said that the RS provided the core structure of the schools and that the schools evolved into social–cultural–religious centers of large outreach.[46] Even more importantly, the schools inserted the Society into the communities in a way nothing else could. Through the schooling of children and young adults, Jesuits in effect could become "a part of the family," cooperating with parents in the raising of their children, and becoming father-figures with whom (in the best of cases) there would be lasting bonds of some kind of gratitude and devotion and a distinctive kind of pastoral presence.

A striking recent expression of the way the RS has stamped the image of the Society can be found in a talk given by Pope Benedict XVI (r.2005–13) to the Society at Saint Peter's Basilica on April 22, 2006. It points to the impact of the Society's educational investments, which cannot be severed from its development and use of the RS. I cite here an extended selection because it is important to note the kind of encapsulation and linkages going on here in what is essentially a thumbnail sketch of the Society:

> St. Ignatius of Loyola was first and foremost a man of God who in his life put God, his greatest glory and his greatest service, first. He was a profoundly prayerful man for whom the daily celebration of the Eucharist was the heart and crowning point of his day. Thus, he left his followers a precious spiritual legacy that must not be lost or forgotten. Precisely because he was a man of God, St. Ignatius was a faithful servant of the Church, in which he saw and venerated the Bride of the Lord and the Mother of Christians. And the special vow of obedience to the Pope, which he himself describes as "our first and principal foundation" (MI, Series III, I, p. 162), was born from his desire to serve the Church in the most beneficial way possible.[47] This ecclesial characteristic, so specific to the Society of Jesus, lives on in you and in your apostolic activities, dear Jesuits, so that you may faithfully meet the urgent needs of the Church today. Among these, it is important in my opinion to point out your cultural commitment in the areas of theology and philosophy in which the Society of Jesus has traditionally been present, as well as the dialogue with modern culture, which, if it boasts on the one hand of the marvelous progress

45 See John W. O'Malley, *The First Jesuits* (Cambridge, MA: Harvard University Press, 1993), 200.

46 See Luce Giard, "The Jesuit College: A Center for Knowledge, Art, and Faith, 1548–1773," trans. Brian Van Hove, *Studies in the Spirituality of Jesuits* 40, no. 1 (Spring 2008): 1–31.

47 MI = *Monumenta Ignatiana*, a subset of the Monumenta Historica Societatis Iesu. The twenty volumes, grouped into four series, are available at http://www.sjweb.info/arsi/Monumenta.cfm (accessed October 3, 2018).

> in the scientific field, remains heavily marked by positivist and materialist scientism. Naturally, the effort to promote a culture inspired by Gospel values in cordial collaboration with the other ecclesial realities demands an intense spiritual and cultural training. For this very reason, St. Ignatius wanted young Jesuits to be formed for many years in spiritual life and in study. It is good that this tradition be maintained and reinforced, also given the growing complexity and vastness of modern culture. Another of his great concerns was the Christian education and cultural formation of young people: hence the impetus he gave to the foundation of "colleges" which after his death spread in Europe and throughout the world. Continue, dear Jesuits, this important apostolate, keeping the spirit of your Founder unchanged.[48]

These words support the present thesis: the tradition of Jesuit education springs from the charism of the founder; it has notably distinguished the Society; and it has served the church, particularly in the areas of culture (or "Letters" broadly understood), philosophy, and theology, the very stages of the RS (explicitly present since the *Fundación* of 1541). The educational involvement has in effect become one of the Society's chief missions.[49] Notice particularly how the last paragraph links "the spirit of the founder" specifically with the colleges and gives the project currency: "*Continue!*"

Why It Is Important to Acknowledge the Foundational Nature of the *Ratio studiorum*

The opening of this essay evoked the importance of foundational moments. On such a basis alone, affirming the foundational nature of the RS stands to have significant implications at many levels, from self-concept to vocation promotion, to formational practices and to apostolic structures, to the fulfillment of missions and to institutional unity and character, and even to choices in governance and in new reformulations that build organically on the core of that which is taken to define Jesuit identity. The metaphor of "the foundational" suggests that there is "something below" that supports everything built upon it. The idea of a "founding moment" means that there is some part of the narrative that has lasting implications, and for that reason it must be remembered.

48 From "Address of His Holiness Benedict XVI to the Fathers and Brothers of the Society of Jesus, Vatican Basilica, Saturday, April 22, 2006"; https://w2.vatican.va/content/benedict-xvi/en/speeches/2006/april/documents/hf_ben-xvi_spe_20060422_gesuiti.html (accessed October 3, 2018).

49 For the implication of the idea of "missions" and its relationship with *doctrina*, see Kevin L. Flannery, "*Circa missiones:* On the Founding of the Society," a talk given to the Loyola Club on September 27, 2007. Available at https://www.academia.edu/844747/CIRCA_MISSIONES_ON_THE_FOUNDING_OF_THE_SOCIETY_OF_JESUS (accessed October 3, 2018).

In the context of an intelligent Jesuit recovery of its origins and the Society's proper adaptation to contemporary culture, there is another level of meaning: the Society cannot be what it is or what Vatican II exhorts it to be unless it knows how it should recover its "original charism"—and first, what that charism really should best be defined to be. The second section of the "Decree on the Adaptation and Renewal of Religious Life (*Perfectae Caritatis*), Proclaimed by His Holiness Pope Paul VI on October 28, 1965" states the following:

> The adaptation and renewal of the religious life includes both the constant return to the sources of all Christian life and to the original spirit of the institutes and their adaptation to the changed conditions of our time [...]. It redounds to the good of the Church that institutes have their own particular characteristics and work. Therefore let their founders' spirit and special aims they set before them as well as their sound traditions—all of which make up the patrimony of each institute—be faithfully held in honor.[50]

It therefore makes a huge difference to what historical moment one will be appealing. Does one simply go to 1534 or 1540 or 1550 or 1558 or later for the fullest normative expression of the idea? How does one avoid selectively applying elements that were already fading away in Ignatius's lifetime (like the importance of moving from place to place)? An argument has been made here that the self-concept of the Society is truncated and distorted if 1599 *and all that it represents* are either omitted or minimized. Some might wish to assert that the Spirit does not stop speaking in 1599 but remains active later, for example in GC 32. Indeed. The Spirit might also be judged active in Martin Tripole's critique of the concepts of GC 32 in his study *Faith beyond Justice*, and in GC 34's qualifications of GC 32, and perhaps in the words of this very essay.[51] Nevertheless, there is still a form, a character, a configuration of traits and practices that define a distinctive and organic tradition; these all help to constitute a meaningfully coherent institute across time. There is still value, therefore, in the idea of foundations, even while the Spirit continues to inspire in various ways.

Careful discernment and good judgment about the details are presupposed. Even though the desire to go the Holy Land was quite a prominent part of the

---

50 The text is available at http://www.vatican.va/archive/hist_councils/ii_vatican_council/documents/vat-ii_decree_19651028_perfectae-caritatis_en.html (accessed October 3, 2018).

51 Martin Tripole, *Faith beyond Justice: Widening the Perspective* (St. Louis, MO: Institute of Jesuit Sources, 1994). It has been reported that the delegates of GC 34 (1995) were each given a copy of this volume. If so, that distribution may help to explain the highlighting of the theme of culture in some of the congregation's decrees, as culture is a key concept in the book's important seventh chapter. See, for example, decree 4, "Our Mission and Culture," in *Jesuit Life and Mission Today: The Decrees and Accompanying Documents of the 31st–35th General Congregations of the Society of Jesus*, ed. John W. Padberg (St. Louis, MO: Institute of Jesuit Sources, 2009), 536–46.

original thinking of Ignatius and then the early companions over a good number of years (at least 1521–37), it was not so important as to amount to a foundational aspect of the order.[52] Availability for mission was the deeper reality. Likewise, we have to distinguish major from minor turns. If someday the Society were to begin establishing monasteries, wearing a common habit, singing the daily office together in choir, and opening female branches under the superior general of the Society, Jesuits would have rather good grounds on which to say, "Well this is something quite other than our Institute." In a similar way, if, instead of adding, someone *removes* something essential, like the vows or the generalate or general congregations or a major formational period or possibly a signature apostolate, then Jesuits would also have good grounds on which to argue that this does not quite seem to be the Institute of the Society of Jesus. The changes may seem good and "called for by God." They may be "practical" and "well advised." But to the extent that the new configuration is really something different in character, there should at the least be an open admission of what has taken place, without prejudice to possible renaissances. A "re-founding" of the Society would call for yet another papally approved version of the *Formula of the Institute*. And it would still be necessary to know what was being re-founded.

The academic underpinnings of the Society were established and confirmed not only through the life of Ignatius but by the fourth part of the *Constitutions* and the history of the Society and the Ratio studiorum. This whole academic dimension falls, I would claim, into the category of what is essential to the Institute. It is something aboriginal and lasting and inescapable. Details can be changed. Practices and structures can evolve. But this entire dimension that is expressed in the RS and its tradition cannot be lopped off or radically diminished without requiring the honest admission that there has been a serious break with the tradition or possibly a deformation of the Institute. The RS is never to be dismissed entirely, any more than the *Constitutions* or *Spiritual Exercises* can be disregarded (adaptable though they are) when it comes to the governance of the Society or the giving of Ignatian retreats. Such dismissals would be tantamount to acts of self-erasure.

Admitting the foundational nature of the RS entails apostolic implications that extend far beyond the domain of that spiritual work of mercy known as "educating the ignorant." Jesuits may perform many types of charitable or catechetical educational services (which may replicate what many other kinds of agencies can perform). Jesuit *studia or* "Jesuit education" as such, however, refers to quite a different endeavor, an organized and high-achieving approach to and style of Christian education. This latter arena is what is most affected by any

52 The idea of going to Jerusalem dates from the earliest days of Ignatius's conversion. See Ribadeneyra, *Life of Ignatius*, no. 19. The group of companions finally left Venice (where they had been waiting for passage to the Holy Land) in 1538.

admission that the RS is foundational. Jesuit *studia* determine *both* the formation of the Jesuits of the future (who are reasonably expected to be able to provide essential leadership in "Jesuit education") *and* the core of Jesuit education in schools that "belong" to the Society in some meaningful sense.[53] The Jesuit educational enterprise bears significantly upon the task of evangelization, on the deepening of the understanding of faith and participation in the church, as well as on the promotion of the common good (knowledgeable *converted* citizens being vital to civic flourishing). This project is itself directly bound up with the core (and unchangeable) missions of the Society: (1) defense and propagation of the faith, and (2) the progress of souls in Christian life and doctrine; both of these require a particular kind of learning and teaching that does not simply coincide with the secular good that is "education." Christians can *also* rightly aspire to provide that secular good, but the Jesuit educational effort *proper* involves questions of faith, religion, justice, culture, and the well-being of all people from a perspective of belief and apostolic and ecclesial commitment. Only by admitting the foundational nature of the RS-tradition will the Society have a lasting basis for a unified and historically based approach in managing "Jesuit education." Otherwise, what will be the defining elements? The RS-tradition stands against the absorption into the standing secular educational projects, just as it stands against *laissez-faire* and the organizational entropy that bring about a fuzziness and lead to a dissolution in a thousand different directions.

The RS does in fact bring along with it goods of a great secular value too, because culture and society at large have many pressing motivations to turn in the direction of the values of the RS: both schools and formational programs are crying for attention, structure, order, and specificity with regard to the most significant high-quality content. The contemporary educational crisis and decline is more than well documented in thousands of books, essays, columns, and formal reports.[54] The Jesuit order, given its historical and institutional background,

---

53 As noted in the arguments above, the RS directed the running not only of the *schools* but of the *formation* of Jesuits. This critical connection between these two domains often seems lost in discussions about the RS.

54 Examples are all too easily found, from Allan Bloom's *The Closing of the American Mind: How Higher Education Has Failed Democracy and Impoverished the Souls of Today's Students* (New York: Simon & Schuster, 1987) to Harry R. Lewis's *Excellence without Soul: How a Great University Forgot about Education* [now subtitled *Does Liberal Education Have a Future?*] (New York: PublicAffairs, 2007) to Anthony T. Kronman's *Education's End: Why Our Colleges and Universities Have Given Up on the Meaning of Life* (New Haven: Yale University Press, 2008) to Derek Bok's *Our Underachieving Colleges: A Candid Look at How Much Students Learn and Why They Should Be Learning More* (Princeton: Princeton University Press, 2008). There are countless shorter pieces, also with very telling titles, for example Daniel Seymour, "Higher Education Has Lost Control of Its Own Narrative," *Chronicle of Higher Education* (November 11, 2016); http://www.chronicle.com/article/Higher-Education-Has-Lost/238321 (accessed October 3, 2018). See also webpages such

seems a most likely agency to refashion a fully organized and integrated edifying, purposeful liberal arts program of studies. Even non-believers can profit from the vision and the competencies and the practices employed in such a course of studies. This potential contribution to the secular sphere and to the "common good" suggests yet another compelling reason why it is important for the Society to recognize the full relevance of the RS. The beneficial civic (secular) impact of a religiously, ethically, and spiritually motivated education is something one might discern in the rise of the very first Jesuit school in Messina (1548).[55]

The Society needs to acknowledge the RS not only to be in a better position to make such a contribution by being what it is but also to be able to do what it more immediately ought to be doing for the church. Consider the domain of obligation directly declared by the pope himself (Paul VI [r.1963–78]):

> Certainly, today the difficulties which a Catholic University faces are grave. But they should not cause discouragement nor lead us to the temptation, either open or covert, of abandoning this field of work and leaving it for others to take up. In this context, we should note that it is certainly praiseworthy and necessary to have the collaboration of the laity and of priests who are not Jesuits for carrying on the work of the university, but it is necessary to be sure that this comes about in such a way that the Society is able to retain the authority necessary to face up to its Catholic responsibilities. *The Society should not, therefore, relinquish its authority in those universities which belong to it. To lose this worthwhile tradition would signify not only losing something of your "identity" but also, and above all, losing something of which the Church has need and which she cannot do without.*[56]

---

as "15 Books That Take American Education to Task"; http://www.onlineuniversities.com/blog/2012/08/15-books-that-take-american-education-task/ (accessed October 3, 2018), which includes Richard Arum and Josipa Roksa's *Academically Adrift: Limited Learning on College Campuses* (Chicago: University of Chicago Press, 2011). The most devastating incisive critique is that written by Christian Smith, "Higher Education Is Drowning in BS and It's Morally Corrosive to Society," Chronicle Review, B6 to B7, in the Chronicle of Higher Education (February 9, 2018; digital version, January 9, 2018; https://www.chronicle.com/article/Higher-Education-Is-Drowning/242195 [accessed October 3, 2018]).

55 See Ribadeneyra, *Life of Ignatius*, nos. 286–87. "Thinking that it would be too little merely to surround his towns with walls and guards, to open the highways after eliminating brigandage, and to establish trust and security in that kingdom, de Vega wanted his subjects' hearts filled with virtue and devotion, and he wanted to make a good start by spreading the divine name. [...] For longer-lasting results, de Vega used his authority to get the town officials of Messina to seek out Ours and call them in, and to set them up in a permanent residence after the founding of a college."

56 "Address of the Holy Father to the Rectors and Presidents, August 6, 1975," reprinted in *Project I: The Jesuit Apostolate of Education in the United States; Agreements and Decisions*, no. 6 (October 1975), appendix 1:35–42, here 38. Published by the staff of the Jesuit Conference as an aid to American Jesuits engaged in the apostolate. Emphasis added.

Though the RS is not explicitly mentioned in these lines, we see in Paul VI's words further strong support for the idea that *the very identity of the Jesuit order* involves its educational presence and leadership, a role well established by the RS and its tradition. Without the right self-concept correctly expressed, one is less likely to fulfill one's expected responsibilities. There is all the greater pressure when one understands that the mission of continuing this tradition is essential for the well-being and vitality of the church itself ("something of which the Church has need and which she cannot do without").

The *Studia*, the *Collegia*, and the *Institutum*: Three Constitutional Corroborations

The citation from Paul VI just presented moves us to a new point in these reflections, one that will retrospectively confirm us in the path originally taken: beyond the RS's foundational nature for which a sevenfold argument has been given, one might simply consider the relationship of the *studia* and the *collegia* to the Society of Jesus in its core idea (*Institutum*), in its formation, and in its apostolic endeavors. Three important constitutional passages should be kept in mind.

First, the colleges as well as the houses are like the members of the Society's very body:

> The authority to abandon or alienate colleges or houses once accepted will belong jointly to the general and the Society. Since *this is like severing a member from the Society's body and is a lasting and important matter*, it is better that the whole Society should be consulted about it.[57]

Second, having already noticed how the *Constitutions* gave so much weight to its fourth part (on the *studia* and *collegia*), we now might also consider how that fourth part begins. It has a special preamble (not present for any other individual part of the *Constitutions*), and this preamble returns the reader to the Society's most essential motivations, linking the idea of the *studia* directly to them:

> The aim which the Society of Jesus directly seeks is to aid its own members and their fellowmen to attain the ultimate end for which they were created. To achieve this purpose, in addition to the example of one's life, *learning and a method of expounding it are also necessary*. Therefore, after the proper foundation of abnegation of themselves is seen to be present in those who were admitted and also the required progress in virtues, *it will be necessary*

Most curiously, only Italian and Latin versions of this address are available on the Vatican website: https://w2.vatican.va/content/paul-vi/en/speeches/1975.index.4.html (accessed October 3, 2018).

57 *Constitutions*, part 4, chapter 2, no. 3 [322]. Emphasis added.

> *to provide for the edifice of their learning and the manner of employing it*, that these may be aids toward better knowledge and service of God, our Creator and Lord. Toward achieving this purpose the Society *takes charge of the colleges and also of some universities*, etc.[58]

Third, the *Constitutions* again highlights the extraordinary importance of studies in the last part, part 10, which is entitled "How the Whole Body of the Society Can Be Preserved and Developed in Its Well-Being." Number 813 stresses that union with God and spiritual means must be considered superior to learning or any natural means of preservation. Number 814 goes on to say that *once that spiritual foundation is in place*, God wants to be glorified by both the divine and the natural means that he gives us as our Creator: "Therefore the human or acquired means ought to be sought with diligence, *especially well-grounded and solid learning*, and a method of proposing it to the people by means of sermons, lectures, and the art of dealing and conversing with men."[59]

Learning is given a very special place here, but notice that it is not just *any* kind of learning but rather learning that is "well-grounded and solid." The RS was designed precisely to guarantee those features.[60] Immediately at this point we see at the start of number 815 a passage that shows how maintaining Jesuit *studia* in the colleges will play a most important role in the preservation of the Society. Here, part 10 of the *Constitutions* explicitly glances back to the academically focused part 4:

> In similar manner, great help will be derived from *maintaining the colleges in their good state and discipline*, by having the *superintendence* over them exercised by those who cannot receive any temporal gain, such as members of the professed Society, which will take care that those who possess the talent for it may receive *formation in life and learning worthy of a Christian*. For these students will be a *seedbed for the professed Society and its coadjutors*. Furthermore, if universities over which the Society exercises superintendence are added to the colleges, they too will aid toward the same end, as long as the method of procedure described in Part IV ["The Universities of the Society," 440–509] is preserved.

The spiritual–educational–institutional–apostolic vision did not simply resonate throughout the Society as edifying discourse; even outside the

---

58 *Constitutions*, part 4, [preamble], no. 307. Emphasis added.

59 This and the following citation are taken from *Constitutions*, part 10, nos. 813–15. Emphasis added.

60 This point suggests that if there is no solid consensus on what kind of learning is well grounded and solid, *there can be no proper Jesuit education or* studia *as such*. Defining and systematically articulating that kind of learning and its repeated optimum delivery of goods necessarily engages a community in an RS-like enterprise.

Constitutions it came to be a formally expressed and well-known principle. The cardinal importance of *docta pietas* along with its institutional and apostolic dimensions was pointedly declared in a 1584 document from a congregation convened by Superior General Acquaviva to begin to prepare the first draft of what would eventually circulate as the RS of 1586:

> There are assuredly two things that constitute our Society's bulwark and mainstay: *the burning zeal of devotion and a surpassing knowledge of reality.* The hinge of our Constitutions swings entirely on these two principles insofar as devotion bereft of the light of learning certainly profits individuals a good bit in private but can contribute almost nothing to help the Church and our neighbors in sermons, in administering the sacraments, in educating the young, in disputations with adversaries of the faith, in giving advice and providing answers in unclear situations, and in the rest of the expected services and functions of our men: these things require learning—*not the well-known common kind but a certain superior kind of learning.*[61]

So it seems clear: both in internal (individual, formational) and in external (institutional, apostolic) ways, the idea and the history and the calling of the Jesuit order are deeply implicated in *studia*; the Society of Jesus cannot be what it is or carry out certain of its key responsibilities without proper attention to the *studia*.

Regarding the issue of responsibility, we might recall at this point the RS's very first rule for provincials: "The provincial should consider himself *obliged to do his utmost* to ensure that our diverse and complex educational labor meets with the abundant results that the grace of our calling demands of us."[62]

We might easily connect this expression of the Society's responsibility not only with Paul VI's 1975 words cited just above ("face up to its Catholic responsibilities") but also with the import of the following passage from the 1995 document "Jesuits and University Life," decree 17 of the thirty-fourth general congregation of the Society of Jesus:

> The complexity of a Jesuit university can call for new structures of *government and control on the part of the Society* in order *to preserve its identity* and

61 *Duo plane sunt Societatis nostrae praesidia ac firmamenta,* ardens pietatis studium et praestans rerum scientia. *In haec duo capita omnis Constitutionum nostrarum vertitur cardo, eo quod pietas, si doctrinae luce orbata sit, singulis quidem privatim prosit non parum: at in Ecclesiae proximorumque utilitatem operam pene nullam conferre possit in concionibus, in sacramentis administrandis, in juventute erudienda, in disputationibus cum fidei adversariis, in consiliis, responsisque de dubiis rebus, et caeteris nostrorum hominum muneribus et functionibus : quae doctrinam,* non vulgarem illam, sed excellentem quandam *desiderant.* Acta Congregationis quae anno 1584, iussu admodum Reverendi Patris Praepositi Generalis Claudii Aquaevivae, habita est de ratione studiorum instituenda. MHSI 129:2. Emphasis added.

62 RS, no. 7. Emphasis added.

> at the same time allow it to relate effectively to the academic world and the society of which it is part, including the Church and the Society of Jesus. More specifically, in order for an institution to call itself Jesuit, *periodic evaluation and accountability to the Society are necessary* in order to judge whether or not its dynamics are being developed *in line with the Jesuit mission*. The Jesuits who work in these universities, both as a community and as individuals, must actively commit themselves to the institution, *assisting in its orientation*, so that it can achieve *the objectives desired for it by the Society*.[63]

According to GC 34, the Society simply cannot give up its responsibilities or its leadership role. It must know how to articulate and how to manage these, and first it has to have a clear idea of its guiding vision as carried through particulars, a sense of what it wants and what it needs to eliminate or adapt. Fully acknowledging the foundational nature of the RS, or acknowledging the foundational nature of the formational-educative dimensions of the Society's Institute (which themselves are *de facto* implicated in the RS-tradition), is a necessary first step on the way to the knowing fulfillment of some of the order's chief obligations and the church's needs. The citations from the *Constitutions* just adduced suggest in addition that such acknowledgment bears directly upon the Society's own proper realization of its purpose, its well-being, and its very survival.

Counter-Arguments

"Well, granting that we must take due account of the RS's institutional genealogy, the investment of the Society in its creation and use, the primordiality of the idea, the constitutive function that it fulfilled, the repeated formal declarations of its status, the authority evoked by its content, and the impact and reception of its consequences for centuries, how can you seriously suggest returning to this curious antique, chained as it is to Renaissance understandings and practices? Whatever authority the RS may have once had, it is now about as useful as a medieval suit of armor in battle."

I respond:

1. But we still do use *something* to protect ourselves in battle, don't we? We don't throw away the idea of bodily protection (helmets, vests, shields, leg-guards). We still try to cover adequately what most needs covering. Just so, *some* guiding document in the mold of the RS, might still be serviceable and even essential: the RS could serve as an exemplary expression of educational genius. We may need to improve, tweak, refine, transpose, transmute, and update

63 See John W. Padberg, ed., *Jesuit Life and Mission Today: The Decrees and Accompanying Documents of the 31st–35th General Congregations of the Society of Jesus* (St. Louis, MO: Institute of Jesuit Sources, 2009), no. 412, #9 (page 631). Emphasis added.

but not eliminate. It is not enough for us merely to have general norms and think primarily in terms of numbers of course-hours rather than in terms of the substance of those courses. The training calls for specific high quality, well-deliberated contents. It needs the right structures, infrastructures, and superstructures. Certain parts cannot be considered merely optional. A specific end might require a certain level of specificity in means. The open-ended pluralism and variability of contents of contemporary college education might have to be judged incompatible with Jesuit education properly conceived.

2. We return to old documents all the time, many of them quite a bit older than the RS: the US Constitution, Ignatius's *Spiritual Exercises*, the *Constitutions of the Society of Jesus*, the Nicene Creed, the Gospels, the Ten Commandments. There are ways of reading, adapting, using what is helpful and not being bound by what is not. People who want to say the RS is simply out of date can seem rather too quick to jettison what can actually be of immense value and relevance.
3. The Renaissance was not the only age to value the long-term canonical greats. Before and after the Renaissance, people returned to many of the same authors: Homer, Sophocles, Plato, Aristotle, Cicero, Virgil, Horace, Seneca, and all the tremendous riches of the Catholic intellectual and spiritual traditions. Now we have more rather than fewer classics, so some type of specific selection, organization, sequencing, competent delivery, and oversight is all the more necessary. Much can be set aside, but that which is perduring needs to be maintained or it will be lost—to our diminishment and to the diminishment of the common good. We can add elements and reconfigure the whole plan without erasing our entire hard drive of the most globally relevant literary culture.

But What Does This Do to Help the Poor?

A yet stronger counter-argument would maintain that this whole tradition lies outside of the contemporary concerns for social justice and on such grounds alone the archaic nature of the RS dooms it to irrelevance. Such thinking fails to see that all social justice issues are significantly at stake in whatever informs and shapes the attitudes, understandings, vision, sensibilities, and powers of judgment of the next generation—and education clearly does that in a significant way, both for the general populace and for its leaders. Education is thus a social apostolate *par excellence*. Its radical relevance has long been known, particularly since the Renaissance's promotion of "civic humanism." The poor will benefit greatly if not immediately from an adequate contemporary elaboration of the RS. At least this is by far the most reasonable working hypothesis. Conversely, it is most reasonable to believe that a truncated, uprooted, and misconceived education will likely lead straight to injustice, first of all to the injustice of depriving the students of their rightful heritage and stunting major parts of their spiritual and moral lives: "Any justification of the promotion of justice as a commitment of the contemporary university must be grounded on the basic conviction that the university exists for the humane growth of its students."[64]

Of course, dysfunctional or misconceived education undoes the cultural unity needed for social stability, so the negative impact is profound and long-lasting in a larger perspective. Without the proper education, leaders and supporters of the best way forward are stymied before they can begin to mature. Social change based on faulty premises or misunderstandings destroys rather than builds. Foolish thinking displaces wise thinking. Consequently, the poor are made all the poorer, and a pathway to social chaos and then tyranny is paved. Classical humanism such as the one purveyed by the RS in fact has *everything* to do with justice.[65]

How to Get There

Let us begin to think through this particular dimension of justice concerns as a way to see what kind of thing needs to be put more widely into place. Let us say that we want a curriculum that appropriately develops in students the best social, political, and economic understandings and powers of judgment, particularly with justice in mind. What needs to be done? First, we have to have a faculty that knows well how to do that, one that has a confidence that it can do it properly, with the right well-deliberated *content*, in a coherent program that is not simply a gathering of the results of monads of "academic freedom," each monad possessing its own point of view (which may possibly be quite faulty or counter-productive or idiosyncratic or shallow or misleadingly bias-ridden) and each monad focused on its own "cause" or career path of publication and promotion. The RS suggests a kind of instrument that allows for the creation and harmonizing of a faculty that can more easily transcend monadic limitations to operate effectively together for certain community ends within a detailed, well-structured framework. The right kind of guide provides for a balanced approach that builds on the greatest corporate wisdom and a larger consensus on what is the most promising way forward.

Admittedly, we have to face something of a chicken-and-egg conundrum here: How to properly form the teachers who might then form the teachers of the next generation? Who forms that first group of teachers—and also the personnel that will provide the adequate oversight of the teachers' performances? This is likely why the RS took so long and so many voices to work out. A consensus on

---

64 Michael J. Buckley, *The Catholic University as Promise and Project: Reflections in a Jesuit Idiom* (Washington, DC: Georgetown University Press, 1999), 113–14.

65 Claude Pavur, "Classical Humanism Has *Everything* to Do with Justice," *Electronic Antiquity* 13, no. 1 (November 2009): 1–25. Available at https://www.academia.edu/700497/Classical_Humanism_Has_EVERYTHING_to_Do_With_Justice (accessed October 3, 2018).

best structures, practices, *and* contents had to be achieved over time, through directed discussion under a competent committee of educators that could then submit to a yet higher authority something that the latter could then institute top-down what had been worked out in detail from the bottom-up. An educational constitution or rationale like the RS, once in place, plays an invaluable role in maintaining the character of a distinctive educational culture.

A start must be made, and it cannot not just emerge miraculously "from below." "Below" does not have authority or administrative sway or budgetary control or staying power as such. "Below" is already quite well occupied in day-to-day demands, sometimes increased "from above." But without "below" and its genuine cooperation, no educational success is possible for the institution. "Below" has to make commitments to follow "above" and actually participate fully in the project. And "above," once it has paid careful attention to the even higher "above" of the Institute, must know both how to listen and how to speak to "below" with the chief ends and foundational understandings in mind.

Leadership should begin to work out details on contents, order, method, curricular design and integration under the guidance of certain basic commonsense insights (e.g., some contents are more important or generally relevant than others; some structures or processes tend toward the unraveling of the fabric of the enterprise). We need to ask questions like the following:

> What authorities do we use to inform and train future educational personnel in, say, for example, political, social, and economic matters that bear so significantly on the details of justice questions today? What are the *specific* books and articles and thinkers used, in what proportion? Who decided them? On what basis and background? How transparent and collaborative and judicious was the choice? How have we avoided simplistic partisanship, tendentiousness, and group bias? How, then, is this political–social–economic part of the curriculum integrated with the parts of the curriculum that focus on cultural history, communication skills, and Christianity?

The last question here points to the all-important larger systematic proportioning that will help to ensure balance, range, and vision.

The area of curricular specifics and structures and procedures is a critical one for Jesuit formation. Indeed, it has for some decades now been needing something like a revamped RS. If studies continue to proceed in a largely *laissez-faire, ad hoc, choice-oriented* fashion, with no *well-deliberated, specific, high-quality relevant content in a well-structured, comprehensive program under competent supervision*, then far less is going to be done for civic society in general or for the poor in particular.[66]

---

66 The latter part of this sentence contains in a nutshell some of the chief good that can be extracted from the tradition of the RS even on a secular basis. Early Jesuits would see these

To go for decades without consensus on particulars of content and structure is neither in the spirit nor the letter of the tradition established by the *Constitutions* and the RS. Consider what might be called "the canon of specificity" (*Constitutions*, no. 359): "Furthermore, it is good to determine in detail the books which should be lectured on and those which should not, both in the humanities and in the other faculties."[67]

Beyond the specifics, the new arrangements are needed, or perhaps old agreements need to be renegotiated, whether formally or informally.[68] Jesuit education may have to attempt to learn how to serve new purposes in this particular moment in cultural history. This cannot happen without a decent knowledge of what has gone into making up that historical moment. It has emerged from *somewhere*. There is meaning in the genesis; a penetrating review of that genesis can lead to the creation of even greater meaning in the current context.

Great Books and Jesuit Education

The RS favors knowing and appreciating certain high points and integrating them into a larger vision of life that is widely appealing (even to non-believers).[69] This is not to say that Jesuit education should simply be a kind of "great books program." It may be worthwhile to sketch out the main differences here to clarify the concept of Jesuit education yet further.

It is true that a great books program would certainly be in some respects closer to the RS than to the current curricular indeterminacy (also known as "smorgasbord," or the following of large generalized content-vague distribution requirements like "Take one course relating to pre-1750 history" or "Incorporate some kind of course on diversity"). The following features speak for the similarities between the two approaches: (1) the curriculum is thought about and

---

features as desiderata only within the context of the moral and religious conversions of the individuals. Letters and good character (*litterae et boni mores*) had to be given equal weight. See also the coda to this essay.

67 *Constitutions*, no. 359. *Et convenit, ad particularia descendendo, qui libri sint praelegendi, tam in humanioribus, quam in aliis disciplinis, qui vero praelegi non possint, constituere.* Part 4, chapter 5, E. The Latin is stronger: "Which books should be presented [...] and which *cannot be* [*non possint*]."

68 The Thirty-Fourth General Congregation spoke to this issue: "The complexity of a Jesuit university can call for new structures of government and control on the part of the Society in order to preserve its identity and at the same time allow it to relate effectively to the academic world and the society of which it is part, including the Church and the Society of Jesus." GC 34, no. 412, decree 17: "Jesuits and University Life," no. 9, in Padberg, *Jesuit Life and Mission Today*, 629–32, here 631.

69 See Claude Pavur, "Ignatian Humanism and Jesuit Higher Education," available at https://www.academia.edu/30313535/Ignatian_Humanism_and_Jesuit_Higher_Education (accessed October 3, 2018).

planned as a whole; (2) high-quality material is carefully chosen; (3) the sectioning off into particular canned "subjects," majors, and minors is avoided; (4) higher values, meanings, and larger visions are brought to the fore; (5) a particular reading of the cultural heritage is appropriated in some fashion, with stress not on reading large quantities but on reading deeply;[70] and (6) "Letters" and philosophy are given prime time (although perhaps theology is often left out of great books programs, Aquinas tending to be taken more as a philosopher); and (7) the achievements of the past (even the distant past) are given great weight.

The RS focused more intently on absorbing certain particular high points really well, especially Cicero, Aristotle, Aquinas, and scripture. Time spent getting deeply familiar with a few highest approved standards of genius and spirit is felt to be a mental and spiritual apprenticeship not easily achieved otherwise. The RS clearly worked within a religious horizon. It did not wish to give equal prime time to every great work and author, but it wanted consistency with the horizons with which it was closely affiliated; it had a particular "lean." The education was never a matter of just *any* Letters, philosophy, or theology. Certainly, proven older material was favored and new material was considered possibly disruptive or confusing. The RS gave much special attention to the individual student's activity (both imitation and creativity) and to their communicational mastery with regard to what they had learned (through the *Actus* or academic performances, the writing of poems and essays, recitations, study-club activities, and the like). The RS was deeply rooted in grammar, language, and rhetoric in a way that great books programs tend not to be. The exemplarity of the teacher was especially important in the RS, whereas the most famous great books exponent, Robert Maynard Hutchins (1899–1977), called his program "teacher-proof" (meaning the books automatically carried certain values even if the teacher was not so effective). Finally, the scope of the RS went from high school to graduate school, with theology at the apex. Not so with great books programs, which are usually conducted during the college years, without the stadial progression from Letters to philosophy to theology. Even if such an order cannot be imitated well today, the idea is that there is a sense of progression with the RS-inspired approach that need not be present at all in a great books program.

70 This is the ancient proverbial advice of *non multa sed multum*. Cf. Pliny the Younger (61–*c.*113), *Letters*, 7.9.15: "They say, after all, that you should read deeply, not extensively (literally, 'many things')" (*Aiunt enim multum legendum esse, non multa*). See also Seneca the Younger (*c.*4 BCE–65 CE), *Letters* 1.2, and Heraclitus (*c.*535–*c.*475 BCE), fragment 40: "The learning of many things does not teach understanding; otherwise it would have taught Hesiod and Pythagoras, and again Xenophanes and Hecataeus" (cited from Diogenes Laertius [fl. third century CE], *Lives of the Philosophers* IX.1).

Some Contemporary Challenges

Our times are abundantly rich and marvelously advanced, but they are also full of violent upheavals, divisions, disruptions, and disturbingly radical changes. What, then, should we do when we encounter the adversarial forces or "wicked spirits" of selective amnesia, dismissive and prejudicial anti-traditionalism, strong secularization, aggressive atheism, ecclesiaphobia, privatizing narcissism, self-righteous and manipulative guilt-inducing indignation, tendentious deconstruction, epistemological despair, postmodern alienation, ideological bullying, technological distraction, scientistic superstition, cynicism, escapism, adolescent wholesale rejection of some substantial authorities accompanied by naïve or self-serving acceptance of others, cultural trivialization and degradation, or paralyzing moral aporia? Working against debilitating historical ignorance, overly simplistic dogmatic impositions, and all kinds of gratuitous negativity and self-destructive behaviors, we need to go to the heart of what is at stake in arguments such as the ones presented here and see what we can do to improve. In the Society of Jesus (as in society at large), the time seems overripe for a large-scale general examen. We might look toward not a "re-founding" but rather a re-awakening, a re-anchoring, and a renewal in what is essential.

It will help to review the whole story carefully and sift the wheat from the chaff. Our own moment occurs after the "Land o' Lakes Statement" of 1967, in which Catholic universities were explicitly taken to be essentially the same kind of species as secular universities, with the addition of certain Catholic accents (like the presence of all theological disciplines and spontaneous Catholic community life).[71] Some critics may say that such a statement was merely the result of a march of history: *studia* are not at all what they were in Ignatius's Christianized early modern Renaissance Europe with its strong medieval heritage. The Enlightenment and the wider historical and cultural knowledge of more recent times have had an impact and must be absorbed. Consensus has broken down on many levels. Pluralism reigns. To this, one response comes quite easily: *These elements are precisely all the more reason* that there should be intense and focused reflection, discussion, distinctions, and guided practice. There is now *all the greater urgency* to make sure that people learn how to read, understand, and discern the wisdom of the ages. Otherwise, one is merely increasing confusion and hastening the entropic diminishment of everything.

Common sense (the prudence that people of at least ordinary levels of insight and intelligence put into play) seems to point us toward certain very obvious perennial values: organized approaches and language mastery; knowledge

71 For the document and its problematical aspects, see Claude Pavur, "The Land o' Lakes Derailment; And a Way to Get Back Homeward in Catholic Higher Education," published at Academia.edu, November 17, 2016; accessible at https://www.academia.edu/30336880/ (accessed October 3, 2018).

of tradition and history; the accurate understanding of key terms and texts and figures and movements; frameworks that assist contextual and conceptual understanding; exposition of the best arguments pro and con; stability and consistency; and so on. And yet there may still be fears of too great a uniformity, consistency, and stability, or even the feeling that these qualities are actually *disvalues* in themselves.

First, we should be completely fair about admitting that the RS allows for *great* variation and creativity. The larger framework is set, and the major content is clearly defined, but many specifics are not, as seen in directives like "take a poet *or* a historian in this period." The teacher at every level must learn and practice the *art* of teaching, making choices and using his native talent. For example: "The students' exercises will include things like imitating some passage of a poet or prose writer; some description (for instance, of gardens, of churches, of a storm) and varying the same expression of similar things in several ways" (and on and on, RS 379). Consider the flexibility implied in something like the following (from RS 384, emphasis added):

> The subject for a poem can also be given in writing *or* orally, *either* by signifying only the theme *or* with the addition of a given saying. And *either* it can be brief, like an epigram, ode, elegy, *or* letter, which might be best done in individual sessions; *or* it can be rather long, so that they construct the poem over several sessions just like a prose composition.

When the RS directs the teacher that he "should see to it that the students get accustomed to distinguishing what stylistically belongs to a poet and what to a prose writer" (RS 352), it is the teacher who has to figure out how to do this.[72]

Second, there simply has to be honest agreement that some uniformity, consistency, and stability are to some extent utterly necessary and helpful positive features. We can distinguish, as the RS did, levels that have their own goals and dynamics and ways to incorporate these values differentially along the way. Greater uniformity seems always much more important at the beginning to ensure the possibility of greater achievement and variety at the end. If each kindergartener were allowed to choose to learn a different writing system to represent the sounds of words (Arabic, Greek, Cyrillic, Latin, IPA, Hiragana, Mycenaean Linear B, Runic, and so on), massive confusion would result. A "free pluralism" would in this case *undermine* unity and coherence and creativity—and it would ultimately fragment the entire society into alternate universes. Just so, in an analogous way at higher educational levels, there needs to be the appropriate, higher

72 To my knowledge, there is as yet no comprehensive study of the various evolutions of the RS in different locales. Some assert that the RS was never followed to the letter anywhere, except perhaps at the Roman College. But it is clear that the drafters expected manifold variations even while maintaining the value of articulating an ideal.

level of uniformity that will create a community of discourse (aiming for, even if never fully achieving a "union of minds and hearts"), a uniformity that will yet enable greater complexity and freedom and a helpful diversity at a later moment.

To a large extent, what is operative here is not so much an *ideological* as a *pedagogical* issue, though much of the reaction against uniformity may derive from ideological concerns. It is simply not fair *not* to teach everyone a common language. Parents would not withhold the alphabet from their children, nor would they complain about uniformity when a single alphabet is taught. RS-inspired practices can be seen as helping to ground and maintain a *community of common discourse that can better discuss and discern the common good.* And where is the common good if there is no longer a real commonality? These unifying practices allow for the development of powers of judgment that will lead, at best, to critiques and transformations that are not wrenchingly self-destructive or socially disruptive. To immediately undercut every idea with an opposite nullifying idea in the name of pluralism produces either alienated cynics or simply very confused individuals who wonder why you are bothering them in the first place. Maturity involves learning to see how *some* particular words, concepts, practices, and formulae are necessary in order for individuals to "get beyond" or "above" those very things.

Education expresses, constitutes, and maintains community and culture. Core elements of the heritage, which include much that is of universal value or that derive from a now "universally" common story or shared past, need to be communicated with a certain stability and continuity. An RS-like approach has this utility and basic good sense. In 1599, having the students of theology learn well the emerging standard, the thinking of Thomas Aquinas, not only allowed the professors to hone their expertise over the years but it also raised a whole community of learners to a higher level of thought and intellectual skill and in the process established a shared language in which a plurality of stances might be meaningfully expressed.

But is such an approach really possible *now*? Yes. Something like Thomas P. Rausch's *Systematic Theology* proves that very helpfully organized comprehensive and systematic overviews can be written, even in this day.[73] More than Rausch does, the tradition of the RS opposes extensive use of very recent materials, and it favors authors and materials of long-proven worth and staying power. Perhaps we should find new ways of vetting and presenting the more recent materials that are so compelling and influential in the culture. In any case, we might easily make use of some such comprehensive introductions as Rausch's and richly supplement them with primary sources taken not in excerpts but in substantial units. Guides like Rausch's could be composed for scripture, the church councils,

73 Thomas P. Rausch, *Systematic Theology: A Roman Catholic Approach* (Collegeville, MN: Liturgical Press, 2016).

moral theology, the social teaching of the church, church history, patristics, and any other relevant area could also be used to great benefit, particularly if they are not just selectively read but mastered. What Rausch does for a particular field (systematic theology) might be expanded to cover an entire curriculum, but only with a pedagogical and institutional intelligence not normally attained within any single discipline. It is the architectonic art so well exemplified by the RS.[74]

Conclusion

The argument made in these pages amply supports the idea that the RS is foundational to the Institute of the Society of Jesus. Should this thesis be accepted, we might expect to see major revisions and restructuring, particularly regarding formational and educational infrastructures, structures, and superstructures. Energies and resources will be allocated differently. A different self-image will emerge in the Society and in its schools. It is conceivable, however, that some might still say that we can agree that the RS is foundational while judging it thoroughly irrelevant now for matters of method and content and structure—that is, that it is as good as abrogated. There should at least be a *bona fide* effort to see what might be living and what might be dead and what, with insight and grace, might be resurrected in a possibly greater form. It would simply not be responsible to admit foundational status and then simply ignore the weight of history, the full configuration of the original inspirations, and the core self-concept. We learn from history. In fact, we need the *repetitio* or we will never *really* learn. One great lesson of the Renaissance is "If you do not go back, you cannot move forward."[75] The very first step might have to be finally waking up and seeing clearly what was there before our leap into postmodern amnesia and do-it-yourself educational schemes under the pressures of partisanship and activism and "individual self-fulfillment." Old remedies might sometimes be the ones we need most. Basics might be best.

I have tried to make the best case for the strongest statement of the thesis. From the skeptical, I welcome a rebuttal. Where precisely do the arguments fail? I do not think that in the aggregate they will so easily be undone. Nor can the whole topic be ignored if we are being responsible: a judgment about the foundational status of the RS is full of consequence since it affects any answer to the question of how the Society's Institute should best be adapted today. One must first properly understand the Institute. Then one can better judge how it should be modified for contemporary circumstances. Of course, like the person

74 For a version of what a new RS might possibly look like in some detail, see chapter 6, "Toward a Revised *Ratio studiorum* for Jesuit Colleges."

75 This is not to say that all we have to do is to "go back." The leap forward in early modernity is certainly unimaginable without the return to and the re-sifting of many ancient works, but creativity and daring and newness played a great role as well.

and utterances of Ignatius himself, that Institute can inspire and direct without requiring a literalistic or fundamentalistic interpretation. But it needs to be adequately understood first, and criteria can emerge that will guide the process.

For example, the spirit of the RS does not prescind from a precise curriculum or a specific order of study. Its way is to decide in a very responsible, focused, consultative but authoritative way the particular structures and contents and methods that the times call for, even while allowing for adaptations according to circumstances. The tradition of the RS would never foreground the principle of subsidiarity and leave to local agents the freedom simply to follow their own creativity and discernment, even while it is not at all averse to such features *within* the system. Without some kind of standard or "universal" concept in mind, something to aim for (if not globally, then at least regionally), the union of minds and hearts would be far more difficult to achieve; parochialism and special interests would be far more likely to emerge and go astray; timely competent oversight would be nearly impossible. Even the RS congregation of 1584 long ago was pointedly aware of this issue.[76]

Against any suspicions that behind this essay there lurks a retrogressive nostalgia, I declare that I am not angling for the reinstatement of an entire classical system of Renaissance-inspired Greco-Latin humanism and Thomistic Scholasticism (though such an intention would not in the least invalidate the argument I have made here). At the same time, I will openly admit that I cannot see how one achieves intellectual–cultural maturity without *some* substantial study of those great traditions.[77] Their presuppositions, their categories, their vocabularies, their points of reference are still with us in some significant ways. They are *now*. We cannot fully enter into "the now" without them. Enlightenment means rejecting self-imposed oblivion, both with regard to the RS for the Society and with regard to our cultural foundations for liberal education in general. The point is not "restoration" but a suitable recovery of that type of apostolic educational genius, useful practice, and breadth and depth of vision the likes of which the world has not often seen and the substance of which it needs more desperately

76 After recalling how solemnly (*gravissime*) the *Constitutions* call for this agreement of minds and hearts (*animorum consensio*), and how the topic was one not yet sufficiently addressed, it gave the following reflection: "For since no order, no common form had yet been prescribed, each person considered himself entitled both to adopt the opinion he wished and to teach his opinion by means of the method he especially approved. As a result Ours occasionally had at least as many disagreements among themselves as with those outside" (*Cum enim nullus ordo, forma nulla communis adhuc praescripta esset, licere sibi quaeque existimavit, et sentire quae vellet; et quae sentiebat, aliis tradere ea methodo, quam maxime probabat; ut aliquando non minus nostri inter se, quam ab externis dissentierent*). MHSI 129:3.

77 There are further points to be considered on the classical elements in older forms of Jesuit education. See Claude Pavur, "The Classical *Ratio* and Jesuit Education," in *Jesuit Education and the Classics*, ed. Edmund P. Cueva, Shannon N. Byrne, and Frederick Benda (Newcastle upon Tyne: Cambridge Scholars Press, 2009), 55–64.

than ever. More precious natural resources are being wasted than are dreamt of in many an economic and social philosophy. In justice, people do have a right to know their own *larger* stories and to be provided with a means of access to all of the most relevant positive aspects of their *whole* heritage. Western/world culture is now a mega-culture that includes, synthesizes, and also transcends all that is merely individual or tribalistic or ethnocentric. Given the character and calling of the Society of Jesus, those who wish to continue the Jesuit tradition should weigh—*knowingly* weigh—which apostolic initiatives should be undertaken today according to its own particular role. May the Spirit speak, and may all allied with the Society's Institute listen both to what Spirit says now *and to what the Spirit has already said again and again in ages past*—for their own well-being and for that of their neighbors.

Coda: Is Organization Everything?

In my graduate studies, a professor once parenthetically mentioned in class: "You know all those Mongolian hordes that swept through Europe in the thirteenth century? It turns out that there were not really that many at all. They were just very well organized." This comment prompted me to think, "Yes, organization is everything." In retrospect, I admit that of course organization is not actually *everything*. Free play, openness to the spirit and inspiration, adaptation to circumstances are equally necessary. But organization is certainly something that seems to make all the difference in many enterprises that we count important. Imagine a symphony, a sport, a theatrical performance, a city's traffic flow without it. Just so for education.

The Latin word *ratio* can mean reckoning, method, plan, system, intelligible structure, order, account, consideration. The full title of the 1599 charter also included the word *institutio*, which might mean "arrangement" or "disposition" while still carrying the connotation of a *formally approved and settled establishment*.[78] It is the *Ratio atque institutio studiorum Societatis Iesu*. The root achievement of the RS was to provide in detail a carefully organized educational plan in service of a larger vision. It was quite practical. It worked. It proved itself by its results. Something like it is needed today. This insight is really quite accessible to common sense. At the end of the first century, the educationist Quintilian (*c*.35–*c*.100) wrote that although he may seem to have recommended far too much to learn in his ambitious program for training the complete orator, it was not beyond the bounds of what is possible: "For systematic organization and proportioning will make everything go faster."[79]

78 The Latin verb *instituere* can mean "to plant firmly in place, establish, fix, institute, found, organize, institute."

79 The passage reads: *Omnia enim breviora reddet ordo et ratio et modus*. Quintilian, *Institutio oratoria* 12.11.14.

This love of structure and organization *as a starting point and as a framework* was a great part of the mystical yet pragmatic mind of Ignatius, who divided up his *Spiritual Exercises* into four set weeks and the *Constitutions* into ten distinct parts. The Society he established concerned itself mightily with the ordering of studies, with much attention to the best contents, methods, and structures for achieving the desired ends. That is why those working under Ignatian and Jesuit inspirations can never entirely escape the idea of the *Ratio studiorum*.

6. Toward a Revised *Ratio studiorum* for Jesuit Colleges

Become what you are, having learned what that is.

—*Pindar*

In the preceding chapters, a case has been made that the *Ratio studiorum* represents something essential for Jesuit education, and indeed for the Jesuit order itself. Why could we not just have gone straight to the question of "What next?" That is what many people most want to know, after all. That is where an interesting discussion can be conducted. The simple answer is that determining "what should be next" requires an informed and discerning understanding. Without being reasonably sure that the right concepts are in play, we would not at all be ready to shape the future. In fact, any conclusions to which we might come would be of questionable validity—and possibly poisonous. Understanding the historical details and the systemic "*a priori*" (that is, the presuppositions, practices, etc., that were in place at the start) changes and clarifies the focus and the boundaries. It alters what counts as a good answer. It directs us toward certain paths and away from others.

Most immediately, historical breadth and depth and insight offer part of the answer to a rather large contemporary problem: namely that the concept of Jesuit education is often all too vague, ambiguous, confused, and unsubstantiated. Thus some conversations end as fuzzily as they began, if not more so. Perhaps some have preferred it that way: a free-floating impressionism certainly helps to support a wider range of options in a more complex cultural situation. It protects the inertial *status quo*. And *laissez-faire* or "free grazing" will always have its attractions. Ordinary prudence, however, suggests the value of operating within more clearly defined parameters when it comes to making effective choices about particulars within a limited timeframe to satisfy pressing needs. We may now find it important to "clarify the broth"—not just for the sake of clarity or good taste but for the sake of authenticity, accurate understanding, good judgments, effective policies, greater concrete results, and ultimately justice for the students who are looking for the highest-order returns on their investment of their prime time and effort (and lives).

After all, the famous imperative "Become who you are" applies to Jesuit schools too.[1] The alternative is inauthenticity, self-alienation, ineffectiveness, and a waste of time and good gifts. The alternative leads to despair in individuals

1 Pindar, *Pythian Ode* 2.72 actually reads "Become such as you are, *having learned* [what that is]." See Pindar. *Olympian Odes: Pythian Odes*, ed. and trans. William H. Race, Loeb Classical Library 56 (Cambridge, MA: Harvard University Press, 1997), 244–45.

and to cultural decline in society. Too much is at stake for us to be content with mere talk—or talk that goes on far too long without positive effective results when there are needs to be met. This is not to say that values, even great ones, do not exist, perhaps impressively and abundantly, in what Jesuit schools are doing today. Yet often, especially in a time of great change and complexity, signals can be confused or contradictory. The most important outcomes cannot be measured, particularly in the short run. But one can notice in the general discourse about education today much disquiet, and sometimes deeply disturbing conclusions. Jesuit education exists within this same climate, with the additional complexity of the theological, spiritual, and ecclesial dimensions that need not be considered in secular institutions. So even within the Jesuit circle of schools, individuals can experience confusion and aimlessness and ambiguity instead of progress in union of minds and hearts toward a clear, shared goal, avoiding the dissociation and dissolution that a naïve hyper-pluralistic diversity can create.

What, then, are some particularities that might emerge as a natural development of the kind of Jesuit education that has been suggested in these pages? Let us go right to the heart of the matter, the place where all students *must* go, that part of the curriculum that is required as "core." All the rest is variable and optional, after all: liturgies, extracurriculars, socials, clubs, service projects, retreats, talks, concerts, plays, sports. Looking to the more universal, we will best be served by rethinking the core of Jesuit college education today in light of (1) the Jesuit Institute, that is, its mission and its organically developing self-understanding and tradition, and (2) contemporary needs and structures (especially those that are social, spiritual, personal, and educational). Here are some first thoughts. They build on many "old thoughts," on long and recent reflections, and on the experiences and observations of several decades, even centuries.

A Necessary, Critical, and Nevertheless Persistently Ignored Distinction

I want to begin by making explicit and foregrounding a distinction that many thinkers disastrously ignore, misunderstand, minimize, or dismiss: the difference between college and university (graduate) teleologies. The former is more *personally* formational, the latter, more *professionally* formational. The former should be the largest part of the undergraduate investment; the latter, of the graduate one. Research interests are not slighted but rather correctly situated when they are primarily connected with the graduate sphere. Questions of personal development and culture are not deprecated when they are primarily connected with the undergraduate one.[2] Collegians are almost always at a time in their lives when they are asking what their lives are going to be about—how will they live, into

2 Of course, if graduate students are going to be hired to teach undergraduates, they too will have to consider the formational aspect of the college endeavor.

what will they put their hearts, in what will they believe, in whom should they trust. College should be markedly helpful to them at this point on their journeys, even if it gives them many things whose value they either never explicitly appreciate or only much later put to use. But to speak this way is misleading, for this education may involve "giving things," but it is all the more a question of *formational growth*, of *becoming*, of assuming greater depth and breadth and quality of *a mature, intelligent consciousness*, of developing *character*.

This distinction is not entirely ignored, but it is virtually so; otherwise, deans from Harvard and Yale would not have had to write books whose titles testify to a sense of what has been lost: Harry Lewis gave us *Excellence Without Soul: How a Great University Forgot About Education* (a critique of Harvard but with wider applicability) and Anthony Kronman authored *Education's End: Why Our Colleges and Universities Have Given Up on the Meaning of Life.*[3] It says a great deal that these books seemed necessary almost forty years after there had been a quite adequate analysis of premature professionalizing specialization in college: *The Academic Revolution* by Christopher Jencks and David Riesman (1909–2002).[4]

In 1969, the year after Jencks and Riesman's work was published, the famous educator Joseph Tussman (1914–2005) was clearly well aware of the important distinction between college and university when he wrote:

> Nor is the college a professional school. It may prepare for, but it does not directly train for, the great professions. It has its own mission: to fit us for the life of active membership in the democratic community; to fit us to serve, in its broadest sense, our common political vocation.[5]

The distinction highlighted here was anticipated 141 (yes, that is *one hundred and forty-one*) years earlier in a report of Yale College, which said:

> By a liberal education, it is believed, has been generally understood, such a course of discipline in the arts and sciences, as is best calculated, at the same time, both to strengthen and enlarge the faculties of the mind, and to familiarize it with the leading principles of the great objects of human investigation and knowledge. *A liberal, is obviously distinct from a professional, education.* The former is conversant with those topics, an acquaintance with which is necessary or convenient, in any situation of life, the latter,

3 Both books appeared in 2007. Lewis's work, now sporting a new subtitle, "Does Liberal Education Have a Future," appeared from PublicAffairs (New York), and Kronman's from Yale University Press (New Haven).

4 (Garden City, NY: Doubleday, 1968).

5 Cited from Joseph Tussman's *Experiment at Berkeley* (New York: Oxford University Press, 1969) in its abridgment in the same author's *The Beleaguered College: Essays on Educational Reform* (University of California: Institute of Governmental Studies Press, 1997), 49–123, here 55.

> with those which qualify the individual for a particular station, business or employment. The former is antecedent in time, the latter rests upon the former as its most appropriate foundation. A liberal education is fitted to occupy the mind, while its powers are opening and enlarging; a professional education requires an understanding already cultivated by study, and prepared by exercise for methodical and persevering efforts.[6]

So the distinction has been known for a long while. And it has been suppressed or ignored, to our great loss. Tussman makes this point in his retrospective reflections on his efforts to establish a proper program of liberal education at the University of California at Berkeley:

> First, I see a fateful conflict between the university and the college, between the graduate school and the undergraduate college. This is a conflict not sufficiently grasped or appreciated. Somewhere, in an apocalyptic mood, I sum it all up by saying that *the university, merely by being what it is, has killed the college.*[7]

So we might begin—no, we *must* begin—by making this distinction. Simply doing that would mark the beginning of a great victory: the resurrection of the college as such.

First Principles for Rethinking the Jesuit Core

Now if we do not agree on some first principles, our discussions will be at cross-purposes and unproductive. I therefore propose the following as a basis:

1. Jesuit college education should have a distinctive style and content. It should be a recognizable educational culture that neither simply reflects the standard college education that is generally available elsewhere nor fails to make appropriate adaptation and use of the best of such an education.
2. Jesuit education today cannot exist without meaningful and substantive connections to its own history and foundations. As soon as one employs the term "Jesuit," a history is evoked, a certain shape of particulars in time. If one demands the freedom to constitute Jesuit education entirely anew without any organic or structural or material or systemic connection to the history and meaning it carried for hundreds of years, then the use of the term is ambiguously problematical at best and deviously misleading otherwise. Why would you use the term if you wish to prescind from all the history?

6 *Reports on the Course of Instruction in Yale College; By a Committee of the Corporation, and the Academical Faculty* (New Haven: Yale College, 1828), part 2, 30. Emphasis added here.

7 Tussman, *Beleaguered College*, preface, vii. Emphasis added. Compare with this his devastating assessment on p. 47, in the conclusion to his first essay in the collection, "A Venture in Educational Reform," 1–47.

And if you want to invent a new meaning for the term, you might be asked to first reveal that you have an accurate understanding of the old one.

3. Even if "realistic" considerations force us to have a variety of "cores," or "core-options," we can nevertheless give prime time, effort, money, promotional effort, and other resources to a well-conceived "Jesuit core," with all necessary incentives for faculty and students—sufficiently to ensure substantial subscription and continuing success. There is therefore no imposition of the program, *but nor is there an institutional indifference or lack of investment and promotion*. It is not therefore the case that it is "total transformation" or nothing at all. But proportionate investment must be made in what one judges to be essential.
4. The root-commitment of the college part of the university is therefore unashamedly and explicitly affixed to the Jesuit core. Otherwise, Jesuit identity and mission will tend to fade off into indistinguishability from other higher education enterprises.
5. The primary *proximate* aim of the core of college education is the well-being and full maturation of the students. It is through them that the common good will be served. The primary aim of the college is not directly the ideologically informed structural transformation of civil society, nor is it directly the promotion of advanced research, nor is it directly the achievement of professional employments or even of some "good works." Jesuit college education seeks its primary aim through significant and sustained attention to the relevant spiritual, ethical, cultural, social, and religious dimensions of human existence.

Proposed Non-negotiables

With agreement on these first principles, we move closer to concreteness with several more specific non-negotiables for thinking through a new Jesuit core curriculum. Again, failure to agree to these impedes our discussions. If there is some disagreement over any of these points, they must be handled up front, before the lines of a new core are worked out or submitted for review.

1. *Specificity of content*. Students need to know specific things. Specific content in the curriculum must be decided upon; we cannot rely on any substantial guidance from the use of general values and categories like "critical thinking" or "cultural diversity." Specific content is a limitation that makes for greater freedom later (just as the learning of the alphabet does). Specific content allows for the building of a community of thought and feeling, perhaps even a union of minds and hearts. Specific content repeated through the years (allowing some variations) enables teachers to (1) know what is being given and (2) attain a high level of expertise in presenting the material. The education can therefore take a distinctive shape as a Jesuit education if the pattern is not reduced to rampant selectivity.

2. *Coherence of content with mission and identity*. The specific content and its presentation should generally work to support the character and direction and mission of the founding tradition. (How could this be controversial?) The purpose is not the protection of "doctrinal purity." Students generally cannot avoid having a pluralistic background and consciousness to start with, and they are better served by learning how they might situate or interpret (not ignore) the boisterous variety that surrounds them. But the curriculum has a particular rhetorical dimension. It aims at persuading and cultivating appreciation in a certain direction, not "in whichever direction." Challenging and diverse material can certainly be used, but the *positive center of gravity* is understood to remain decidedly with the voices most consonant with the nature and mission and vision of the school: for example, the interest remains with learning how to appreciate C. S. Lewis (1898–1963) over Jean-Paul Sartre (1905–80); Kierkegaard (1813–55) over Nietzsche (1844–1900); John Lennox (1943–) over Christopher Hitchens (1949–2011); Christopher Dawson (1889–1970) over Oswald Spengler (1880–1936); Blaise Pascal (1623–62) over Voltaire (1694–1778); Gerard Manley Hopkins (1844–89) over Rimbaud (1854–91); Augustine (354–430) over Marcus Aurelius (121–80). There is nothing at all wrong with knowing both sides of these oppositions, but the school's *primary* mission is more heavily invested in learning the virtues of the first in each pair. It furthers the union of minds and hearts to construct the program's content along those lines.

Furthermore, there has to be a lively sense of the spiritual impact of the reading chosen. If the students are asked to dwell with nihilists and nay-sayers and depressed cynics and really troubled psychologies, then they themselves are likely going to be in a far different place than if they had read deeply consoling, edifying, positive, faith-filled, happy, and magnanimous authors. You become like your company. Teachers may not fully realize the powerful formational impact that the curricular contents *necessarily* carry. They are formational agents, whether that is spelled out in their contracts or not.

This is not at all to say that major figures who have helped to "make" the late modern view have to be avoided, or lesser figures substituted for them. Thinkers like Marx (1888–83), Darwin (1809–82), and Freud (1856–1939) have had epochal impact. They *ought to* be intelligently encountered by all educated persons. And the leading most substantial critiques of such figures should be engaged as well.

3. *The core is not subject to electivization.* "Core" means "so important that you do not leave it out." Therefore, we must not allow abundant parallel electives that can be taken to supposedly fulfill the "same" core requirement. This is a point that would go without saying were it not violated so widely.

4. *The major historical domains or stages of Jesuit education (Letters, philosophy, theology) are organizing principles of the curriculum.* One thing that cannot be left out of Jesuit education is some appropriate correlative to the stages of Letters,

philosophy, and theology. If you change what was the major content for at least four hundred years, then you should just admit that you are doing something else. But these three areas were traditionally staged in successive periods, stretching from high school to graduate school classes. A new kind of synthesis will have to be worked out for a college since the older structures have changed: a college today does not typically have any direct control of its students' earlier high school nor their subsequent graduate school programs.

Letters

Eloquence, language, literature, composition, and rhetoric must be given due weight throughout the program. The study of foreign languages, preferably including some experience of at least one classical language, is a very high value, carrying as it does the development of important vocabulary and large cultural–historical–geographical frameworks for understanding. There is also an importance in the careful attention to expression. From the study of language come important insights into both the content and the medium of thought and communication in culture, philosophy, and theology. Close reading and imitation of models of high-quality literature (including essays and articles) help bring students to rhetorical maturity. But, especially at the start, the program's greater stress on "listening," that is, the deep absorption of some quality materials, should not be lost through a high number of writing assignments.

The domain of Letters is also that of "culture," especially literary culture in all its genres. Culture shapes spirit and it is shaped by spirit. The classical heritage and an understanding of its medieval, modern, and contemporary impact must retain some place in the core. In traditional Jesuit education, a wide and deep cultural appropriation took place as students tried to master Latin and Greek. Their focus may have been on language mastery, but, along with their reading of classical content, they were imbibing content and values and modes of thought and expression relevant across the range of human experience. This classical humanist heritage rightfully belongs to the world. It holds a place as one of later modernity's "major ancestors" and cannot be entirely disowned. It has a universal aspect. We are all everyday in its debt. It is foundational for the cultural and political structures of meaning that have appeared and that have been adapted over time. No major cultural group is unaffected by this tradition today. It is therefore an essential element of self-knowledge and world-knowledge for everyone, proportionately to a greater extent for all those natively speaking European languages. But the ambit of "classical humanism" embraces works and classical traditions that are not Western (e.g., Confucius and the Bible): this tradition began as an open canon and it continues as such.

A concise rationale for foreign language study: Study of a foreign language is something that grounds deep perspectives on philosophy and theology partly through an increasingly well-tuned sense of what the medium of the word can or cannot do, the need for and the value of hermeneutics, an appreciation of ambiguity and rhetoric, the complexities of meaning lost in translation, and the like. Some kind of language study is essential for an understanding of scripture. It also opens upon a large world of cultural meaning. A foreign language is a tool that should be mastered earlier rather than later. Once students have abilities in a given language, their worlds and their possibilities expand, and they have a far deeper grasp of the importance and vastness of language itself and also of the range of human diversity. Language study is also something that can unify the curriculum and the student's experience since it should be a constant over each of the college years.

Philosophy

Philosophy is the eager pursuit of wisdom as a guide for living. Wisdom requires knowledge of reality and also of the limitations we have in knowing that reality. Historically, the Jesuit emphasis was tied to the systematic thinking of the Aristotelean tradition. Jesuit philosophy included, but was never limited to, what is now called "science" (natural philosophy). Now there is a confusing array of approaches, subdivisions, self-concepts in philosophy: surveying these approaches ought to be part of the philosophical course. For a Jesuit core today, some knowledge of the sciences must be included. But the aspect of philosophy that transcends scientific domains might well be understood as more closely related to spirituality than merely to systematic thought or rigorous argument. The history of philosophy does not consist in a sequence of timeless propositions nor is it a mere infrastructure for theology but rather engages the entire story of spiritual–cultural–intellectual journeys and explorations of humanity. It is not a subject like other subjects. It asks questions about human beatitude and purpose. It shares with theology an architectonic status insofar as it seeks to cover the whole range of human experience and meaning.

Theology

Again, traditionally the emphasis was on systematic thought deriving from a well-considered reflection on theological sources. The writings of Thomas Aquinas provided a norm and a very high standard of excellence. Scripture was the apex of the graduate studies in Jesuit education. Now, given historical changes in the status of that (traditionally graduate-level) systematic approach to theology and given the rise in the importance of scripture for appreciating Christianity, the Jesuit college core should attend more to the sources. *Profound understanding of the gospels is the core of the core.* The texts must be studied and returned to over the course of the college years. A mature confrontation with the meaning and impact of the Gospels is the *sine qua non* of Jesuit college education today. It is its special and distinctive mark. If there are to be any requirements about anything, they are to be imposed in this area. It is the bottom line. Those unwilling to accept this should simply not matriculate at a Jesuit college nor seek employment there.

5. *Sequencing*. The order of studies remains important: do not do "Christian ethics" before reading the New Testament, or the Enlightenment before the medieval period. The most challenging and complex material should be given later rather than earlier.

6. *Conversion*. The issues of conversion (aesthetic, intellectual, moral, religious) should be kept continually in mind and raised where appropriate, according to the occasion and the pedagogical artistry of the teachers. Conversion is at the heart of Jesuit formational concerns. Jesuit education above all seeks to have *a spiritual impact on the students*: it aims to teach the relevant disciplines "in such a way that they are thereby aroused to a knowledge and love of our Maker and Redeemer" (*Ratio studiorum*, no. 7). Seeing the importance of the true, the good, the beautiful, and the holy, learning how the turn to the true value of these transcendentals makes all the difference in life—this transformation is one of the primary things that this education is most about. Whatever leads students away from wonder and gratitude and faith or toward cynicism, relativism, amoralism, skepticism, despair, and so forth, is not to be cultivated. Of course, this is not to say that spiritual dysfunctionalities cannot be engaged. There is a helpful way of using the image of what is wrong to highlight the desirability of what is right. The practical point here is that teachers need to choose materials and lead discussions wisely and appropriately, considering the potential contribution to be made to the well-being of the students.

7. *Avoiding ideologies*. While current political, social, and economic problems should be directly considered, especially in the last two years of a four-year program (that is, only after a good deal of "listening" and learning of specific content have taken place), teaching ought to be trans-ideological and non-partisan: the aim is to develop in students an ability to critique ideologies and partisan views, and to become aware of distortions as they are communicated in policies, public discourse, the academy, and the media. Adversaries of certain positions should not simply be turned into straw men for the sake of easy dismissal. The disputation/dialectic must be handled skillfully so as not to leave students adrift in radical skepticism or cynicism.

8. *Active oversight and cooperation*. Governance and steady oversight and adjustment by knowledgeable, competent, committed, experienced, credentialed professional Jesuit educators are essential. A new kind of administrative board of such individuals ought to be established as a standing, independently funded entity. Final judgments must be made by people who are in a position to lead

the mission. Judgments by skilled professionals using prudence and insight should not be diminished by an excess of forms and bureaucratic documentation. Teachers understand from the beginning that their teaching is not solely their own creative project but part of a larger scheme that has some important *directive and constitutive power* with regard to what they have been hired to do in their classrooms.

9. *Professional norms.* Hiring, promotion, and tenuring procedures at the college level must not allow extrinsic academic norms to override the mission. Concerns for mission and identity always take priority over the academy. Publishing good material in fine outlets is certainly praiseworthy but not of the essence. Publication should never outweigh the effort to teach, learn, and manage the curriculum in a responsible and collegial way. *In signing on, faculty and students accept this understanding.* Accreditation is best be done by agencies who fully understand and agree with the mission and identity of the institution.

Curricular Innovations

Jesuit education traditionally (1) gave students entrée into the high cultural discourse of the times and (2) allowed for the absorption of critically important cultural contents (formerly via Cicero, Aristotle, Thomas, and scripture above all) that led to deeper understanding. What will do the same today? Certainly, these two aspects seem impossible to achieve without some familiarity with the discourses of a range of sciences (natural and social) and "arts." How can one possibly claim to be well educated without some knowledge of scientific, economic, cultural, historical, political, and religious terms, categories, and ways of thought? But there must also be some kind of large-scale integrative discourse, not just a list of vocabulary items to be mastered.

The problem is the profusion of disciplines and sub-disciplines. If we consider that the average college school year of two semesters has ten courses a year for four years, there are only forty (three-credit-hour) courses to work with, and often major programs usually take a large part of that.

First Curricular Innovation: one-hour units. Break apart the constraining three-hour credit units and allow one-hour credit units in order to have many more "pieces" to work with. This is somewhat like having more pixels on a computer display for images. There is less "blockiness" and more "smoothness." A one-hour credit unit is the equivalent of fifteen class hours (one hour per week) in a given semester. Frequently, fifteen hours of class time in a particular area is more than enough to give a person a very good introduction to basics.

Second Curricular Innovation: restructure the place of the core and the place of the major. Put all major courses into years three and four. Most of the core would take up all of years one and two, after which students would be in a better position to know which direction they might like to take up for their majors. It stands to reason that without some knowledge of a particular study, even at an introductory level, students would have a hard time realizing its possible appeal and suitability as a life-choice. There would still be some core courses in the upper years because returning to core issues and raising new, more complex ones as maturation proceeds are essential for the students' integration and growth. Their sophistication in handling the larger questions should be increasing. The major should not be emphasized any more than is appropriate for an undergraduate education rightly conceived as something *anterior* to the project of acquiring professional expertise.

Third Curricular Innovation: exclude electives in the first two years. Core means essential, and therefore non-optional. The building of a community depends upon marking out an educational "common ground" and sharing a language. The language is given to everyone; everyone tours the same common ground.

The Jesuit core can highlight certain key domains of thought and try to integrate them with larger-order questions: When and why did the various disciplines and intellectual/cultural enterprises arise? How did they develop? What are their strengths, weakness, limitations, possibilities? How do they bear upon human well-being or work against it? So students will have some clear ideas about what we get out of the study of history, art, various social and natural sciences, and so on. Integrative works that expeditiously but competently survey large fields and present a compelling narrative can help greatly with this task of integration.

Tentative Core Curriculum (United States)

Typical semesters carry fifteen credit-hours. Using a one-hour standard unit, that seems to amount to fifteen possible "courses" per term, but the hours can be combined in any suitable way so that this need not happen. For example, the four hours of the Greco-Roman heritage could all be done in the first term. The proportions of the hours indicated below have to be negotiated by the faculty. This scheme is merely a starting point for reflection.

A Possible Two-Year Curricular Scheme

A. Four hours: heritage includes culture in the largest sense (science, law, philosophy, theology, art, religion). These courses amount to twenty credit-hours total over the first two college years.
   1. Greco-Roman heritage
   2. Judeo-Christian heritage (includes scripture)
   3. Medieval heritage
   4. Modern heritage
   5. World heritage

B. Three hours. These cover nine credit-hours total.
  1. English literature
  2. Composition/rhetoric
  3. Contemporary issues (poverty relief, ecology, crime, inequality, family, addictions, ideologization, partyism, activism, civility, entertainment, education)

C. Two hours. These cover eight credit-hours.
  1. American history and government
  2. Economics, business, finance, marketing, banking, taxes, employment
  3. Ethics and the blessed life
  4. Media, computers, and the digital age

D. One hour: focusing on the major ideas, personalities, books, moments, categories, methods, and achievements. These cover eleven credit-hours.
  1. Philosophy of science and major questions (creation/evolution/design argument/scientism/faith and reason)
  2. Chemistry
  3. Physics
  4. Biology
  5. Mathematics
  6. Sociological thinking
  7. Psychology
  8. Ecology, meteorology, geography
  9. Anthropology
  10. Health, wellness, medicine
  11. Law and legal systems

E. Twelve hours: foreign-language study, including at the least some minimal exposure to the fundamentals of Latin and/or Greek.

Unfinished Business

This schema does not propose what the upper-level core courses will be or how major programs might best be handled. The most complex and sensitive issues might well be left for the upper part of the core curriculum. There should be some way to review and carry forward what was taken earlier and also a way to introduce material that prepares the students spiritually and conceptually for adult family and professional life and for the responsibilities of citizenship. Finally, there should be some place for large systematic overviews and syntheses. Thus, the domains of philosophy and theology should at least be mapped out and their interrelationships presented. For example, in theology, there are areas like fundamental theology, Christology, soteriology, ecclesiology, sacramental theology, moral theology, and so on. You do not have a good idea of the subject of theology if the logic and scope of such areas are not at least surveyed.

This proposal should be understood as a call to collective pedagogical solidarity and artistry. The college faculty as a whole has a shared fiduciary responsibility to give the students the best and most appropriate educational foundation they can. The faculty needs to cultivate a moral unity, a singleness of vision and purpose, and actual professional expertise under the best available guides and authorities, learning from their experiences. This is their mission as "Jesuit educators."

7. Jesuit Education in a Hundred Words

To many people, the term "Jesuit education" is quite a meaningful phrase but nevertheless one whose reference is still relatively vague. One only has to ask "How precisely would you define Jesuit education?" and then "On what are you basing your understanding?" to bring about a quick end to the conversation. Since our age has been indulging in secularism, pluralism, and diversity, and combining these with a selective activism, amnesia, and decentralization, we could only have expected some confusion. Furthermore, not all Jesuit teaching activity amounts to "Jesuit education" as such. Nor do spiritual mottos like "persons for others" or "faith that does justice" seem adequate to the subject at hand. They can be employed in a way that is all too reductivistic, non-distinctive, and open-ended to be able to provide the concrete guidance that is wanted. What, then, might we propose as a schematic starting point for understanding the term "Jesuit education"? I tentatively offer here some core definitions for confirmation, adaptation, expansion, correction, or reasoned rejection. The organizational and apostolic importance of achieving a shared foundational understanding of "Jesuit education" should be obvious: this is by no means purely an academic exercise. At the very least, these attempts offer an occasion for the clarification of differences, even if not for their resolution.

First Proposed Concise Definition of Jesuit Education (Ninety-Eight Words)

Historically understood, Jesuit education is one that is structured, content-specific, well planned, and disciplined but not rigid; it cultivates definite, high-quality, proven material; it has oversight mechanisms that significantly include competent Jesuit leadership, with published directives for achieving its goals as articulated in the relevant documentation of the tradition and that tradition's organic evolution; its primary aim is to support from a Christian basis the students' spiritual, intellectual, moral, and religious conversions as well as competence, maturity, and integration in those areas; its core is built on an appropriate, well-deliberated selection and study of Letters, philosophy, and theology.[1]

---

1 "Conversion" here does not apply to denominational adherence but to a re-orientation of consciousness that becomes ("turns") more deeply and accurately and knowingly appreciative of the realities that are operative in the given domains of the true, the good, and the holy. Other transcendental categories might also be added here, such as the intelligible, the beautiful, the just, the merciful. "Letters" in capitalized form means not just "epistolary literature," but humanistic studies based originally on the study of Latin and Greek grammar, syntax, philology, translation, "erudition" or scholarly knowledge, composition of prose and poetry, rhetoric, and great edifying humanistic literature or "authors" (in several genres, for example, history, oratory, drama, philosophy, epic, lyric, and so forth, including "letters" as epistolary literature as well).

Second Proposed Concise Definition of Jesuit Education (Fifty Words)
Jesuit education is structured, content-specific, well planned, and disciplined but not rigid; it cultivates rhetoric and analysis through high-quality, proven material, with a view to students' spiritual, intellectual, moral, cultural, and religious conversions; its core consists in an exercise-based study of Letters, philosophy, and theology, with special attention to the scriptures.

Third Proposed Concise Definition of Jesuit Education (Thirty-Four Words)
Jesuit education is a structured and content-specific program that exercises students primarily in Letters, philosophy, and theology from a Christian basis and with a view to their spiritual, intellectual, moral, cultural, and religious conversions.

Fourth Proposed Concise Definition of Jesuit Education (Twenty-Five Words)
Jesuit education exercises students in a structured program of quality content in Letters, philosophy, and theology to promote their conversions and their appreciation of Christianity.

Fifth Proposed Concise Definition of Jesuit Education (Thirteen Words)
Jesuit education is the appropriation of structured Christian humanistic content promoting *docta pietas.*

Sixth Proposed Concise Definition of Jesuit Education (Nine Words)
Jesuit education is a *ratio studiorum* for *docta pietas.*

Seventh Proposed Concise Definition of Jesuit Education (Eight Words)
Jesuit education is the *Ratio studiorum*, rightly adapted.

Afterword: Recovering the Fullness of Ignatian and Jesuit Spirituality

The reader may now understand more clearly how it happened that a religious order that had not been founded to run schools but rather to travel about on diverse missions in diverse places according to diverse instructions from diverse popes nevertheless had a particular kind of *studia*—both the learning and the teaching—so much in its mind and heart and blood that its spirituality, its history, its idea, its self-concept, its Institute, and its impact cannot be fully understood apart from that academic element—no, that integral academic *dimension*—which came to an inspired fruition so soon in its administration of schools—schools of a new order, we might say—as well as later in its prominent intellectual and cultural leadership in early modernity.

Joseph de Guibert (1877–1942) studied the spirituality of the Society in a nearly seven hundred-page "sketch" entitled *The Jesuits: Their Spiritual Doctrine and Practice; A Historical Study*.[1] His impressive achievement failed to incorporate the above insight. If we ask what weight de Guibert gave to the *studia* of the Society, we would have to answer "almost none at all." The index contains no entry for *Ratio studiorum* or studies or universities; the entry on schools has to do with "schools of spirituality" rather than anything academic.[2] The text largely ignores the Society's extensive investment in educational projects, treating the colleges very tersely and dismissively in the context of the humanistic atmosphere that surrounded Ignatius but that did not, in de Guibert's opinion, reach his heart.

It is true, the author says, that humanists were found in the early Society, but as for Ignatius himself: "The study of humanities which he prescribed for the members of his order interested him only as a means necessary for better apostolic work."[3] In another place, he mentions the apostolate of teaching in the colleges where the work, he says, we must suppose could only have been sustained by "the maintaining of a noteworthy tenor of spiritual life."[4] The wording betrays how he seems to separate the apostolic service from some underlying spirituality, one that was able to support an ascetical perseverance in those less than glorious classroom arenas. He does not seem to consider how, for Ignatius's Society, the

1 Joseph de Guibert, *The Jesuits: Their Spiritual Doctrine and Practice*, trans. William J. Young, ed. George E. Ganss (St. Louis, MO: Institute of Jesuit Sources, 1964). The original was published posthumously eleven years earlier as *La spiritualité de la Compagnie de Jésus: Esquisse historique* (Rome: Institutum Historicum Societatis Iesu, 1953).

2 De Guibert in fact explicitly distinguishes spiritualities from speculative theologies early in his work. Ibid., 4–5.

3 Ibid., 164.

4 Ibid., 290.

pietas was necessarily expected to be *docta*, learned. This modification made a huge difference, a foundational one in fact, for the core spirituality of Ignatius and his Society. So these pages have argued.

Toward the end of his study, de Guibert asks how far the *Spiritual Exercises* "do or do not contain the entire spiritual tradition of Ignatius's order."[5] He answers negatively:

> Has all this been tantamount to saying that we have everything in this little book [of the *Spiritual Exercises*]? We have seen that in it we do not have even the entire personal spirituality of Ignatius. So much the more must we state that we do not have in it all the spirituality of the order he founded.[6]

He cites, for example, "the special place given to obedience in the life of the religious of the Society," the elimination of an obligation to the hours of choir, and the importance of the Sacred Heart devotion in the order in more recent times.[7]

If the essays here have been persuasive, we know that we must add one other aspect, one so important that without it we must miss the nature and heritage and full spirituality of both Ignatius and the Society: that entire dimension and dynamic of *docta pietas*. "Learned devotion" had in fact been something of age-old and general importance in the life of the church, so Ignatius was far from being a revolutionary innovator. In his day, the Dominicans were its greatest exponents, and the universities had widely popularized such an ideal.[8] But long before there were universities, from the very beginning, devout Christians had been invested in the Greek equivalent of *ratio*: *logos*—that is to say, word, speech, reckoning, reason, rhetoric, communication, and Letters in the large sense, not to mention the *logos* that is order, an ordered account, and also the Sacred Order, appearing now as God's Word (*Logos*) Incarnate (John 1). A very early writing says: "He chose to give us birth *through the word of truth*, that we might be a kind of firstfruits of all he created" (James 1:18). Presenting that quickening word of truth required that attention be given to order in the presentation and in the understanding: Luke narrates "an ordered account" (Luke 1:3) and the apostle Paul seeks to find and set forth a coherent understanding of the Christ event and the "plan of salvation."

But this old attention to *logos* writ both large and small was taking on an unprecedented and vibrant form in Ignatius's times, as his world was spinning in the wake of the high university culture; advanced Scholasticism; fresh humanistic

5 Ibid., 527.

6 Ibid., 539.

7 Ibid., 542–43.

8 Astrik L. Gabriel, "The Ideal Master of the Mediaeval University," *Catholic Historical Review* 50, no. 1 (April 1974): 1–40. Gabriel gives as the first feature expected of an ideal master "a combination of profound learning and excellent virtue, a proper balance between intellectual and ascetic performance" (9). The other six features that Gabriel lists likely also influenced Ignatius's own conception of what a "master" should be (9–10).

researches and perspectives; the return of Greek literature and learning from the East; reformational yearnings and rumblings; intense spiritual currents like the *devotio moderna*; and daring global explorations. The past was being recovered and read with new eyes, enlivening illuminations, and audacious energies. Both new worlds and old ones were having an impact, electrifying Ignatius's historical moment, even as the older heritage provided an indispensable ballast.

Ignatius and the Jesuit order represented a new configuration, balance, and synthesis. And *docta pietas* was very much involved in a new way. Perhaps the best way to clinch the argument for its importance in the Society is to dwell again on those words of the 1584 congregation convened to set in motion what ultimately became the great *Ratio* of 1599:

> There are assuredly two things that constitute our Society's bulwark and mainstay: the burning zeal of devotion and a surpassing knowledge of reality. The hinge of our *Constitutions* swings entirely on these two principles insofar as devotion bereft of the light of learning certainly profits individuals a good bit privately, but it can contribute almost nothing to help the Church and our neighbors in sermons, in administering the sacraments, in educating the young, in disputations with adversaries of the faith, in giving advice and providing answers in unclear situations, and in the rest of the expected services and functions of our men: these things require learning—not the well-known common kind but a certain superior kind of learning.[9]

Learning, not just *any* learning, but *a certain superior kind* of learning, has here been put on a par with devotion; they are the two-part hinge on which the Society's *Constitutions* entirely swings. The tremors generated by this radical statement should be felt under our own feet at this very moment. And anyone who is adequately aware of late modernity's landscape might easily realize how the spirituality of *docta pietas* is needed now more than ever it was, both in secular and religious modes. We, like Ignatius, live in a supercharged, electrified moment. We too need not just passionate commitments (*ardens pietatis studium*) but also clear, valid, well-informed thinking and a superior grasp of reality (*praestans rerum scientia*). Both elements are essential. Everywhere there are movements, approaches, and schools of thought deserving of critical review and either refinement and integration or censure and elimination.[10]

---

9 Acta Congregationis quae anno 1584, iussu admodum Reverendi Patris Praepositi Generalis Claudii Aquaevivae, habita est de ratione studiorum instituenda. MHSI 129:2.

10 Scientism is one example, with its simplistic, fundamentalistic rejection of religious truth. See, for example, Austin L. Hughes, "The Folly of Scientism," *New Atlantis* 37 (Fall 2012): 32–50. Also Terry Eagleton, "Lunging, Flailing, Mispunching," *London Review of Books* 28, no. 20 (October 19, 2006): 32–34, a review of *The God Delusion* by Richard Dawkins (London: Bantam, 2006).

This vision conditions the very sustainability of our civil societies. It greatly affects the lowest as well as the highest levels in human communities. Such is the understanding given in Pope Benedict XVI's *Caritas in veritate*:

> Paul VI had seen clearly that among the causes of underdevelopment there is a lack of wisdom and reflection, a lack of thinking capable of formulating a guiding synthesis, for which "a clear vision of all economic, social, cultural and spiritual aspects" is required. The excessive segmentation of knowledge, the rejection of metaphysics by the human sciences, the difficulties encountered by dialogue between science and theology are damaging not only to the development of knowledge, but also to the development of peoples, because these things make it harder to see the integral good of man in its various dimensions. The "broadening [of] our concept of reason and its application" is indispensable if we are to succeed in adequately weighing all the elements involved in the question of development and in the solution of socio-economic problems.[11]

In the conclusion of this encyclical, we read: "The greatest service to development, then, is a Christian humanism that enkindles charity and takes its lead from truth, accepting both as a lasting gift from God."[12] This Christian humanism is exactly what a fuller, more concrete idea of the Institute of the Society of Jesus should lead it and its allies boldly to profess, support, develop, maintain, defend, and strengthen over against all and any opposition.

Development of the Society of Jesus on the basis of *docta pietas* will be far more roundly coherent not only with *Caritas in veritate* and with the history and documented self-concept of the Society but also with the essential spirituality of Ignatius himself. He was not just the Ignatius of Manresa; he was equally the Ignatius of Paris. In fact, we should be careful about making too much of that opposition. It is easy to see that the scholastic Ignatius of Paris was eager to live in *pietas*—he was almost punished publicly for allowing his devotional life to interfere with classroom order.[13] But conversely, the Ignatius of Manresa was more than the simple poor pilgrim praying and doing penance and good works. It is better to think that, even at Manresa, Ignatius was in a way *already on the road to Paris* in search of God's word of truth and a "surpassing knowledge" of the way things are. He was questing for a spiritual enlightenment and a full understanding that had begun to take definite shape back at Loyola castle during his recovery and conversion. That same dynamic continued on at Manresa where he

---

11 *Caritas in veritate*, encyclical letter of Pope Benedict XVI, June 29, 2009, no. 31. Notice how the title of this encyclical parallels the cardinal elements of the Society's Institute: *caritas* (charity) and *pietas* are inseparable, as are truth and "a surpassing knowledge of reality."

12 Ibid., no. 79.

13 Pedro de Ribadeneyra, *The Life of Ignatius of Loyola*, trans. Claude Pavur (St. Louis, MO: Institute of Jesuit Sources, 2014), nos. 106–9.

was attending carefully to lessons that he felt God was giving him. His spirituality embraced not just prayer and works of charity, but the path of a decidedly deep and expansive kind of learning that went far beyond matters of his own interiority and penitential needs. Without both these dimensions, we simply do not have the complete Ignatius. From the start, Ignatius wanted both "knowledge and love of the Maker and Redeemer" (RS, no. 7). A revealing moment in his so-called autobiography is quite direct:

> God treated him at this time just as a schoolmaster treats a child whom he is teaching. Whether this was because of his lack of education and of brains, or because he had no one to teach him, or because of the strong desire God himself had given him to serve him, he believed without doubt and has always believed that God treated him in this way. Indeed if he were to doubt this, he would think he offended his Divine Majesty.[14]

This idea of the schoolmaster is not merely some vague metaphor. Ignatius is speaking of *actual learning*. He was being taught and led to real insights into true realities. His service-oriented *pietas* is palpable, but so is his path of learning and his hunger to understand correctly God's world and his will. Ignatius goes on in his account to illustrate his emphatic statement in five points, the last of which is the vision at the Cardoner. We have already noted that Ignatius compared what he received on the riverbank to his other learning—the vision gave far more but it was not qualitatively incommensurable or unrelatable to his other illuminations or scholarship. Ignatius's fourth point ends by saying that he was strengthened in his faith by his illuminations and that he often thought to himself "if there were no Scriptures to teach us these matters of faith, he would be resolved to die for them, solely because of what he has seen."[15] Again, there is content being learned here: it is like what the scriptures teach.

Therefore, it is this Ignatian spirituality of heart *and* mind, the flame that is heat *and* light, that we should identify as the living core of "Jesuit spirituality." What, then, will the Society make of *docta pietas* today? We find ourselves in a vastly more confused and complicated cultural setting. Not only are old molds broken but the manner of making molds seems to have changed substantially, and some relevant old arts seem to have been lost (e.g., unified and integrated architectonic curricular planning). The project of a feasible *ratio moderna*—even one that does not take on the same kind of "universal form" that it previously assumed—is therefore all the more overwhelming—yet just so is it all the more needed. It is hard to imagine that progress will occur without some well-deliberated, stable, guiding plan.

---

14 Ignatius of Loyola, *A Pilgrim's Testament: The Memoirs of Saint Ignatius of Loyola*, trans. Parmananda R. Divakar (St. Louis, MO: Institute of Jesuit Studies, 1995), 39.

15 Ibid., 42.

At the very least, we can make some small beginnings: we can begin to think out a new framework for learning and teaching, and we can identify the most important elements that have emerged in the course of long centuries. It will be a vitally important help to have some shared design for any given region. The Jesuit fathers of the 1584 *Ratio* congregation

> considered it a settled and confirmed opinion among them that nothing could be either more useful for maintaining and advancing the classes, or better designed to attain favorable influence and hold on to a position of high esteem, than for everyone to keep and follow just one and the same norm and prescription in cultivating natural talents and in managing academic responsibilities.[16]

Might there not be perennial values here for us to emulate, not for the glory they might bring but rather for their intrinsic advantages?

So then, agreeing on all that can hardly be denied and praying for the gift of timely insights and the prudence to enact them well, let us begin our discussions and our *disputationes*. We also need that spirit of urgency that drives us not just to talk but actually to begin to provide in a timely way at least some of what has been so desperately needed for decades.

Above and Below: A Final Word

And yet it is hard simply to end there, even with the importance of *docta pietas* potentially restored to its rightful place in the spirituality of Ignatius and the Society of Jesus. Two brush strokes must be added. There is still something standing under and something standing over this concept of learned devotion, things that deserve a mention here. They help to situate the domain of *docta pietas* between the ground of its emergence and the goal of its yearning.

1. Lying beneath the *studia* of the Society is ultimately a deep spiritual quest for "right order."[17] And here the *Spiritual Exercises* and the RS agree: we must eliminate disordered affections and disordered educational approaches. The drive for rightly ordered feelings and motivations and for rightly formulated ideas and actions should rule. De Guibert notes how Jesuit theology was notably doctrinal

16 *Cum fixum ac ratum id apud se haberent, nihil esse posse vel ad scholarum conservationem promotionemque utilius, vel ad gratiam comparatamque existimationem retinendam accomodatius, quam uniusmodi omnes normam praescriptionemque in excolendis ingeniis gubernandisque scholasticis muneribus tenere ac sequi.* Acta 1584, MHSI 129:5.

17 I say this is an "underlying" or deep structure because it seems a universal human reality, possibly rooted in biological/sociological/psychological mechanisms inherited from distant primeval origins and expressed across many cultures in various symbolizations of a "Sacred Order." See, for example, Francis MacDonald Cornford, *From Religion to Philosophy: A Study in the Origins of Western Speculation* (London: Longman, Green & Co., 1912), which discusses the universal (though variously conceived) idea of a Sacred Order.

rather than speculative.[18] One can understand this as a natural outcome to a basic orientation to the right kind of order within the living engagements of the church. Order requires accepting and understanding hierarchical arrangements and knowing where in that system one can best contribute. It is not just a matter of content (*doctrina*), but of *pietas* as well.

This love of proper order and harmony can be seen behind the "Rules for Thinking with the Church" that Ignatius added to the *Spiritual Exercises* possibly as early as his studies in Paris (1528–35).[19] *Sentido*, often understood as "thinking," points to more than intellection: it refers to thinking that is deeply held over time, thinking with an emotional component; it therefore involves both *pietas* and *doctrina*.[20] One item in Ignatius's list most directly links the *Spiritual Exercises* and the learning that Ignatius expected of his followers:

> We ought to praise both positive theology and scholastic theology. For just as it is more characteristic of the positive doctors, such as St. Jerome, St. Augustine, St. Gregory, and the rest to stir up our affections toward loving and serving God our Lord in all things, so it is more characteristic of the scholastic teachers, such as St. Thomas, St. Bonaventure, the Master of the Sentences, and so on to define and explain for our times the matters necessary for salvation, and also to refute and expose all the errors and fallacies. For the scholastic teachers, being more modern, can avail themselves of an authentic understanding of Sacred Scripture and the holy positive doctors. Further still they, being enlightened and clarified by divine influence, make profitable use of the councils, canons, and decrees of our Holy Mother Church.[21]

Here, Ignatius explicitly draws attention both to how the positive doctors "stir up our affections toward loving and serving God our Lord in all things" (*pietas*) *and* to the intellectual services and resources of the Scholastic doctors (*doctrina*).

2. Lying above the domain of the Society's *studia* and *docta pietas* are the Gospels, scripture, revelation, and ultimately the subject of those texts, namely Christ. Again, the RS and the *Exercises* both testify to this deep orientation: at the top of

---

18 De Guibert, *Jesuits*, 582.

19 Ibid., 162.

20 See George E. Ganss's edition of the *Spiritual Exercises of Saint Ignatius* (St. Louis, MO: Institute of Jesuit Sources, 1992), 163–64n164. In addition, behind the Spanish word *sentido*, the Latin usage of *sentio/sensus* combines both feeling and thinking. Elsewhere, Ganss notes that the title "Thinking with the Church" is not directly from Ignatius, but a fair summary of his longer title. Ganss renders the opening of the title as "Rules for Thinking, Judging, and Feeling with the Church." See George E. Ganss, "Thinking with the Church: The Spirit of Saint Ignatius's Rule," *The Way*, Supplement 20 (1973): 72–82.

21 Ganss, *Exercises*, no. 363.

the Jesuit educational scheme stands scripture,[22] and the *Exercises* are essentially a deep personal appropriation of the core of the scriptures in the Gospels, even to the point of a living encounter with the Lord. The former, study, may speak more to the head, and the latter, prayer, to the heart, but ultimately one cannot achieve a valid spiritual order without the heart's learning and devotedly following the idea, the "word of Truth" that comes with the Gospels.

A mere week before he died, Ignatius—being even then still interested in the academic formation of young Jesuits and also being even then *perceived* by others as one who still had this interest—wrote to a young independent student of theology looking for advice on what to study. Ignatius mentioned several authorities and texts either to avoid or to emphasize, including some of the doctors, Chrysostom (d.407), Bernard (1090–1153), and Jerome (*c*.347–420), who are good for preaching and conversation. "Finally," he added, "you should devote more study to Scripture than to anything else."[23] Note that the reading of scripture is *not* put totally in the domain of private piety and religious devotion: scripture is a teaching text that stands with and yet above those others included in theological programs.

With the Gospels and revelation, we find ourselves back at the idea of the teacher. Deep in the religious DNA of Christianity is the ancient Hebraic idea of *Torah*, which, we must always remember, does not so much mean law (Greek *nomos*) as *instruction*, *direction*, *teaching*, *doctrine*. Ignatian and Jesuit spirituality in their fullness must be appreciated along these lines. "Where there is no revelation, people cast off restraint; but blessed is the one who heeds wisdom's instruction."[24] May we all be so blessed.

---

22 For a visual illustration of the hierarchy of Jesuit subjects, see the arrangement given on the "Roll of the Roman College, 1696–1697," in Paul F. Grendler, *The Jesuits and Italian Universities 1548–1773* (Washington, DC: Catholic University of America Press, 2017), 328–29. The scripture course (on the book of Genesis) is placed at the very top.

23 To Stefano Baroello (Rome, July 25, 1556), in *Ignatius of Loyola: Letters and Instructions*, ed. Martin E. Palmer, John W. Padberg, and John L. McCarthy (St. Louis, MO: Institute of Jesuit Sources, 2006), 699–700.

24 Proverbs 29:18 in the NIV translation. The RSVCE has "Where there is no prophecy the people cast off restraint, but blessed is he who keeps the law."

Appendix 1: A Timeline for Jesuit Education

This timeline attempts to give some important educationally related moments in the history of the Society of Jesus. It can only suggest—it cannot fully represent—the vast academic and scholarly energies and the manifold educational connections and concerns that have characterized the Society. Second, the timeline points to some helpful works for further research. What appears here is often a synthesis from several sources. The main works are abbreviated in the timeline itself and the bibliographical data are given in the reference list that follows it. For an excellent summary table presenting the university educational experience of some leading early Jesuits see the table in Paul F. Grendler's *The Jesuits and Italian Universities 1548–1773* (Washington, DC: Catholic University of America Press, 2017), 22.

~

1491–1521 Iñigo López de Loyola (later known as Ignatius of Loyola) is born to a noble Basque family in Guipúzcoa (Gipuzkoa), Spain. Perhaps as early as 1506, he goes to Arévalo to be raised by Juan Velázquez de Cuéllar (d.1517), the royal treasurer of King Ferdinand II (1452–1516, r.1479–1516). He becomes a gentleman-courtier (not ever a professional soldier), likely gaining some familiarity with the library of that house (Dalmases, 31–32). In 1517, he is in the service of the duke of Nájera, Antonio Manrique de Lara (d.1535), the viceroy of Navarre.

1521 Recovering at Loyola castle from wounds received defending Pamplona against French forces on May 20, Ignatius reads from of *Life of Christ* by Ludolph the Carthusian (c.1295–1378) and the *Flos sanctorum* (lives of the saints drawn from the *Legenda aurea* (The golden legends) of Jacobus de Voragine [*c*.1230–98]). He experiences a conversion that leads him toward a life dedicated to God, first making pilgrimage to the Holy Land and then living a penitential life somewhere, perhaps in a monastery.

1522 Ignatius leaves his family household (end of February) and goes to Montserrat, Spain (March 21–25). There, he divests himself of everything and formally dedicates himself to the Lord's service. For about a year, he lives in the nearby town of Manresa, doing good works, begging alms, praying long hours, confessing his sins, doing penance, engaging in spiritual conversations, receiving the sacraments, and hearing sermons. He has an overwhelming mystical vision at the Cardoner River during this period (perhaps in August or September). This vision is the greatest one of his entire life; it carries insight into the Trinity, the creation of the world, the Eucharist, the humanity of Christ, and other spiritual and doctrinal matters. Since his days of recovery at Loyola, he has been taking note of his inner illuminations, consolations, and desolations. At Manresa, he begins to compose his book of "spiritual exercises."

1523 Ignatius leaves Manresa in mid-February and makes his way to the Holy Land. The Franciscan authorities there compel him to leave because of the dangers for visiting foreigners.

1524 Ignatius returns to Spain "with the idea that he would devote his attention to his education in language and literature" (Rib., no. 73). At thirty-three years of age, he begins to study Latin under Jerónimo Ardévol (d.1551), a devout schoolmaster in Barcelona, with the financial assistance of a benefactress, Isabel Roser (d.1571) (Rib., no. 73).

1526 Ignatius takes classes at the University of Alcalá, Spain, and attracts several companions who follow him in his way of life (Rib., 78). He feeds the needy with alms he collects, fosters people's devotional life with spiritual exercises, and explains the basics of Christian doctrine to the uneducated (Rib., no. 77). Under suspicion for his teaching about spiritual matters, he is arrested and impeded in his ministries by local authorities (Rib., no. 79). When he is forbidden to teach about the Christian mysteries for four years (when he will have had more education), he leaves for the university in Salamanca.

1527 Ignatius studies at the University of Salamanca, Spain, where, again with companions drawn to his way of life, he falls under the suspicion of the Dominican community, who wonder how he can speak about vices and virtues without formal education (Rib., no. 82). Partly on the basis of rumors about his teaching and way of life, he is again arrested, investigated, and cleared. Ignatius is instructed not to teach about the distinction between mortal and venial sin without four more years of education (Rib., no. 90). He decides to leave for Paris by way of Barcelona.

1528–35 Ignatius studies at the University of Paris where he cultivates his life of faith with some fellow-students. He is impressed by the style of education as he experiences it in his college, the *modus Parisiensis*. He finds it much more rigorous, ordered, efficient, and productive than what he had experienced elsewhere, with regular lectures, exercises, exams for advancement, and a professional concern for the progress of the students (Padberg, 82). Ignatius also organizes his own studies better, now undertaking separate academic efforts in sequence rather than jumbling them all together. He starts by reviewing his Latin humanistic literary studies in 1528 and 1529 at the Collège de Montaigu. On October 1, 1529, he begins the arts (philosophy) course at the Collège de Sainte-Barbe.

1534 At a chapel in Montmartre, Ignatius and six companions, all students at the University of Paris, take vows "to renounce all things (apart from travel provisions) until an appointed day, to care for the spiritual wellbeing of their neighbors, and to sail to Jerusalem" with the understanding that if they could not go to the Holy Land or live in it, they would put themselves at the pope's disposal for the care of souls (Rib., no. 112).

1535 Ignatius receives the title of master of arts on March 14 at the University of Paris after taking a rigorous examination. He had received a license in arts on March 13, 1533 (Rib., no. 68n8). He makes a return home to Azpeitia, Spain (April to July); at the end of the year, he goes to Venice.

1536–37 Ignatius, hoping to complete four years of theological study, reads theology at Bologna and Venice (Larrañaga). On October 14, the faculty of theology at Paris sends him a diploma declaring that he had studied theology for one year and a half. He had attended Dominican lectures at the convent of Saint-Jacques and Franciscan ones given in another location not far from there (Dalmases, 122).

1537 In January, his companions come from Paris to join Ignatius in Venice. Ignatius is ordained with some of the others (June 24). In October, he goes to Rome with Pierre Favre (1506–46) and Diego Laínez (1512–65) while the others wait in Venice, hoping for passage to the Holy Land. On the way, Ignatius experiences a vision at La Storta (about ten miles from Rome): "I will be favorable to you in Rome" (Rib., no.140) or "I will be with you" (*Io saró con voi*, Dalmases, 152). This vision is considered a confirmation of the Society of Jesus, "a supernatural event [...] of enormous and lasting importance both for the spiritual life of Ignatius and for the foundation of the Society of Jesus" (Dalmases, 151).

1537 In April, Pope Paul III (r.1534–49) receives the companions (except for Ignatius who remained in Venice) and asks them to engage in a theological discussion at the Castel Sant'Angelo (Rib., no. 129).

1537–39 Impressed by what he had heard in their disputation before him, the pope appoints Favre and Laínez to the University of Rome, where they freely offer lectures over the next two years in the Palazzo della Sapienza (Wisdom Hall). Favre lectures on scripturally based positive theology, and Laínez on Gabriel Biel's (*c.*1410–95) *Canon of the Mass* (*Epitoma expositionis canonis Missae* [Tübingen: Johann Otmar, for Friedrich Meynberger, 1499]). Alfonso Salmerón (1515–85) was also academically active at the University of Rome, possibly in 1539–40 (Grendler, 29).

1538 Plans for going to Jerusalem are abandoned as travel becomes impossible because the Venetians have broken off their relations with the Turks. The companions reunite in Rome. Ignatius, after postponing his first Mass to be able to say it in the Holy Land, celebrates it on December 25 at Santa Maria Maggiore in Rome.

1539 Deliberations are held on the religious institute the companions hope to found. They compose the *Formula of the Institute*, which encapsulates the core idea and self-understanding of the order. On September 3, the *Formula* is given oral approval by the pope, who says "Digitus Dei est hic" (The finger of God is here; Exodus 8:19).

1540 The Society of Jesus receives official written approval from Pope Paul III (r. 1534–49) as a religious order. A revision of the companions' 1539 *Formula* is included in the papal charter *Regimini militantis ecclesiae*, stating the order's chief purpose as twofold: "The progress of souls in Christian life and doctrine" and "the propagation of the faith by the ministry of the word, by spiritual exercises and works of charity, and specifically by the education of children and unlettered persons in Christianity." The *Formula* states explicitly that the members "may [...] set up a college or colleges in universities capable of having fixed revenues, annuities, or possessions which are to be applied to the uses and needs of students" (CN, no. 8). The *Formula* insists on the authority of the Society in managing all aspects of these colleges and on not diverting the use of any of their goods elsewhere, except to provide for the needs of the scholastics (CN, no. 8).

1541 Upon his election as general, Ignatius takes on the role of community cook and begins teaching children the rudiments of the faith in the church of Our Lady of the Way (Rib., no. 219–20).

1541 "Fundación de collegio" (The founding of a college) is composed to give directives for establishing (residential) colleges for those who are to enter the Society but who need academic training to fulfill the mission of the Society (MPSI 5, introduction, 2–3). Since they are to travel to various places at the command of the pope, preach, hear confessions, and catechize, it seems appropriate and necessary that these be persons of upright life and adequate education (*personas de buena vida y de alguna suficiencia de letras*). Because it is hard to find these people already well formed and still willing to take on the demanding labors that are envisioned, the Society chooses these colleges as the way to preserve and expand their Institute. Before a person enters such a college, he must undergo certain probations, after which he promises to enter the Society upon the completion of his studies. This document already indicates the stadial structuring of Jesuit education that would last until approximately 1966: Letters, philosophy, theology (*despues de seer bien fundados en gramática, estudiar súmulas, lógica y philosofía, graduándose en artes liberales, y después por quatro años en theología expeculativa y positiva*; MHSI 63:57, no. 13). The shape of the studies follows the needs of the church; they are ordered to the help of souls (*tamen que todo estudio sea para el provecho y salud de las ánimas*; MHSI 63:57, no. 13).

1541–42 King João III of Portugal (r.1521–57), partly concerned to provide successors for the missionary Francis Xavier (1506–52), is "the very first to decide to found a college for our Society to be a kind of seedbed for spreading it in Portugal" (Rib., no. 227). This college is founded at the University of Coimbra (which had been opened in 1537).

1542 The bishop in Goa, India, asks that two Jesuits in a diocesan seminary teach reading, writing, and some Latin to children.

1543 Claude le Jay teaches at the university at Ingolstadt, in the important theological chair left open at the death of Johann Eck (1486–1543) (Bangert, 23). Le Jay is offered a chair and doctoral status, but he is soon sent to Augsburg, then to Dillingen where he promotes the founding of colleges to defend the faith. The bishop of Augsburg calls him to the Diet of Worms (1521) (Ravier, 79).

1543 Xavier reports on the college in Goa where humanities and Christian doctrine are being taught to local and to Portuguese children. Ignatius saw this school as a model he would like to see the Society establish in Europe (Farrell, 16).

1543–56 Ignatius drafts and revises the *Constitutions*. Part 4 (covering academic matters) receives contributions by Juan Alfonso de Polanco (1517–76), Laínez, and André des Freux (*c.*1515–56).

1544 Jesuits are studying in their own residential colleges at universities in Paris, Coimbra, Padua, Louvain, Cologne, Valencia, and Alcalá. In Lent of this year, Francisco de Borja (1510–72) "offers to endow a college for the Society at Gandía" (Farrell, 16).

1544–45 The "Fundación de collegio" of 1541 is revised. Now entitled "Para fundar colegios," it states that the founders must provide not only for administrators (as in the 1541 document) but for teachers as well (*preceptores*)—a significant innovation (Lukács–Ganss, 129). The document also indicates that the particulars of the education and the order to be followed by every college will be worked out later (MHSI 63:58–59). This passage is echoed in the *Constitutions* (4.13n2, A; CN, no. 455), looking ahead to the *Ratio studiorum* of 1599.

1545 On March 14, 1545, Ignatius accepts Borja's offer (forwarded by the Spanish provincial Antonio de Aráoz [1515–73]) to found a college in Gandía. It opens on November 16. Since there is no larger university to which it is attached, Jesuits must teach. It opens as an endowed establishment for the formation of Jesuit scholastics, but Borja is particularly motivated by an interest in the Christian education of the local Agarenes, descendants of Christian apostates to Islam in the seventh century, some of whom had recently converted to Christianity (Lukács–Ganss, 130).

1545 *Constitutiones Collegii Patavini* (Constitutions of the Paduan College) are composed after it becomes obvious that more specific directives are needed (MPSI 1:introduction, 9). Ignatius asks Laínez to draft an outline for the college at Padua that might serve as an example for others. The first part outlines the structure of the academic training. It includes a "Parisian" kind of emphasis on academic exercises. Scholastics sent to Padua in September of 1546 take with them an Italian copy of these rules (MPSI 5:introduction, 3). This year is an important pivot in the Society's approach: it is at this point that it clearly realizes that the standard lectures at the university need to be supplemented for more efficient, speedy, and solid progress such as Ignatius had experienced in Paris (O'Malley, 203).

1546 The rector of the college in Gandía, Father Andrés de Oviedo (1518–77), invites lay students into the philosophy classes (the "arts course"), and it becomes the first *Jesuit* college where some non-Jesuit students are being taught. This school may have had the greatest impact on Ignatius and his thinking about this apostolate (Farrell, 16).

1546 With Salmerón as his companion, Laínez is sent by the pope as papal theologian to three periods of the Council of Trent (1545–63). Laínez gives an important speech on justification (October 26, 1546).

1547 The pope raises the college in Gandía to university status. Borja's endowment there and the beginnings of plans for a university in Messina turn Ignatius's interests to the idea of universities (Farrell, 145). Civil authorities keep Ignatius from establishing "a college seminary for Jesuits and externs" in Paris, and in Dillingen in 1548 and at Ingolstadt in 1549 (Lukács–Ganss, 131).

1547 At Ignatius's request, his secretary Juan de Polanco works on the *Constitutiones collegiorum* (more detailed than the *Constitutiones Collegii Patavini*) and the *Industriae*, which foreshadows the contents and structure of the *Constitutions* of the Society, including the material on studies. It is clear that some Jesuits will be *litterati* and have a more intense academic training than others. The *Constitutiones collegiorum* is not circulated, likely because its matter soon appears in drafts of *Constitutions* and because the late 1540s saw a new model of Jesuit studies arising: one incorporating non-Jesuits (MPSI 1: introduction, 14). Even in these earliest drafts of the *Constitutions*, Ignatius clearly had non-Jesuit students also in mind.

1547 The new viceroy of the Kingdom of Sicily, Juan de Vega (1507–58), seeks to institute a general moral and civic reform there. Knowing the Society from his time in Rome as a representative of Holy Roman Emperor Charles V (r.1519–58), he persuades the officials at Messina to write to the pope and to Ignatius to found a college and set up a permanent residence there (Rib., no. 286–87). Vega himself writes to the pope and to Ignatius to the same effect.

1548 The school in Goa is put entirely under the management of the Society. The college that the Portuguese had set up for Christian converts "was entrusted to Ours so that they might take care of the youth who were to be given religious training, receive their own brothers coming from Portugal, and test local candidates for the Society" (Rib., no. 229).

1548 Opening of the college of Messina (April 25), primarily for externs (non-Jesuits). According to Father Hannibal du Coudret (1525–99), it was here that the Society "first undertook the task of educating youth, and initiated its system of dividing the pupils into distinct classes with lessons accommodated to their individual capacities. From here the first *ratio studiorum*, written for the Roman College, was sent to the other colleges which had been instituted according to its norm" (cited in Farrell, 48). Six Jesuit students were also sent to Messina; in the following years, Ignatius would not accept colleges unless provisions were made for Jesuits to study there as well. "*Otherwise there seemed no means of providing the knowledge of doctrine and skill in teaching it which was needed by members of the Order*" (Farrell, 134–35). The *Ratio studiorum* of 1599 still reflects this dual coverage: it is a plan both for the formation of Jesuits (*ad intra*) and for education of others in "public classes" (*ad extra*), both groups following the *studia Societatis Iesu*. Perhaps already by the end of this year Ignatius has spoken with Laínez about the idea for a Roman college (MPSI 1: introduction, 18).

1548 Jerónimo Nadal (1507–80), rector at Messina, and Andrés de Oviedo, rector at Gandía, both ask Ignatius for rules by which they might organize their respective schools. Ignatius answers that they should write them up and send them to Rome for approval. Nadal's document becomes the essential core of all later plans for Jesuit education. It seems to have been used for the school in Palermo (1549); soon requested by Father Aráoz in Spain; and later given important attention and use by Ignatius in Rome (MPSI 5: introduction, 4).

1549 On October 4, Salmerón, le Jay, and Peter Canisius (1521–97) are awarded doctorates at the University of Bologna. This allows them to accept chairs in Ingolstadt, on the request of William IV of Bavaria (1493–1550). They arrive there on November 13 (Grendler, 428–30).

1549–50 Statutes of the University of Gandía are drawn up by Fathers Andrés de Oviedo (1518–77), Antonio Aráoz (1515–73), Diego Mirón (1516–90, rector at Valencia), and Francisco de Rojas (d. after 1556, superior at the residence in Saragossa). They use the constitutions of the university in Valencia, adapting them to the "Parisian style." The main concern here is not for a plan of studies or method, but issues concerning examinations and academic advancement (MPSI 5: introduction, 4).

1550 The Society's general *Constitutions* appear for the first time. Part 4 is "The Learning and Other Means of Helping Their Neighbor That Are to Be Imparted to Those Who Are Retained in the Society." It calls for a formal *ratio studiorum* (plan of studies) that will provide a detailed treatment of (1) the lecture-times, their order, their method; (2) exercises in compositions and in disputations; and (3) delivering orations and reading verses publicly (*Constitutions* 4.13. n2, A; CN, no. 455).

1550 Still a duke but already collaborating significantly with Ignatius, Borja, seeing the potential impact of a Jesuit college in Rome, "had a college founded at Rome, with Ignatius's encouragement and advice" (Rib., no. 395).

1551 On February 18, Father Jean Pelletier (*c.*1520–64) and fourteen Jesuits open the Roman College. Ignatius wanted to make it "the center and model of the Society's educational work" (Farrell, 69), both for Jesuits and for others. The tablet on the front door reads: "SCHOLA DI GRAMMATICA, D'HUMANITÀ E DOTTRINA CHRISTIANA, GRATIS" (School of grammar, humanistic studies, and Christian doctrine, free). Using his earlier *Constitutiones collegiorum*, Polanco composes *Regulae rectoris Collegii Romani* (Rules for the rector of the Roman College), and it is sent out to provincials and rectors of Jesuit colleges.

1551 Father Hannibal du Coudret, at the instruction of Rector Jerónimo Nadal, writes up and sends to Rome the plan for the school at Messina. Polanco entitles the document "Ratio studiorum collegii Messanensis" (Plan of studies for the college in Messina). It covers in great detail the structure of the classes, the daily schedule, the authors taken, and the academic exercises (MPSI 1: introduction, 23). This is followed (perhaps in early 1552) by Nadal's *De studiis Societatis* (On the Society's studies), which looks to a full university program (Farrell, 54).

1551 Ignatius states to various college rectors that "no rule of studies was to be considered fixed or final until a program applicable to all the schools could be drafted and approved" (October 31, 1551, cited in Farrell, 47 [MHSI vol. 28 (Mon. Ignat. 1 ser., 3): 703–6]). The summary of the Italian original to André des Freux in Venice actually speaks of "public devotions and letters": "Che avisi del modo di procedere nelle devotioni publiche et lettere, et in questo mezo che non metta usanze che sia immobile, insin a tanto che si faccia l'ordine che si ha da servare in tutti li collegii" [He informs him of the manner of proceeding in public devotions and letters, and in this matter he should not introduce any fixed custom until the creation of an order that has to be followed in all the colleges]).

1551 On December 1, Ignatius writes to the Spanish provincial Antonio Aráoz a letter that has been called "in many points a remarkable epitome of Ignatius's spirit in the work of education" (Ignatius, Letters, 360). The letter covers the way a college is founded; the educational decorum, procedures, and subjects; the advantages for Jesuits; the benefits for the non-Jesuit students.

1552 Nicolas Bobadilla (1511–90) gives forty lectures on the book of Jonah in Naples. This is but one example of an ongoing ministry of the Society. See O'Malley, 104–26, for this event (107) and for a larger presentation of the "ministries of the Word" in sacred lectures and in publications.

1552 The (residential) German College is established through the efforts of Cardinal Giovanni Morone (1509–80) working with Ignatius to care for the future of the church in Germany. The college is put under the direction of the Society, and the Roman College soon (1553) begins to offer the higher courses in philosophy and theology, partly for the sake of these students.

1553 *Regulae de scholis* (Rules concerning classes) makes Nadal's organization of studies "universal in the Society" and "truly the nucleus of the entire plan of studies" (MPSI 1: introduction, 17).

1553 Nadal is chosen as a "commissary" (authoritative representative) to organize and direct the rapidly expanding educational work (Farrell, 188–216). He has the power to "collate and communicate the existing legislation of the Society, to found and organize colleges, approve and revise local customs, and in general to direct the manifold undertakings of the Order" (Farrell, 221).

1554 In a letter of August 13, Ignatius advises Canisius that an "excellent means for helping the Church in these travails [i.e., the confusions and conflicts arising from reformational movements] would be to multiply colleges and schools of the Society in many lands, especially in places where it is thought there would be a large number of students" (Ignatius, Letters, 506).

1555 Ignatius sends Laínez and Nadal as papal theologians to the diet of Augsburg (O'Malley, 255).

1555 The Royal College of the Arts in Coimbra is entrusted to the Society and operates in connection with the university there. The institutions at Gandía and Coimbra and the plans for a university at Messina (which never became a Jesuit university, although the college continued to operate there) occasion the study of academic constitutions that are already in use at other universities. The "Society's universities" are first mentioned in 1553 or 1554. "University" usually indicates institutions that have a faculty of theology in addition to the arts faculty that defines a "college"; a "gymnasium" focuses on the study of Letters (that is, language and literature).

1556 In January, Pope Paul IV (r.1555–59) grants the Roman College the right to confer philosophy and theology degrees, thereby raising it to the level of a university. (Some such courses had been offered as early as 1553.)

1556 In a letter of February 14 to Philip II, king of Spain (r.1556–98), Pedro de Ribadeneyra (1527–1611) expresses the idea that the Society has involved itself in teaching because "all the welfare of Christianity and of all the world depends upon the sound education of the young" (*todo el bien de la cristiandad y de todo el mundo depende de la buena institución de la juventud* [MPSI 1:475]).

1556 Ignatius of Loyola dies on July 31. He had opened or accepted as many as forty-six colleges (this number including some that were exclusively for Jesuit formation; MPSI 2:introduction, 43). His last official business had concerned a house purchased for the use of the Roman College (Rib., 479n110).

1558 The *Ratio studiorum* of the Roman College, composed by the teachers there at the request of Superior General Diego Laínez (in office 1558–65). This document included rules for the prefect of studies, the teachers, and the students.

1558 Publication of the *Constitutions* of the Society of Jesus.

1560 Laínez, through a letter to Jesuit superiors drafted by Polanco on August 10, makes teaching a standard part of the formation and apostolic activity of Jesuits ("tutti haveran da spendere qualche tempo in questo essercitio tanto importante al divino servicio et al ben commune" [MHSI, 50:165–67]). This is the beginning of a standard part of all Jesuit scholastic formation, "regency" (Latin: "magisterium").

1560 Laínez commissions a letter through Polanco declaring that "generally speaking, there are [in the Society] two ways of helping our neighbors: one in the colleges through the education of youth in letters, learning, and Christian life, and the second in every place to help every kind of person through sermons, confessions, and the other means that accord with our customary way of proceeding" (Letter of August 10, 1560, cited in O'Malley, 200). The colleges were becoming "the principal centers for all Jesuit ministry" (O'Malley, 206).

1562–63 Nadal writes *Ordo studiorum germanicus* (German order of studies) for the schools in Germany, adapting the rules from those written for the Roman College.

1563 Diego de Ledesma (1519–75), prefect of studies at the Roman College, asks Superior General Laínez that Nadal write a document covering in detail the entire educational plan and method for each class.

1562–75 "Painstaking examination and revision of every element contained in [the early formulas used for school organization]" (Farrell, 153).

1564 Faculty of the Roman College issues a revision of the rules they had done in 1558. The distribution of prizes at Rome in this year was not the first such event, but it had a wide impact, through the rules composed by Father Pedro Juan Perpiñá (1530–66), an outstanding teacher of rhetoric. These rules appear in the *Ratio* of 1599. The first Marian sodality is created, accepting the best students. Similar sodalities are eventually adopted at many other locations (MPSI 2: introduction, 21).

1565 Earliest reference to the *Summa sapientia* (Highest wisdom) in the documents of the Second General Congregation (Farrell, 221–22). Named after the opening words, it was a collection of rules and guidelines written in service of formulating a comprehensive educational plan.

1568 Father Cipriano Soares's (1524–93) *De arte rhetorica* (On the art of rhetoric) is published. It becomes the standard rhetoric textbook in Jesuit schools.

1569 Ledesma's *De ratione et ordine studiorum Collegii Romani* (On the plan and order of studies) ("perhaps the most substantial contribution to the development of the Jesuit code of education" [Farrell, 169]) is issued by Superior General Borja (in office 1565–72). Known as "the *Ratio Borgiana*," it was the first "common and universal Ratio," in effect until the 1591 *Ratio* was issued for trial use.

1572 Ribadeneyra's *Life of Ignatius of Loyola* is published in Latin, later rewritten in Spanish (1583), and then expanded in its Latin form (1586). It explains the Society's origins and Institute, giving an extended reflection on "Why the Society Has Colleges for Educating

Youth" (Rib., nos. 351–87). It also surveys the beginnings of many of early Jesuit educational institutions.

1573 The third general congregation proposes that *Summa sapientia* be examined, revised, and made normative for the entire Society.

1575 Publication of Manuel Álvares's (1526–82) Latin grammar, *De institutione grammatica libri tres* (Grammatical education in three books), the Latin grammar prescribed in the *Ratio studiorum* of 1599 (RS, no. 46).

1575 Juan Bonifacio (1538–1606) publishes the earliest Jesuit educational tract, *Christiani pueri institutio adolescentiaeque perfugium* (The education of the Christian child and a shelter for adolescence [Salamanca: Mathias Gastius, 1575]). To this author is attributed a famous motto of Jesuit education, *Puerilis institutio est renovatio mundi* (The education of the youth is the renewal of the world). This expression is taken cited from Bonifacio's *De sapiente fructuoso, epistolares libri quinque* (On the productive wise person, five books of letters [Burgos: n.p., 1580]).

1577 Superior General Everard Mercurian (in office 1573–80) codifies instructions and rules for particular officials involved in running schools. He seems intent on comprehensive legislation (Farrell, 222), but he dies before the work can be done. "The Society is working more at its form than at its reform, since it has not yet been brought to the fullest actuality of its Institute" (Statement attributed to Mercurian: see the epigraph to Thomas McCoog, S.J., ed., *The Mercurian Project: Forming Jesuit Culture (1573–1580)* [St. Louis, MO: Institute of Jesuit Sources, 2004]).

1581 Superior General Claudio Acquaviva (in office 1581–1615), very soon after his election, appoints a committee of twelve to compose "a formula of studies."

1582 Pope Gregory XIII (r.1572–85) endows a new and magnificent building to house the Collegio Romano "as a seminary of all nations" (Rib., no. 399). It is inaugurated on November 5, 1584. It is later known as the Pontificia Università Gregoriana in honor of this benefactor.

1584 A congregation, called to provide for a fully finished plan of studies, says the following:

> There are assuredly two things that constitute our Society's bulwark and mainstay: the burning zeal of devotion and a

> surpassing knowledge of reality. The hinge of our Constitutions swings entirely on these two principles insofar as devotion bereft of the light of learning certainly profits individuals a good bit privately, but it can contribute almost nothing to help the Church and our neighbors in sermons, in administering the sacraments, in educating the young, in disputations with adversaries of the faith, in giving advice and providing answers in unclear situations, and in the rest of the expected services and functions of our men: these things require learning—not the well-known common kind but a certain superior kind of learning. (MHSI 129:2)

Acquaviva appoints an entirely new committee of six to carry on their work: Juan Azor (1535–1603; Spain); Gaspar González (d.1590; Portugal); James Tyrie (1543–97; Scotland); Pierre Busée (1540–87; Netherlands); Antoine de Guise (1537–94; Flanders); Stefano Tucci (1540–1597; Sicily). These work from December 8, 1584 until the summer of 1585, meeting three hours a day, spending the rest of the time "examining correspondence and ordinances from various Provinces, the statutes of noted universities, the fourth part of the *Constitutions*, and other documents relating to studies, local customs, and discipline" (Farrell, 225).

1586 The first *Ratio studiorum* is issued for review only (not use). Written critiques are requested from committees of at least five fathers in each province. There are two major parts: the *Delectus opinionum* (Selection of opinions) (including particular propositions that were to be taught or that were prohibited) and the *Praxis et ordo studiorum* (Practical guide and plan of studies) (structured by the subjects to be studied from sacred scripture down to the grammatical studies of the lowest classes).

1586–91 Responses from the provincial committees are examined and work on a new edition is begun. Fathers Tucci, Azor, González continue to work on it, along with professors from the Roman College: Fathers Robert Bellarmine (1542–1621), Francisco Suárez (1548–1617), Benedetto Sardi (1544–86), Benedetto Giustiniani (1550–1622), Pietro Parra (1531–93), Benet Perera (1535–1610), Francesco Benci (1542–94), Orazio Torsellini (1545–99), and (probably) Fulvio Cardulo (1529–91).

1591 The second *Ratio* is issued as binding for three years. At the end of that period, written critiques will help the committee prepare for the definitive version. The structure is now not by classes but by rules for the distinct offices and units, from the provincial to the schools' "academies" (organized study groups).

1599 Promulgation of the "definitive" *Ratio studiorum* on January 8. The cover letter ends with a solemn call to the superiors "to strive with greatest possible personal involvement to get everyone to enthusiastically and faithfully follow this undertaking that is so strongly called for by our *Constitutions* and expected to produce such abundant results for our students." The scope of the document covers the modern equivalents of high school, college, and graduate work in the large stages of Letters, philosophy, and theology, with the first stage of humanistic studies corresponding to four years of high school and two of college.

1608 Decree 18 of GC 6 finally resolves all doubts about whether the Society could licitly run schools for non-Jesuits. There had been scruples about whether the Society and its members could live on the fixed revenues of a school if it was not, according to the papal charters, supporting a seminary for the Society (Lukács–Ganss, esp. 164–66).

1623 Lord Francis Bacon (1561–1626) famously comments, "As for what concerns pedagogy, the shortest way to put it is 'Consult the schools of the Jesuits': for nothing better than these has appeared" (*Ad Paedagogicam quod attinet, brevissimum foret dictu, consule scholas Jesuitarum: nihil enim, quod in usum venit, his melius*). This statement appears only in the Latin version of his *The Advancement of Learning* (*De dignitate et augmentis scientiarum*, libros 9 [London: Haviland, 1623], here book 6, chapter 4). The English text had appeared in 1605.

1623 *Protrepticon ad magistros scholarum inferiorum Societatis Iesu* (Exhortation to the teachers of the lower classes of the Society of Jesus) by Francesco Sacchini (1570–1625).

1625 *Paraenesis ad magistros scholarum inferiorum Societatis Iesu* (Advice for the teachers of the lower classes of the Society of Jesus), also by Sacchini.

1639 Superior General Muzio Vitelleschi (1563–1645, in office 1615–45), writing to the entire Society, speaks of the educational work of the Society in these terms: "There is no doubt that the sound education of the young is foremost among the helps that God's providence has granted the Society to promote good moral behavior in the common life of humanity. This mark and, as it were, badge of honor is so distinctive for our family that it not only distinguishes us and sets us apart from other religious orders but it also wins for us celebrity and good repute with almost all Christian leaders, who on this account have eagerly and graciously called us to their lands, and we see that this has happened no less to the glory of God than to the increase of our order" (cited in MPSI 1:1n1).

1703 Jesuit Father Joseph de Jouvancy's (1643–1719) *Ratio discendi et docendi* (The way to learn and the way to teach) is published pursuant to decree 10 of GC 14 (1696). It is a guide for professors of humanistic studies (the "lower classes"), both for their own progress in learning and for their advancement in pedagogical effectiveness. The text is formally attached to that of the *Ratio studiorum.*

1773–1814 The Society of Jesus is officially suppressed by Pope Clement XIV (r.1769–74) with a papal brief (*Dominus ac Redemptor*). The Society has 845 educational institutions at this time. It survives in Russia, where the brief is not promulgated, largely because of the high regard of Empress Catherine the Great (r.1762–96) for the Jesuit colleges. A full restoration of the Society's status, even if not of its former properties, occurs in 1814, through the papal bull *Sollicitudo omnium ecclesiarum*, issued by Pope Pius VII (r.1800–23).

1832 A trial version of a revised *Ratio studiorum* is issued with contemporary adaptations. Superior General Jan Roothaan's (1785–1853, in office 1829–53) cover letter presents a rationale for a contemporary turn to vernacular literature, mathematics, and natural sciences, provided that there is great care to preserve what had been done in the *Ratio studiorum* of 1599: "[This new formulation was not] a matter of having to fashion a new order of studies [...] [but] of adjusting the very same venerable text to our times [...] that work that had been composed by the very best men after a long process of gathering a great body of advice, well tested by the successful experience of almost two centuries, and often recommended by the praise even of the very enemies of the Society" (Pachtler, 229; a translation of the entire letter is available in Mesa, 178–84).

1903 Father Robert Schwickerath (1869–1948) publishes *Jesuit Education: Its History and Principles Viewed in the Light of Modern Educational Problems* (St. Louis, MO: B. Herder, 1903), a magisterial survey of Jesuit education. It includes an overview of its achievements and challenges in the nineteenth century.

1934 The Jesuit Educational Association (United States) is founded by Superior General Włodzimierz Ledóchowski (1866–1942, in office 1914–42) to provide leadership for Jesuit education (secondary and higher) in the United States.

1938 *Jesuit Educational Quarterly* (JEQ) begins publication under the auspices of the Jesuit Educational Association. It produces 130 issues before being closed in 1970.

1938 Father Allan P. Farrell (1896–1976) publishes *The Jesuit Code of Liberal Education: Development and Scope of the* Ratio studiorum (Milwaukee, WI: Bruce Publishing Company, 1938).

1943 François Charmot's (1881–1965) *La pédagogie des* jésuites: *Ses principes, son actualité* appears (Paris: Aux Éditions Spes, 1943; 2nd ed. 1951). It is a large and thorough survey of the entire Jesuit pedagogical tradition.

1948 "Instructio pro Assistentia Americae de ordinandis universitatibus, collegiis, ac scholis altis et de praeparandis eorundem magistris" (Instruction for the American assistancy on organizing its universities, colleges, and high schools and on preparing their teachers) (New York: Jesuit Educational Association, 1948).

1954 Father George E. Ganss (1905–2000) publishes *Saint Ignatius' Idea of a Jesuit University* (Milwaukee, WI: Marquette University Press, 1954; 2nd ed. 1956). Ganss believes that the educational vision of Ignatius rests chiefly in the *Constitutions* rather than in the *Ratio studiorum*.

1954 *Ratio studiorum superiorum Societatis Iesu* (Rome: Apud Curiam Praepositi Generalis, 1954), instructions for "higher studies" in Jesuit formation, is one of the last universal documents to evoke the phrase "ratio studiorum" in its title.

1957 General Congregation 30 declares that "all should know well and greatly esteem the *Ratio Studiorum*; and its method and rules should be carefully observed in the education of our young men."

1962 *Veterum sapientiae* (On the promotion of the study of Latin), an apostolic constitution, is promulgated by Pope John XXIII (r.1958–63), mandating continued use of Latin: "No one is to be admitted to the study of philosophy or theology except he be thoroughly grounded in this language and capable of using it." The traditional curriculum is to be restored. "Should circumstances of time and place demand the addition of other subjects to the curriculum besides the usual ones, then either the course of studies must be lengthened, or these additional subjects must be condensed or their study relegated to another time."

1965–92 László Lukács, S.J. (1910–98) produces for the MHSI seven volumes of thoroughly annotated critical editions of early Jesuit pedagogical material. These are known as the Monumenta Paedagogica. They supersede in method, scope, and presentation the earlier Monumenta Paedagogica volume from 1901 (MHSI, vol. 19).

1966 General Congregation 31 declares: "To ensure that the intellectual formation of Jesuits is ordered to meet the needs of the times, the entire *Ratio Studiorum* shall be revised. Considering the great diversity of regions and circumstances, this *Ratio* shall determine only general norms" (Decree 9, "The Training of Scholastics, Especially in Studies," no. 15).

1966 In the United States, the Society's formational period known as the "juniorate" (two years of language, literary, and other studies after the novitiate) begins to be generally discontinued; the classical languages are no longer maintained as a required part of the scholastics' training. Latin ceases to be the medium of instruction in philosophy and theology.

1967 First "separate incorporation" of a Jesuit university in the United States (St. Louis University): the board of trustees is reconstituted with a predominance of lay membership. The Jesuit community becomes a corporate entity legally distinct from that of the university. The president of the university (who may be required by charter to be a Jesuit and who is to be hired and evaluated by the board of trustees) has an entirely separate office from that of the Society-appointed rector of the Jesuit community. Other Jesuit colleges and universities in the United States soon follow this pattern.

1967 In July, administrators from leading Catholic universities, including strong Jesuit representation, draft and approve at a rural retreat in Land o' Lakes, Wisconsin, a document entitled "Statement on the Nature of the Contemporary Catholic University." It declares that "the Catholic university must have a true autonomy and academic freedom in the face of authority of whatever kind, lay or clerical, external to the academic community itself." The immediate reception and impact of the document is unclear, but to many it comes to represent a significantly new stance even though its preamble limits the document's scope considerably.

1970 The first full official English translation of the Society's *Constitutions* appears: Saint Ignatius of Loyola, *The Constitutions of the Society of Jesus*, translation, introduction, and commentary by George E. Ganss (St. Louis, MO: Institute of Jesuit Sources, 1970). Fr. Ganss had founded the Institute of Jesuit Sources in 1961 to make significant Jesuit historical sources and studies available in English.

1970 The Association of Jesuit Colleges and Universities (AJCU) is founded, replacing the Commission on Colleges and Universities of the Jesuit Educational Association (JEA). Part of it becomes the Jesuit Secondary Educational Association (JSEA). The *Jesuit Educational Quarterly* ceases operation.

1973 Superior General Pedro Arrupe (1907–91, in office 1965–83) gives a major address at the European Alumni Congress: "Promotion of Justice and Education for Justice." It becomes known as the "Men for Others Address" (reprinted in Mesa, 215–62).

1975 General Congregation 32 issues a decree entitled "Our Mission Today: The Service of Faith and the Promotion of Justice." The same congregation declares: "Studies in the Society are governed by the common law of the Church and by Decree 9 of the 31st General Congregation [...] All the decrees of previous General Congregations which are contrary either to this decree or to Decree 9 of the 31st General Congregation or to the *General Norms for Studies* are definitively abrogated. These *General Norms* which Father General promulgated in place of the previous *Ratio Studiorum* are to be continually revised and adapted to new needs" (decree 6, "Formation of Jesuits Especially with Regard to the Apostolate and Studies," no. 37).

1975 "Project 1: The Jesuit Apostolate of Education in the United States; Agreements and Decisions: A Step on the Way" (Washington, DC: Jesuit Conference, 1975) presents a concluding summary report. Project 1 had been a year-long effort to examine and think through issues of Jesuit education in the United States. Among the conclusions: "There is still need for much more development and clarification in regard to the nature, scope, and objectives of a corporate Jesuit apostolate on the local, provincial, and national levels" (Project 1:12, no. 4). The provincials state their commitment to "the mandate of the 32nd General Congregation," and they "affirm that the service of faith and the promotion of justice, as a single focus must be fundamental to the secondary education apostolate" (Project 1:4, no. 4). Likewise, universities' rationales should give a central place to "the Society's apostolic focus on the promotion of faith and justice as decreed by the 32nd General Congregation" (Project 1:12, no. 6).

1975 Pope Paul VI (r.1963–78) addresses the rectors and presidents of Jesuit universities, saying that collaboration with non-Jesuits is a great value "but it is necessary to be sure that this comes about in such a way that the Society is able to retain the authority necessary to face up to its Catholic responsibilities. The Society should not, therefore, relinquish its authority in those universities which belong to it." Losing such a tradition would mean losing something of the Society's identity and also "something of which the Church has need and which she cannot do without" (Project 1:38).

1980 Superior General Pedro Arrupe at a symposium on the "Apostolate of the Society in Secondary Education" a paper entitled "Our Secondary Schools: Today and Tomorrow" (reprinted in Mesa, 263–86).

1987 "Go Forth and Teach: The Characteristics of Jesuit Education" (Washington, DC: Jesuit Secondary Education Association, 1987; reprinted in Mesa, 287–366).

1989 Assembly 1989: Jesuit Ministry in Higher Education. Over six hundred Jesuits and non-Jesuits meet at Georgetown University for a conference on issues related to Jesuit higher education. Superior General Peter-Hans Kolvenbach's (1928–2016, in office 1983–2008) address to this gathering is available online and in print ("Assembly 1989: Jesuit Ministry in Higher Education" [Washington, DC: Jesuit Conference, 1989]).

1990 *Ex corde ecclesiae*, an apostolic constitution, is issued by Pope John Paul II (r.1978–2005). It seems to answer the Land o' Lakes statement of 1967, asserting the relevance of episcopal authority for Catholic colleges and universities, their identity having been born "from the heart of the Church." In one paragraph (no. 13), it cites *L'université Catholique dans le monde moderne* (Document final du 2ème Congrès des Délégués des Universités Catholiques, Rome, November 20–29, 1972, §1) to highlight the following as essential characteristics of every Catholic university:

> 1. A Christian inspiration not only of individuals but of the university community as such; 2. a continuing reflection in the light of the Catholic faith upon the growing treasury of human knowledge, to which it seeks to contribute by its own research; 3. fidelity to the Christian message as it comes to us through the

Church; 4. an institutional commitment to the service of the people of God and of the human family in their pilgrimage to the transcendent goal which gives meaning to life.

1992 *Conversations* magazine, created as a result of Assembly 1989, begins publication. Its first issue declares that it wishes to promote discussions "which can help clarify and promote the identity of each college or university." The journal is one of the purposes of the National Seminar on Jesuit Higher Education, which is jointly sponsored by the Jesuit Conference Board (the ten provincials of the United States) and the Board of the Association of Jesuit Colleges and Universities (AJCU).

1993 Father Michael Buckley writes about the next large phase in the development of Catholic higher education: "If Catholic institutions of higher learning are to develop in what they are, the next stage must exhibit the increasing realization of the mutual and inherent unity between the religious and the academic" ("A Collegiate Conversation," *America* [September 11, 1993]:18–23, here 21).

1993 "Ignatian Pedagogy: A Practical Approach" (Rome: International Commission on the Apostolate of Jesuit Education, 1993) proposes the "Ignatian Pedagogical Paradigm" (IPP) (reprinted in Mesa, 367–423).

1994 Father Martin Tripole publishes *Faith Beyond Justice: Widening the Perspective* (St. Louis, MO: Institute of Jesuit Sources, 1994). It critiques the formulations and understandings of justice in GC 32, proposing instead the formulations "faith and culture" or "evangelization and culture" (128). His book is distributed to all members of GC 34 the next year.

1995 General Congregation 34's fourth decree is entitled "Our Mission and Culture." It states that "Our educational institutions, in particular, have a crucial role to play in linking Christian faith to the core elements in contemporary and traditional cultures" (d. 4, no. 125, see JLMT, 546). GC 34's decree 17 on "Jesuits and University Life" speaks of the possible need for "new structures of government and control on the part of the Society in order to preserve its identity [in Jesuit universities]." The institution should be accountable to the Society. Jesuits, as community and as individuals, "must actively commit themselves to the institution, assisting in its orientation, so that it can achieve the objectives desired for it by the Society" (decree 17, no. 9).

1995 GC 34 also issues *Complementary Norms* to accompany the *Constitutions* of the Society of Jesus. These include directives on the academic formation of scholastics in the Society (CN, 131–90, *passim*):

> Since the purpose of studies in the Society is apostolic, through their studies our members should acquire that breadth and excellence in learning that are required to achieve this end. The Society confirms its proper option for a profound academic formation of its future priests—theological as well as philosophical, human, and scientific, persuaded that, presupposing the testimony of one's own life, there is no more apt way to exercise our mission" (no. 81.1–2).

1998 Father Michael J. Buckley, director of the Jesuit Institute at Boston College, publishes a collection of well-researched, far-reaching essays on various aspects of Jesuit and Catholic education: *The Catholic University as Promise and Project: Reflections in a Jesuit Idiom* (Washington, DC: Georgetown University Press, 1998). He states: "Any justification of the promotion of justice as a commitment of the contemporary university must be grounded on the basic conviction that the university exists for the humane growth of its students" (113–14).

1999 Celebrations of the quadricentennial of the *Ratio atque institutio studiorum Societatis Iesu* lead to a re-awakening of a sense of the document's importance. Several vernacular translations continue to appear in the wake of László Lukács's 1986 critical edition in MPSI 5 (MHSI, vol. 129): Spanish, 1986; French, 1997; Polish, 2000; Italian, 2002; English, 2005; Japanese, 2008; Ukrainian, 2008; Portuguese, 2009.

2000 Superior General Peter-Hans Kolvenbach delivers a public lecture at Santa Clara University: "The Service of Faith and the Promotion of Justice in American Jesuit Higher Education" (reprinted in Mesa, 477–95).

2006 At St Peter's Basilica, Pope Benedict XVI (r.2005–13) addresses the Society of Jesus for the jubilee celebration for Ignatius, Xavier, and Favre. He identifies the urgent needs of the church today as something to be addressed by the Society's long-standing "cultural commitment" in theology and philosophy as well as in "the dialogue with modern culture" (paralleling the traditional stages of Jesuit academic formation: Letters, philosophy, and theology). The traditionally intense and thorough Jesuit formation should be "maintained and reinforced." Following Ignatius's concern for Christian education and cultural formation, the Society should continue "in this important apostolate, keeping the spirit of your Founder unchanged."

2010 "Depth, Universality, and Learned Ministry: Challenges to Jesuit Higher Education Today," an address by Superior General Adolfo Nicolás (1936–, in office 2008–16) at the conference "Networking Jesuit Higher Education: Shaping the Future for a Humane, Just, Sustainable Globe" in Mexico City (reprinted in Mesa, 534–54).

2012 In March, Superior General Adolfo Nicolás forms "an *ad hoc* International Commission to reflect on the intellectual formation of our men during their course of studies and to propose possible changes in the Society's program of philosophical and theological studies."

2012 The International Colloquium on Jesuit Secondary Education issues a vision statement, "Jesuit Education—Our Commitment to Global Networking, 2012" (reprinted in Mesa, 570–72).

2013 "Some Characteristics of Jesuit Colleges and Universities: A Self-evaluation Instrument" (Washington, DC: American Jesuit Colleges and Universities, 2013).

2014 Superior General Nicolás issues the report of the International Commission formed in 2012: "The Intellectual Formation of Jesuit Brothers and Scholastics: Initial Formation." His cover letter of March 3 states:

> The Church and the world continue to ask of the Society a service that is "learned": that is, a service that is always characterized by a depth of reflection that allows us to understand reality more deeply and thus to serve more effectively. The challenges we face cannot be responded to with superficiality. Our mission continues to "require all the learning and intelligence, imagination and ingenuity, solid studies and rigorous analysis that we can muster" (GC 34, December 26, no. 20).

Father Nicolás asks for (1) a review and evaluation of the current programs of Jesuits in initial formation, and (2) appropriate modifications within three years. In a letter of October 24, the Jesuit Conference of the United States announces that: "While Fr. General's letter emphasizes intellectual formation, the provincials of Canada and the US prefer to broaden the renewal to all aspects of formation."

2014 The Institute for Advanced Jesuit Studies opens at Boston College, incorporating the Institute of Jesuit Sources from St. Louis. Its focus is on Jesuit educational heritage and pedagogy along with Jesuit history and spirituality.

2014 International Seminar on Ignatian Pedagogy and Spirituality, meeting in Manresa, Spain, produces a vision statement (reprinted in Mesa, 573–77).

2015 The Jesuit Secondary Educational Association is renamed the Jesuit Schools Network (JSN) and given a standing office at the Jesuit Conference in Washington, DC.

2015 "Our Way of Proceeding: Standards and Benchmarks for Jesuit Schools in the 21st Century" is published by the Jesuit Schools Network.

2017 In June, a report on the future of Jesuit formation (in response to Fr. Nicolás's directive in 2014) is proposed by the Jesuit Conference of Canada and the United States. It prescinds from specific academic contents, sequencing, and structure. These it leaves to local authorities "in keeping with a principle of subsidiarity."

2018 On July 10, in Bilbao, Spain, Superior General Arturo Sosa (1948–, in office 2016–) addresses the general assembly of the International Association of Jesuit Universities: "The University as a Source of Reconciled Life." He says:

> For the university institutions run by the Society of Jesus it is not enough to reach the intellectual depth to develop knowledge and transmit it as an element of overall human education. The real challenge is that it should be an apostolate, that is, a way to more effectively announce the Good News of the Gospel, to learn to grasp the presence of God in the world and the action of his Spirit in history in order to join in it and contribute to human liberation.

Abbreviated Timeline References

Bangert = Bangert, William V. *A History of the Society of Jesus*. Revised ed. St. Louis: Institute of Jesuit Sources, 1986.

CN = Padberg, John W., ed. *The Constitutions of the Society of Jesus and Their Complementary Norms: A Complete English Translation of the Official Latin Texts*. St. Louis, MO: Institute of Jesuit Sources, 1996.

Dalmases = Dalmases, Cándido de. *Ignatius of Loyola, Founder of the Jesuits: His Life and Work*. Translated by Jerome Aixalá. St. Louis, MO: Institute of Jesuit Sources, 1985.

Farrell = Farrell, Allan P. *The Jesuit Code of Liberal Education: Development and Scope of the* Ratio studiorum Milwaukee, WI: Bruce Publishing Company, 1938.

Grendler = Grendler, Paul F. *The Jesuits and Italian Universities, 1548–1773*. Washington, DC: Catholic University of America Press, 2017.

Ignatius Letters = Palmer, Martin E., John W. Padberg, and John L. McCarthy, eds. *Ignatius of Loyola: Letters and Instructions*. St. Louis, MO: Institute of Jesuit Sources, 2006.

JLMT = *Jesuit Life and Mission Today: The Decrees & Accompanying Documents of the 31st–35th General Congregations of the Society of Jesus*. St. Louis, MO: Institute of Jesuit Sources, 2009.

O'Malley = O'Malley, John W. *The First Jesuits*. Cambridge, MA: Harvard University Press, 1993.

Larrañaga = Larrañaga, P. Victoriano. "Los estudios superiores de San Ignacio en Paris, Bolonia y Venecia." In *San Ignacio de Loyola: Estudios sobre su vida sus obras su espiritualidad*, 19–40. Zaragoza: Hechos y Dichos, 1956.

Lukács–Ganss = Ganss, George E. "The Origin of Jesuit Colleges for Externs and the Controversies about their Poverty, 1539–1608." *Woodstock Letters* 91 (April 1962): 123–66. Reprinted in Thomas H. Clancy, *An Introduction to Jesuit Life: The Constitutions and History through 435 Years*, 283–326. St. Louis, MO: Institute of Jesuit Sources, 1976. Ganss's article is an adaptation and condensation of a two-part article by László Lukács: "De Origine Collegiorum Externorum deque Controversiis circa eorum Paupertatem Obortis, 1539–1608." *Archivum Historicum Societatis Jesu* 29 (1960): 189–245 and 30 (1961): 3–89.

Mesa = Mesa, José, ed. *Ignatian Pedagogy: Classic and Contemporary Texts on Jesuit Education from St. Ignatius to Today*. Commissioned by the Secretariat for Education of the Society of Jesus. Chicago: Loyola Press, 2017.

MPSI 1 = Lukács, László, MHSI vol. 92, Monumenta Paedagogica Societatis Iesu, 1 (1540–56). Rome: Institutum Historicum Societatis Iesu, Via dei Penitenzieri 20, 1965.

MPSI 5 = Lukács, László, MHSI vol. 129, Monumenta Paedagogica Societatis Iesu, 5: Ratio Atque Institutio Studiorum Societatis Iesu: 1586, 1591, 1599. Rome: Institutum Historicum Societatis Iesu, Via dei Penitenzieri 20, 1986.

MHSI = Monumenta Historica Societatis Iesu. 157 vols. Madrid, Rome, 1894– .

MPSI = Monumenta Paedagogica Societatis Iesu. A subset of MHSI, covering volumes 92, 107, 108, 124, 129, 140, 141. An early volume, 19, was also titled Monumenta Paedagogica, but it is not part of this series edited by László Lukács.

Pachtler = Pachtler, G. M. [Georg Michael]. *Ratio studiorum et Institutiones Scholasticae Societatis Jesu per Germaniam olim vigentes collectae concinnatae dilucidatae*. Edited by Karl Kehrbach. Tomus 2. Ratio studiorum ann. 1586, 1599, 1832. Monumenta Germaniae paedagogica 5. Berlin: A. Hofmann & Company, 1887.

Padberg = Padberg, John W. "Development of the *Ratio studiorum*." In *The Jesuit* Ratio studiorum: *400th Anniversary Perspectives*, edited by Vincent J. Duminuco, 80–100. New York: Fordham University Press, 2000.

Project 1 = *Project 1: The Jesuit Apostolate of Education in the United States; Agreements and Decisions; A Step on the Way*. No. 6 (October 1975). Published by the Jesuit Conference, 1717 Massachusetts Ave., N.W., Washington, DC 20036. Appendix 1 (pp. 35–42): "Address of the Holy Father to the Rectors and Presidents of Jesuit Universities, August 6, 1975."

Ravier = Ravier, André. *Les chroniques Saint Ignace de Loyola*. Paris: Nouvelle Librairie de France, 1973.

Rib. = *The Life of Ignatius of Loyola by Pedro de Ribadeneyra*. Translated by Claude Pavur. St. Louis, MO: Institute of Jesuit Sources, 2014.

RS = *The Ratio studiorum: The Official Plan for Jesuit Education*. Translated by Claude Pavur. St. Louis, MO: Institute of Jesuit Sources, 2005.

Appendix 2: Jesuit Colleges Operating at the Time of Ignatius's Death

(Adapted from Dalmases, *Ignatius of Loyola*, 301–2)

1540 Paris
1542 Padua
1542 Lisbon
1542 Coimbra, College of Arts, 1555
1542 Louvain
1543 Goa, India, college for Indian boys
1543 Goa, India, college for Jesuits
1544 Valencia
1544 Cologne
1545 Gandía, raised to a university in 1547
1545 Barcelona
1545 Valladolid
1546 Bologna
1548 Messina
1548 Alcalá de Henares Salamanca
1548 Basein, India
1549 Palermo
1549 Cochin, India
1549 Quilon, India
1550 Tivoli
1550 Burgos
1551 Venice
1551 Roman College
1551 Ferrara
1551 Medina del Campo Ofiate
1551 Evora
1551 Vienna
1552 Florence
1552 German College, in Rome
1552 Naples
1552 Perugia
1552 Modena
1553 Monreale
1553 Cordoba, moved to Granada l556
1553 Sao Vicente, Brazil
1554 Argenta
1554 Genoa
1554 Avila
1554 Cuenca
1554 Plasencia
1554 Granada
1554 Sevilla
1554 Piratininga, now Sao Paulo, Brazil
1555 Loreto
1555 Siracusa
1555 Murcia
1555 Zaragoza
1555 Salvador de Bahia, Brazil
1556 Bivona
1556 Catania
1556 Siena
1556 Monterrey
1556 Billom
1556 Prague
1556 Ingolstadt

Index